Democratization, Liberalization & Human Rights in the Third World

Democratization, Liberalization & Human Rights in the Third World

Mahmood Monshipouri

LYNNE
RIENNER
PUBLISHERS

BOULDER
LONDON

Published in the United States of America in 1995 by
Lynne Rienner Publishers, Inc.
1800 30th Street, Boulder, Colorado 80301

and in the United Kingdom by
Lynne Rienner Publishers, Inc.
3 Henrietta Street, Covent Gardens, London WC2E 8LU

Library of Congress Cataloging-in-Publication Data
Monshipouri, Mahmood, 1952–
  Democratization, liberalization, and human rights in the Third
  World / Mahmood Monshipouri.
  Includes bibliographical references and index.
  ISBN 1-55587-529-7 (alk. paper)
  ISBN 1-55587-550-5 (alk. paper, pbk.)
  1. Democracy—Developing countries. 2. Human rights—
Developing countries 3. Developing countries—Economic policy.
4. Economic stabilization—Developing countries. I. Title.
JF60.M66   1995
320.9172′4—dc20
                                                    94-31377
                                                        CIP

British Cataloguing-in-Publication Data
A Cataloguing-in-Publication record for this book
is available from the British Library.

Printed and bound in the United States of America

The paper used in this publication meets the requirements
of the American National Standard for Permanence of
Paper for Printed Library Materials Z39.84.

5 4 3 2

In memory of my father, Abdul-Kareem,
and dedicated to my mother, Sara

Contents

Preface

Democratization, Liberalization, and Human Rights in the Third World
provides college students, social science theorists, policymakers, and general
readers with insights into the intricacies of democratization and the protection
of human rights in Third World countries. These intricacies include fundamental institutional, structural, operational, and situational obstacles to effective
democratization and to the realization of human rights. Studies of democratization and human rights have been symbiotic and have closely analyzed new
developments in post–Cold War politics. As democratization has become the
legitimate and central focus of world politics, many new questions regarding
the pace, strategy, timing, and implementation of democratization programs
have surfaced. The very feasibility of democratization in some Third World
societies is an issue. The fashionable prescription of guidelines based on East
European experiments with democratization needs to be reassessed with
respect to its utility in the Third World. East European "shock therapy" and
radical political reforms are germane in certain areas, but their overall
relevance in many Third World countries is highly questionable.

I believe that a new path must be sought to secure a sustainable transition
to democracy in the Third World. Such a path must address the primacy of
these countries' socioeconomic ills. Gradual economic and political liberalization, as a legitimate stage between fast-track democratization and traditional
authoritarian governance, could in the long run expand the civil society,
promote democratization, and protect human rights. They need to be applied
incrementally and in tandem.

This volume was inspired by a National Endowment for the Humanities
summer seminar at the State University of New York at Buffalo during
June–August 1992, directed by Professor Claude Welch Jr. of the Political
Science Department and Professor Newton Garver of the Philosophy Department. The seminar readings incorporated many related and valuable contributions made in the field prior to the 1989 global democratic revolution. It
occurred to me that a collection of case studies from different Third World

regions on the subject of democratization and human rights in the context of the post–Cold War era would neatly supplement those readings. By the end of the seminar, I was convinced that it was time to theorize about democratization, the turbulence accompanying it, and its effect on human rights in the Third World.

A study of democratization and human rights in the Third World poses several problems. Its premises need to be inspected carefully and comparatively. I embarked on this project with the hope of bringing a comparative assessment of the prospects for democratization/human rights to the attention of students, academics, politicians, and a wider public. There are no simple solutions to these problems, but if progress is to be made against authoritarianism and the abuse of human rights, the policies developed must combine serious commitment to economic and human development with other ideals. I hope this book will be seen as a contribution in this direction.

* * *

David P. Forsythe of the University of Nebraska provided me with excellent ideas and suggestions that have guided me throughout my work. Professor Forsythe's comments on the draft of Chapter 1 helped enormously in sharpening my thesis. I also wish to express great appreciation to Manochehr Dorraj of Texas Christian University for his contributions. His meticulous investigation of and comments on the entire manuscript bolstered it immensely and reflect his deep commitment to the study of democratization and human rights. I would also like to thank Martha Peacock and the staff of Lynne Rienner Publishers. Without their assistance this project could not have been completed.

My sincere thanks go to Peter Koper of Central Michigan University and Carl Mentley of Alma College who provided me with careful readings and valuable suggestions about the style and substance of the manuscript. Finally, I would like to extend my appreciation to the following colleagues and students for the time and care they took to help me with this project: Ronald Massanari, Burnet Davis, Tracy Luke, Gina Petonito, Sergion I. Chávaz, George Gazmararian, Barb Tripp, Arlene Nyman, Lori Shemka, Tomas Moore, Tanya Shire, Phil Warsop, Donna Adams, Mary Battaglia, Alan Crowley, Peter Dollard, Larry Hall, Priscilla Perkins, Susan Beckett, Mary van den Bergh, Kristin Vogel, Diane Bradley, and Amy Bluem.

—*Mahmood Monshipouri*

Introduction

The study of democratization in the Third World is not new, but a broad consensus has not emerged, not even regarding the utility of democratization in these countries. There are theoretical and conceptual confusions about the subject. This is partly due to the extraordinary turbulence that permeates many Third World nations in these early years of the post–Cold War era. The so-called global democratic revolution has produced upheaval, uncertainty, and fluctuating policies, as well as essential yet unresolved questions concerning the viability of Third World democratization.

As the process of democratization spreads, most Third World governments agonize over the selection of policies for political change and economic reform. Increasingly, they lean toward market-oriented solutions and economic liberalization to address their economic crises, convinced that state-run and mixed economies fail to provide optimal solutions. In the wake of the bankruptcy of centrally planned economies, public and private sectors alike are searching for alternatives in the free-market domain.

Given the dramatic, liberalizing transformation of Eastern Europe and the former Soviet Union, a study of the nature and persistence of economic reforms in the Third World must begin with an examination of the term *liberalization*. It is not necessary to accept uncritically liberal democratic traditions and understandings as universally valid in order to examine the relevance of liberalization for the economic and political issues facing Third World countries.

Liberalization has economic and political dimensions. This study addresses two questions: Are these economic and political processes separate or interrelated (or even sequential)? And can economic liberalization lead to a process of political liberalization, and vice versa? Prospects for achieving economic and political gains are hard to examine in the abstract and need careful study within any given country's political, economic, and social contexts.

Judgments regarding the successes or failures of policies are based on the

1

policies' actual long-term results. Leaders' foresight, commitment, and sound policymaking are often decisive for a policy's success. Structural constraints that set limits on democratization and choices made by leaders will largely influence the outcome of liberalization programs; and while there is no evidence that liberalization will automatically generate democratization, it is plausible to argue that the former, if properly conducted, will expand the civil society, undermine authoritarian economic and political structures, and promote internal and external pressures on a state to open up both economy and polity in the future. Liberalization can, in certain circumstances, deprive authoritarian states of a panoply of coercive tools. South Korea, Taiwan, and Chile are examples where gradual economic and political liberalization have led to an increase in democratization.

The complex connections between economic and political liberalization, democratization, and the problems of governance require case-by-case investigation. This book focuses on Algeria, Pakistan, Peru, and El Salvador—cases where experiments with democratization have either been reversed or have proved destabilizing. By taking a historical and comparative view of the evolution of democracy in these countries, I attempt to draw some conclusions concerning the impact of internal, external, and situational factors shaping democratization in the Third World.

Notwithstanding the basic realities of Third World countries, a leader's skill and choices can be pivotal. This book is concerned with an appraisal of both *structure* and *choice* as well as an assessment of the modus operandi of governments pursuing liberalization and democratization. Two other variables—the role of the armed forces and external actors—figure prominently in this analysis. Historically, nationalism has perpetuated the legacy of praetorian rule. In all the cases reviewed here, the participation of military leaders in wars of independence was the route by which they became involved in politics. The detachment of the colonial aristocracy from such wars left the military as the sole arbiter of each country's political destiny for many years. Today, the military's active support or acquiescence is the key to any viable, sustained transition to democracy.

In each case examined in this book, the country's society and politics have been considerably influenced by external forces. Ever since these countries won independence from colonial domination, bilateral and multilateral foreign influences have penetrated their economy and politics. The tendency to make foreign aid conditional on the holding of elections has risks. Pressing nations to conduct either restricted and closely monitored elections or to administer democratic elections can itself imperil the process of democratization.

Traditionally, foreign aid was the most significant external influence in the shaping of a country's economic and political conditions. Recently structural adjustment has become an important force in this regard, substantially shaping events. Structural adjustment is the package of reforms or conditions that Third World countries must adopt in order to be eligible for loans from the International Monetary Fund (IMF) and World Bank. Balance-of-payments assistance or development loans have, at times, been based on conditions that require strong government actions and imposition of heavy-handed economic programs.

Structural adjustment has the potential to promote a gradual and measured process of economic liberalization. However, its execution thus far has failed to deal effectively with social welfare in the Third World and has routinely imposed unbearable and unjust burdens on the most powerless people: the wretchedly poor, women, and children. The utility of structural adjustment hinges upon its actual outcome, and before its further use there must be a period of evaluation to assess the gains and costs associated with it. There is mounting evidence that the immediate impacts of poorly planned structural adjustment programs aimed at fostering economic reforms are hindering Third World economic development.

In the long run, the main concern need not be the promotion of more stable democracies in the Third World, but rather the creation of conditions that can sustain a steady transition. The importance of properly planned structural adjustment must not be underemphasized. Furthermore, since building democracy and a free market at the same time may be impractical in tumultuous Third World politics, it may be necessary to afford economic liberalization a higher priority than democratization. Protracted crises of debt and lack of growth pose enormously difficult problems for a successful transition to democracy.

Human rights in Third World countries will most likely be improved if transitions from authoritarianism are preceded by processes of economic liberalization and expansions of civil society. The choices that leaders make are critical because systemic and social constraints are so inflexible that abrupt democratization often fails fundamentally to alter these countries' human rights situations. Rather, it produces social chaos and cyclic repression. The process of economic liberalization can indeed provide a legitimate median between fast-track democratization and traditional authoritarian rule. Such an intermediate stage is warranted as a source of the gradual expansion of civil society. The relations between democratization, human rights, and liberalization explain the frequency with which democratic processes in the Third World have been aborted. This book offers a comparative assessment of the failure of these processes in some of the fledgling, frail democracies.

Organization of the Book

The key analytical questions in this book are not just what structural changes and reforms are required but also how adaptable Third World countries are to transition and to the pace and effects of change. Contemporary theories of democratization are overly sanguine about the possibilities of regime transformation and the promotion of Western-type democracies in the Third World. These theoretical frameworks in general are still quite underdeveloped, especially in their endeavors to link human rights studies with those of democratization. These studies have not accounted for the dynamic between liberalization and the historical, economic, cultural, and political components in each nation-state. There is a great deal more to be said and done on the subject. This book is a contribution to this work.

The first chapter of this book offers a review of the literature; introduces conceptual, theoretical, and ideological orientations; and assesses this study's significance. In Chapter 2, I survey different categories of constraints on human rights and fragile democratic governments. Historical realities and contemporary setbacks are thoroughly discussed. Chapter 3 focuses on the global changes and opportunities of the post–Cold War era. Opportunities to renew civil society, to promote human rights vis-à-vis sovereign rights of the states, and to take other actions (bilateral and multilateral) aimed at improving human rights conditions in Third World countries are discussed. Chapters 4 through 7 explore the prospects for democracy and guarantees of human rights in the four countries listed above. Chapters 4 through 6 discuss Algeria, Pakistan, and Peru. The experiences of these countries in recent years illustrate how a sudden democratization has resulted in political instabilities, government turnovers, and military and executive coups. The objective of these chapters is to identify the destabilizing conditions that these countries have faced and explain ways to enhance their prospects for constructive social change. Chapter 7 explores the historical evolution of civil-military relations in El Salvador, and includes discussion of the peace process that began in 1992. Recent elections and the prospects for change are briefly discussed with a view to assessing the impact of the electoral process on economic and political reforms. I argue that if stable and effective democratization is to unfold in El Salvador, such reforms are indeed necessary.

Finally, Chapter 8 is a comparative analysis of the interaction between choice, structure, and other factors affecting political change. To this end, the military's political role, the influence of foreign elements on electoral politics, human development conditions, and reform strategies will be examined. I close with a brief note on the prospects for democratization and human rights in our vastly altered world.

CHAPTER 1

Toward an Understanding of Liberalization, Democratization, and Human Rights

The recent experiences of many Third World countries with liberalization and limited democratization have raised serious questions regarding the readiness of these countries to experiment with democracy. Although a growing number of Third World countries have in the last few years turned to economic liberalization, and although many now accept democracy as standard, their brief experiments in these areas have been disruptive and tumultuous. Such experiences have culminated in military takeovers (Algeria, Haiti, Nigeria, Sudan), democratic volatility and government turnovers (Pakistan), the reversal of the government's declared policies (Côte d'Ivoire, Morocco, Peru, Tunisia), and a return to blatantly repressive political measures and violence in the face of soaring legitimate dissent (Congo, Egypt, Guatemala, Kenya, Venezuela, among others). These problems have led to charges that the West—by becoming actively involved in promoting democracies where its interests dictate—has found new ways of meddling in the internal affairs of Third World countries. Frustrated with their diminishing capabilities and faced with mounting popular demands to liberalize and democratize, Third World governments face formidable tasks and dilemmas.

The dilemmas of liberalization, democratization, and human rights protection raise several questions: Can Third World countries reasonably be expected to adjust their views on democratization in the wake of evolving global standards? If so, what pace and form will these adjustments assume, given the wide array of societal and structural constraints standing in their way? And, in the fragile socioeconomic and political contexts of these countries, are the process of democratization (with its complicated structures and institutions) and the protection of basic human rights compatible?

This book develops three propositions. The first is that democratization is logically preceded by economic liberalization and by the building of a civil society. Given the distinction that (later in this chapter) I draw between economic and political liberalization, I argue that encouraging economic liberalization and some form of political liberalization, however restricted, serve as a transition for countries moving toward democratization. In light of the prevailing socioeconomic, political, and cultural conditions of these countries, such a proposition is not only logical but prudent.

The second proposition is that the pace and scope of liberalization are shaped by de facto socioeconomic and political conditions. The pace and scope of liberalization is determined by the specific realities of any given country. In some cases, liberalization may be effective if it is implemented gradually and incrementally. In other cases, a swift and thorough liberalization with quick results will better serve the transitional objectives.

The third proposition is that cultures historically are dynamic and adjustable to changing conditions. Currently, cultural constraints in many Third World countries are among the principal impediments to democratization. There are neither logical nor empirical reasons to assume that such constraints are permanent curbs on the evolution of cultural change in these societies.

This book seeks to identify the constraints to and opportunities for the protection of human rights and development of democracy in the post–Cold War era. I focus on Algeria, Pakistan, and Peru as examples of vexatious and troublesome transitions toward democracy and on El Salvador as an example of the enormous difficulties involved in an authoritarian electoral experience. In this chapter, I discuss (1) the theoretical approach and conceptual framework of this study; (2) the logic and methodology of the case selection and comparative study; and (3) the analytical framework adopted.

Theoretical Treatments

The literature concerning democratization process offers different theoretical perspectives. For practical purposes, I focus on two dominant approaches: the structural approach and the agency approach. The latter involves the so-called transition theories.

The Structural Approach. This approach, also known as macrohistorical perspective, suggests that long-term and deep structural changes (economic development, urbanization, increased literacy rate, political participation, and so on) are prerequisites for a stable and effective democracy. This approach has traditionally been associated with the work of Seymour Martin Lipset (1959).[1]

The Agency Approach. This approach, also known as "the choice model," emphasizes the significance of the strategic choices, policies, and interactions of the ruling elites for transition. It has been identified with the work of Guillermo O'Donnell, Philippe Schmitter, and Laurence Whitehead (1986).[2] From a human rights perspective, a volume edited by David P. Forsythe (*Human Rights and Development: International Views,* 1989) has also underscored the importance of the ideas and policy choices of leaders in the mix of variables affecting human rights and the expansion of political space.[3]

More recently, the contributions of Larry Diamond, Juan Linz, and Seymour Martin Lipset (1988),[4] Huntington (1991),[5] and Haggard and Kaufman (1992)[6] have attempted to bridge the gap between these two approaches by emphasizing the significance of both the structural forces (e.g., economic growth, external influence, the state) and political leadership. Moreover, the question of which strategy works best in Third World countries—gradualism or fast-track liberalization and democratization—remains at the heart of these contributions and an ongoing debate about how to promote political and economic liberalization.

Answer to: what is liberalization.

In keeping with these perspectives and their value, I argue for liberalization, a process of gradual economic adjustment and renewal of civil society, on the assumption that an abrupt transition from authoritarianism to democratization often relapses into nondemocratic processes. Haggard and Kaufman seem to imply, although not in all cases or circumstances, a somewhat similar logic when they maintain that "sharp economic shocks are likely to lead to widespread demands for public assistance and possibly changes of regime. Long periods of slow growth, by contrast, do not necessarily produce destabilizing political responses."[7] Economic freedoms plus a gradual relaxation of civil (and finally political) restraints could lead to a stable and mature democracy. If the socioeconomic structures are to be established that will support democracy over time, leaders must commit to gradual economic and political reform.

My central argument, as is further elaborated later in this chapter, is that abrupt democratization in Third World countries does not always result in enhanced human rights. Human rights in fledgling democracies are most likely to be improved if the transition from authoritarianism is preceded by a process of economic liberalization, which works as a prelude to a gradual expansion of civil society. To guard against the simplistic notion that the trajectory from authoritarianism to democracy is solely predicated on economic liberalization, I argue, as do many scholars, that there is no automatic link between economic liberalization and democratization.[8] Rather, for economic liberalization to pave the way successfully for stable democratization, two primary conditions must be fulfilled: (a) the pace and strategy of change must be suitable; and (b) political liberalization, however confined in its initial stages and scope, must simultaneously be pursued.

A comparison of the recent experiences of China and Russia, despite stark differences in their economic structures, shows that democracy and radical free-market reforms and economic "shock therapy" do not necessarily go together. Whereas the Chinese economy is booming at an annual rate of 13 percent, Russians are constantly aware that democratic elections, though much touted in Washington, have been followed by plummeting living standards.[9] While not shrinking from the inevitable concern over the human rights situation and the lack of political liberty in China, many observers emphasize the role of economic development and expanded trade in democratization and the improvement of human rights. For instance, Marshall Goldman argues that "if true democracy comes to either of these countries, it will come to China first" since China stands a better chance of building a middle class in the long run.[10]

Over time, however, the commitment of leaders to gradual political reforms is a necessary condition for democratization. Many authoritarian regimes have prolonged their longevity by introducing economic liberalization programs at the exclusion of political reforms. Caution must be exercised not to confuse promoting economic reforms with presaging an overly optimistic scenario regarding the withering away of authoritarianism in the Third World. In the last analysis, genuine and vigorous commitment by leaders to political reforms and necessary political structures and institutions could prove to be the missing link in the actual realization of democratization. Political reforms must go beyond instrumental means of achieving mere economic objectives.

Liberalization invites Third World societies and regimes to undertake change with appropriate pace, procedures, modes of adjustment, and institutional frameworks. The encouragement of sharp changes in regimes, in the absence of institutions that provide linkage between the demands of civil society and existing social conditions, carries unpredictable and costly risks. The position of the liberalizers in the government is often jeopardized and the process may never be completed. Initially, building operations, habits, and institutions that support civil society can be more important for the long-term development of democracy than such nominally democratic activities as early elections. Once developed, civil expectations could convince or compel an authoritarian regime either to tolerate or to cooperate with reforming democratic forces.

Liberalization may ensure a regime's survival by increasing the flexibility of its existing authoritarian structures. Usually illegitimate and rigid, authoritarian regimes naturally find it difficult to change in ways that would expedite their destruction. Liberalization, by reducing tensions and solving some problems, will extend the life of some regimes. Therefore, democratization will not automatically follow liberalization in every case (more on this later). The transition from liberalization to democratization is not a linear process. But, because liberalization has a better chance than premature democratization in culminating in some form of permanent move toward stable democracy, it is morally and practically defensible.

Furthermore, with the changing global environment of the post–Cold War era, where populist political movements and interethnic tensions are on the upsurge, it seems imperative to account for two variables: external pressures and the military. The prospects for democratization in many Third World countries in the post–Cold War era appear to be increasingly a function, inter alia, of these two variables. Whether or not civil and military bureaucracies can reach a consensus on how to rule could very well determine the extent to which international actors are willing to offer long-term and effective support to these countries. In the troubled democracies of Central America (Guatemala,

Honduras, Nicaragua), the armies are on the march again in the wake of economic doldrums, legislative corruption, judicial abuses, and political instability. The oustings from political power of Guatemalan President Jorge Serrano Elias, Brazilian President Fernando Collor de Mello, and Haitian President Jean-Bertrand Aristide serve as grim reminders that the presence of the armed forces in the politics of Latin America remains a thorn in the side of democratic movements.

The people's turn to the army in the absence of any other alternative marks the ebb of fervor for democratization. The interaction between the military and the civilian sectors can be greatly influenced by the economic predominance of transnational institutions like the United States–dominated International Monetary Fund (IMF) and the World Bank, the European-led Bank for International Settlements, or the European Monetary System. Liberalization, as a process, can be facilitated by policies recommended by the World Bank and the IMF. The issue regarding reform proposals and conditions that Third World countries must meet in order to get development assistance is discussed thoroughly in Chapter 3.

Methodology

In this study I examine four nations—Algeria, El Salvador, Pakistan, and Peru. The samples display profound similarities and marked differences. Algeria and Peru have failed in their efforts to democratize by way of electoral competition and widespread voting participation. While Algeria's President Zeroual has welcomed negotiations with opposing groups and organizations, Peru's President Fujimori, relying on his regime's relative success in curbing inflation and terrorism, has remained reluctant to enter into any negotiations with the opposing groups.

In the post-Zia era (since 1988), Pakistan has had several elections without making consistent progress toward stable democratic conditions. El Salvador has experienced several elections since 1982 but has achieved little in the way of enhanced living conditions for its people. Although Pakistan's Benazir Bhutto, in her second term, has shown more acceptance of democratic principles and the commitment to negotiate with the opposition party, it is too early to describe her regime as an example of democratic stability. The same conclusion can be drawn for El Salvador. Despite El Salvador's first peacetime elections, the new civilian police force has been undermined by the military, and the country is far from democratic stability.

The four countries display differences in per capita incomes. Three are in the lower-middle income category (Pakistan $350, El Salvador $820, and Peru $1,130 GNP per capita); one is in the upper-middle income category (Algeria, $2,570 GNP per capita).[11] Not all of these countries are ethnically diverse. The percentage of homogeneity is high in El Salvador (83 percent), low in Algeria (57 percent), and even lower in Peru and Pakistan (41 and 36 percent respectively).[12] Two of these countries are predominantly Muslim. The percentage of Muslims in Algeria is 98.6; in Pakistan it is 96.8.[13] The two other nations are predominantly Christian (Roman Catholic). The percentage of Christians in the population of Peru is 95; in El Salvador it is 81. All four countries are in the lower-middle category of PQLI (Physical Quality of Life Index, averaging infant mortality, literacy rate, and life expectancy): El Salvador is ranked at 74, Peru at 71, Algeria at 62, and Pakistan at 43.[14] Two of these four nation-states gained independence in the twentieth century (Pakistan in 1947 and Algeria in 1962). El Salvador and Peru have been independent since 1821.

These nations illustrate three situations: (1) democratic uncertainty (Pakistan) and chaos (Peru); (2) the return to and consolidation of authoritarianism (Algeria); and (3) authoritarian electoral politics (El Salvador before 1994). In each of the four nations, the military alliance with and subordination to the elected civilian government is an important issue. The sharp differences displayed by these four cases is of paramount concern. In Algeria, an authoritarian regime has returned, after a brief period of political liberalization and democratization, with the military at the helm. In Peru, an authoritarian civilian regime has the strong backing of a unified military. In Pakistan, the military has cooperated closely with the civilian regime. In El Salvador, some uncertainty surrounds the armed forces' subordination to the elected civilian government.

In the Muslim countries, Algeria and Pakistan, the political activity of the Islamist groups has increased extensively, posing many, and sometimes formidable, challenges to these regimes' long-established secular Islamic identities. In Peru, a Maoist guerrilla group, the Sendero Luminoso or Shining Path, has posed a major threat to the stability of the regime. In El Salvador, since December 15, 1992, the leftist groups (e.g., the Farabundo Martí National Liberation Front—FMLN) have been gradually incorporated into the political structure following twelve years of civil war.

In situations where a civilian government has the tacit or explicit backing of the army, an attempt to experiment with the democratization process has a fairly realistic chance of improving a society. The significance of a balanced relationship with the army has been underscored as sine qua non for the political longevity of many Third World civilian governments. Myron Weiner observes, with considerable evidence, that "sections of the military must be won over, and for democracy to be sustained military acquiescence to democratic civilian rule must continue."[15] Adam Przeworski's explanation of the role of the military in the transition to democracy is poignant and standard: "Military tutelage may be preferred by some civilian political forces as a protection from demands for greater representation, to ward off pressure from those who seek a social as well as a political revolution."[16] Further, the role of the military in these countries, except for Algeria, is what Alfred Stepan called "redemocratization initiated by the civilian or civilianized political leadership."[17] In this subtype, the army is neither the preponderant actor nor the chief institution in calling the political shots, but rather a significant ally.

In cases where the army continues to be either a superior partner in the state structure or has actually confiscated the government apparatus (as in Algeria, where it maintains a strong secular posture vis-à-vis the Islamist and fundamentalist groups), any hope of returning to democracy for the foreseeable future seems farfetched. Furthermore, the consequence of a failed democratization is turmoil, civil war, or worse. Despite their differences, the cases studied in this book lend credence to the idea that democratization needs to be incrementally adjusted to indigenous conditions and that overt democratization often needs to be preceded by a measured, and if necessary protracted, process of liberalization.

The purpose of this and the following chapters is to make the case for gradual liberalization. Toward this end, this book's principal theoretical position and its underlying theme is, in sum: The contribution of economic liberalization to the eventual growth of democracy is directly and positively associated with the gradual expansion of the civil society and political institutions. In the absence of such association, economic liberalization is most likely to sustain, or even invite, authoritarian forms of rule. Drastic political reforms are more apt to complicate economic reforms and liberalization, especially in those Third World countries that have neither the experience with democratization nor the needed civil society and institutions to sustain such reforms. An abrupt democratization may not serve as an immediate solution for the socioeconomic ills of Third World societies. Rather, gradual and deliberate economic and political liberalization programs, if applied incrementally and in tandem, could prepare these societies for a sustainable drive toward democracy in the long run. Thus, the more gradual and consistent the tendency to experiment with economic liberalization and civil society, the more stable and steady will be the transition from authoritarianism. Conversely, the more drastic and radical the political reforms, the less stable will be the move toward steady macroeconomic policies.

The bottom line is, of course, the performance of government and a successful operation of economic adjustment. Avoiding widespread economic deprivation, inequality, and social dislocation for the mass of the people is the key to long-term success of government policies. A useful corrective to economic adjustment is a reduction of economic frustrations caused by distributional inequalities. This entails the right package of social compensation.[18] The creation of a political climate conducive to the expansion of civil society is also an imperative for sustainable democratization. In the end, political change is a vital component for economic liberalization to lead to successful democratization. As Haggard and Kaufman contend, the long-term sustainability of policy choices regarding economic adjustment will depend on elite preferences, ideas, ideology, and coherence, as well as political institutionalization.[19]

"Small Number" studies, according to comparativists, have proven to be the success story of comparative politics in recent decades.[20] This book, taking the four nations listed, looks for similarities and differences in historical traditions, ethnic makeup, the governing coalitions, the military, state institutions, the nature and pace of transition, the role of international factors, and external intervention. My conclusions respond to the questions: (1) How do these countries differ in their reactions to transitional necessities? (2) How likely are the chances in these countries of recovery from authoritarianism, whether chronic or episodic? Such information is crucial for understanding the prospects for constructive social change in the Third World.

Notes on Conceptualization

The core concepts in this book are *liberalization* and *democratization*. They are related but significantly different concepts. Liberalization has been used to denote a wide range of policies, from governmental reduction of all forms of repression and exploitation to simply allowing the formation of autonomous organizations. At its broadest level, liberalization represents a strictly political characterization: political openings initiated from above to deflect political tensions and to coopt opposition, perceived or real. In Huntington's account, "liberalization . . . is the partial opening of an authoritarian system short of choosing governmental leaders through freely competitive elections."[21]

Similarly, Przeworski defines liberalization using the terms *opening, decompression, renewal, reconstruction,* and *remodeling*. These terms, he adds, describe policies of change carried out within strong limits.[22] The distinctions between economic and political liberalization are enormously important for the practical welfare of societies.

By *political liberalization,* I refer to a process of gradual expansion of civil society. Embedded in political liberalization is the idea of "making the society more free" for a gradual transition from authoritarian rule. Hence, political liberalization can be defined in terms of protecting and promoting civil rights such as freedom from torture and degrading punishment, arbitrary arrest, and imprisonment; freedom of speech, faith, opinion, and assembly; and also the right to life, security, and the ownership of property. A broader definition of political liberalization includes the right to seek or nominate for public office and the right to form and join political parties through an orderly electoral process. Thus conceived, political liberalization means democratization. This definition is not employed here. Rather, my thesis is that political liberalization in the narrow sense, defined as increases in civil rights, is often more feasible for Third World nations than liberalization as democratization in the long run.

By *economic liberalization,* I refer to a process leading to the implementation of privatization and a free market economy. This process involves economic restructuring, such as removing tariffs and other barriers to trade, providing incentives for foreign investment and tax reforms for exporters,

liberal. to author [handwritten margin note]

reforming the financial system, deregulating the labor market, privatizing public enterprises, and protecting private property. Properly implemented, economic liberalization leads to the emergence of new, functionally interrelated centers of economic power and decisionmaking. When these centers mature, they cannot be controlled for long by authoritarian governments. Economic liberalization is thus closely connected to the possibilities for political liberalization.

Economic liberalization and political liberalization are interrelated processes. Some scholars have argued, however, that the link between the two processes cannot be determined precisely and that it is not clear which process is consistently more important. Haggard and Kaufman argue that if economic and political liberalization are *sequenced,* this does not always make for clarity about what are the choices and that governments may be pushed toward a given sequence by circumstances beyond their control.[23] In examining contemporary economic and political liberalization in the Middle East, David Pool writes that there are different sequences of economic and political liberalization and that both processes sometimes strengthen the position of authoritarian political elites relative to other classes.[24] In the cases of Turkey and Egypt, two states with significant experience of political and economic change, Pool detects a general pattern followed by the liberalizers:

> Economic liberalization sets constraints on political liberalization, and although a degree of political liberalization can facilitate the introduction of economic reform measures, the social and political consequences of such measures put limits on the extent of political reform. As a result of this symbiosis and dialectical tension between the two processes, economic liberalization is marked by progress and regress and political liberalization is authoritarian, cautious and controlled.[25]

Whether to assign higher priority to economic liberalization to the exclusion of political liberalization or vice versa is a dilemma for many authoritarian Third World countries. One concern is the role of the state in the early stages of economic restructuring. It is understandable that it seems vital to have a strong state at the initial stages, because market irregularities, distributional imperatives, and political instabilities keep the state heavily involved in the economy. All past cases of effective economic development have involved some type of state intervention. However, those states whose leaders are flexible and favor the gradual expansion of civil society find themselves in a better position to survive the usually tumultuous transition from authoritarian rule.

Another dilemma presents itself when economic liberalization is implemented without corresponding political openings. This typically leads to an alliance of political elites, the military, and economic elites. This alliance, while pursuing its interests, inevitably encounters resistance from economically deprived and politically excluded segments of the society. The result, in most instances, is political instability. In the long run, political liberalization becomes inevitable if national accommodation, compromise, and consensus are to take shape.

Political liberalization without tangible economic improvements presents the converse dilemma. There, economic frustrations are likely to restore public confidence in authoritarian regimes (as in Peru), or in the military's credibility (as in Sudan), or in revived regional, political, economic, and ethnic divisions (as in Pakistan). Such reversals of national attitudes are often reflected in the inconsistency of economic orientation. Frequent shifts from orthodox to unorthodox strategies and vice versa is a well-documented fact in the Third World.

It appears that the fate of political liberalization hinges, to a considerable extent, upon the outcome of economic liberalization. Failure in programs of economic liberalization results in various destabilizing (yet predictable) outcomes. Three possible outcomes are: (1) a resort to political liberalization to defuse or preempt disorder; (2) a return to stricter authoritarianism; (3) the abandonment of the liberalization measures. The first outcome has proved to be short-lived and, with regard to further economic liberalization, at times counterproductive. The second outcome has been justified in the name of economic reforms and political stability. The third of these possibilities has, where applied, proved costly. It is not recommended—a view supported by the failures of dominant public sector and command economies. Which of these outcomes (or combination of them) will be pursued, and how the tensions between political and economic liberalization are resolved in the longer term, depends on the relationship between political and social forces and classes. David Pool's observation in this connection is apt:

> Even though there have been societal pressures for reducing authoritarian controls, the process of political liberalization has been state-induced, and the state retains a considerable degree of management over the process. In its turn, economic liberalization has changed and is likely further to change the political balance between classes, shape new social inequalities and create different patterns of access to the state. It is the volatility of these latter processes which is likely to determine whether political liberalization is maintained in its current partial form, extended into a process of democratization, or ushers in a new period of authoritarianism.[26]

While economic-cum-political liberalization is almost certainly a prolonged and difficult process, often it is a necessary part of a sustainable drive toward democratization. Rapid transitions to electoral politics without the state's effective retreat from some economic and political spheres and without national reconciliation and accommodation are bound to be unstable.

A broadening of civil society in an evolutionary process precipitates the transformation of authoritarian regimes. Therefore, those polities that liberalize over time offer reasonably better prospects for constructive change than those that do not make incremental preparations. Liberalized authoritarian societies will not be converted into democracies if political liberalization leads to a polarization of the society or if the process is not reconciled with the broader interests of the key actors in the state, society, and economy. In recent years, there have been many efforts at political opening in the Third World. Some have led to severe political repression (Algeria, Egypt, Kenya, Nigeria, Peru, Zaire); others show signs of taking root in their societies (Chile, Jordan, South Korea, Taiwan).

Definition of Democracy

The definition of *democracy* is problematic. One view emphasizes the existence of socioeconomic equity in society as a fundamental condition for the successful functioning of democracy.[27] Another definition includes popular participation in free-and-fair elections as well as measures for substantial protection of minorities. So defined, democracy is based on limits on majority rule that ensure pluralism and stability. Some contemporary theorists view contestation *and consent to outcomes of the contest* as the essential characteristics of democracy. Adam Przeworski asserts that "in a democracy, no group is able to intervene when outcomes of conflict violate their self-perceived interests. . . . It is this very act of alienation of control over outcomes of conflicts that constitutes the decisive step toward democracy."[28]

Other theorists in defining democracy regard participation and contestation as the operative variables.[29] Robert A. Dahl's definition, known as the procedural minimum, emphasizes the procedures that must be present for the effective operation of modern political democracy. They are: frequent and fair elections, the right to vote, and the right to form relatively independent associations and organizations. Dahl considers the relative influence of the average citizen as the basic definition. The tendency to focus on the holding of elections—known as electoralism—has been strongly criticized by those who maintain that, if such a characterization of democracy is adopted, the militarized countries of Central America easily fit this definition. One such critic, Terry Lynn Karl, notes that an effective definition of democracy must go beyond the holding of elections to include other components: participation of the citizenry through associational and collective actions, the accountability of rulers, and civilian control over the military.[30]

This book employs a definition of democracy that includes both procedural and substantive dimensions. This definition of democracy would encompass a set of institutional arrangements; e.g., elections, political parties, and an independent judiciary designed to safeguard popular participation and contestation; minority rights; and the rule of law. Democracy in this definition also has a set of structures and processes for the promotion of socioeconomic justice. Thus conceived, democracy involves more than a multiparty system and/or electoral laws: it also includes structures that promote socioeconomic opportunity. *Democracy,* as conceived here, has applications in the economic, social, and cultural spheres: it implies some degree of equality.

Unlike classic liberalism (such as the nineteenth-century version represented by John Stuart Mill) and modern conservatism (as represented by Irving Kristol), both of which embrace the notion that egalitarianism detracts from the effective operation of democracy, I maintain that some degree of formal equality (in the political-legal sense) and equality of opportunity and condition (in the socioeconomic sense) are desirable and necessary for the successful working of democracy. Such a definition limits the number of countries that can be called democratic, but it is more accurate than less stringent definitions. Because some authoritarian regimes in the Third World have adopted forms of democracy as a cloak for repressive policies (Pakistan, Sri Lanka, Turkey . . . to name only a few) a concept of democracy encompassing more aspects can be meaningful in assessing Third World countries.

As noted earlier, *democratization,* is generally defined in terms of rules and procedures for the implementation of competitive and free-and-fair elections. This definition fails properly to reflect the complexity in the implementation of democratization. By *democratization,* I refer to a highly complex process involving successive stages of transition, endurance, and consolidation. This process ultimately leads to both institutionalization and consolidation of structures and conditions conducive to structural transformation and regime change from authoritarian rule. The contemporary transitions include cases of democratization initiated from within the authoritarian regimes (as in Latin America) as well as cases largely triggered by external forces (as in Eastern Europe).[31] In both cases, transitions are imposed from above: they are clearly not mass-based.[32] Democratization has also been defined in terms of consent to procedural rules and of compliance with the outcomes of the process, "an act of subjecting all interests to competition, of institutionalizing uncertainty. The decisive step toward democracy is the devolution of power from a group of people to a set of rules."[33]

It seems plausible to argue that as liberalization grows, so do demands for democratization (as in Chile, South Korea, and Taiwan). In many Third World countries without well-entrenched processes of liberalization, sudden democratization has been destabilizing. Examples are legion: Algeria, Côte d'Ivoire, Pakistan, Peru, Sudan, Tunisia. The assumption in this book is that it is better first to liberalize, both in the economic and political senses discussed earlier, than suddenly to apply democratization "shock therapy." The hurling of a regime into the democratization process risks relapse into an even more strict form of authoritarianism. Abrupt democratization in the face of a moribund economy, weak political institutions, and crumbling social structures renders subsequent democratic consolidation difficult and makes regression to authoritarianism inescapable. All things considered, a liberalized authoritarian regime is more likely to generate democratization than an authoritarian electoral reform. The success of center-right governing coalitions in initiating the process of "controlled" liberalization in the 1970s in Brazil is

partial evidence of this.[34] It should be noted, however, that gradual liberalization does not preclude the return of military rule (e.g., Turkey and Nigeria).

The validity of this proposition can be seen in the outcomes of experiments
with liberalization and democratization in various Third World countries—in
their political, ethnic, demographic, economic, cultural, and social conditions.
This book differs from other works in the field in the extent to which it
differentiates liberalization and democratization. It treats liberalization and
democratization as different variables—at the same time recognizing that they
are closely related.

Definition of Human Rights

The concept of *human rights* also defies easy definition. The Western World
refers to the rights enunciated in the Universal Declaration of Human Rights
(UDHR) as its point of departure, for the most part emphasizing the declaration's first twenty-one articles. The contents of these articles are based on
civil-political rights: rights to life, privacy, a fair trial, and humane treatment;
prohibition of torture and slavery; freedom of movement and residence; the
right not to be arbitrarily arrested or detained; freedom of thought, conscience,
religion, expression, association, political participation, and equal protection
under the law.

Third World countries, on the other hand, tend mainly to emphasize the
remaining articles (XXII through XXX), the substance of which is based on
economic, social, and cultural rights: the right to work and to just and favorable
conditions; the right to strike, to social security, and to an adequate standard
of living; and the right to physical and mental health, education, and participation in cultural life, and to benefit from scientific, literary, or artistic production. An increasing number of Third World countries are now pressing for a
so-called "third generation" of rights (sometimes referred to as "solidarity
rights"). These include the rights to development, to a healthy environment, to
peace, to humanitarian aid, and to the benefits of an international common
heritage. Some Western states have questioned whether such concerns should
be regarded as a matter of human rights.

These two viewpoints are reflected in scholarly work. Many Western
scholars emphasize the primacy of civil-political rights.[35] Whereas growing
numbers of Third World observers rate socioeconomic and cultural rights as
equally important,[36] others reject a dichotomy between political and economic
rights.[37] Still others maintain that the concept of cultural relativism, which is
used by traditionalists and communitarians as a defense of their "way of life"
against the individualism of liberal currents of thought, is actually a concept
of cultural absolutism. In this view, culture is believed to be of more value than
the internationally accepted (but Western in origin) principle of human rights.
In fact, this group argues that cultural absolutists are the real ethnocentrists for
they deny their citizens the right to use their reason to consider transcendent

ethical norms.[38]

In the World Conference on Human Rights (held in Vienna, June 1993), the Asian and Muslim nations argued that human rights legislation has failed to respect their cultural and regional traditions and that it has interfered in their internal affairs. They also maintained that developing nations should be allowed to emphasize economic development over human rights.[39] The United States and other Western countries opposed the weakening of human rights legislation. U.S. Secretary of State Warren M. Christopher, speaking at the conference, stressed the "universality" of human rights, saying: "We cannot let cultural relativism become the last refuge of repression."[40] The conference ended with several basic disagreements over cultural relativism and the right-to-development claim of the developing countries.[41]

To avoid the pitfalls of cultural relativity, I subscribe to the view that these categories are interactive and not sequential. Nonetheless, I recognize the urgency and the immediate relevance of socioeconomic and cultural rights in Third World countries. To many, the concept of human rights remains an elusive notion about which no universal consensus has emerged. I have chosen to use the concept in a broad sense, including both notions of the exercise of free choice and personal autonomy (civil-political rights in connection with negative rights) and notions of social justice (socioeconomic rights in relation to the positive injunction on government to provide those rights). My view takes into consideration the complexities involved in observing human rights in the Third World. The adoption of either of the narrow definitions of human rights significantly distorts the investigation. For many Third World countries, the central question continues to be whether or not change will in the foreseeable future bring them economic development and social justice.

While the official rhetoric of Third World governments is in conformity with the UDHR and its ensuing two covenants, the actual extent of the protection of human rights is largely determined by the customs, legal traditions, and cultural forces of these societies. One human rights scholar aptly summarizes the point: "Human rights make up such a complex, multifaceted and intricate matter that divergences are inevitable, when it comes to the implementation of those rights."[42] Despite the democratic revolutions sweeping the world, the recognition and practice of human rights in many Third World countries have yet to approach the universal standards enunciated by the UDHR.

At both the conceptual and empirical levels, Third World states and their societies continue to rely in practice on nativistic approaches to human dignity and equality. While it is possible to claim certain universal human rights and moral standards, it is critical to understand different cultural perspectives if we are to reach consensus on how human rights can effectively be implemented.[43] The evolution of human rights as well as the process of democratization have necessitated an intercultural dialogue on how to forge such a universal understanding. Some insist that "non-Western contexts" have conceptions of human dignity but lack concepts of human rights.[44] I contend that human dignity and human rights are related. Those societies that recognize human dignity have some conceptions of human rights, however normatively different they may be from Western counterparts.

It should be noted that certain standards of human rights must be recognized and observed, irrespective of the historical, cultural, economic, and political conditions of the Third World countries. A consensus is emerging on a set of universal standards. Genocide, racial discrimination, torture, and the denial of people's right to self-determination are breaches of this consensus. Increasingly, albeit gradually, points of convergence on a wide range of rights are developing.[45] There is a proper role for regional and international factors (of both governmental and nongovernmental types) in preventing egregious violations of human rights and in pressing authoritarian governments and groups (sectarian or otherwise) to observe certain basic and internationally recognized human rights standards.[46]

Definition of the Third World

Finally, the term *Third World* needs some clarification. As a generic term, *Third World* describes those nations of Africa, Asia, Latin America, and the Middle East that lack developed economic and political institutions and social structures.[47] There are extensive and obvious variations among these societies, but Third World countries nevertheless typically share underdeveloped economic conditions, a colonial legacy, and structural dependence on the developed countries. In narrow economic terms, Third World countries have little if any capital, technological base, production capacity, or access to international markets. Some writers refer to Fourth or Fifth Worlds to emphasize the wide differences in development among countries that fit these criteria. To the extent that the term *Third World* helps us to identify some common and salient features within this bloc, it can be fruitful.

The problem with the term *Third World* is that there are enormous differences between the countries of the Third World. Countries are at different plateaus of socioeconomic and political development. They also confront today's world from entirely different cultural milieus and political histories. To disregard history and culture in these countries would be a critical mistake.

In the process of emerging as nation-states, however, many countries have dealt with virtually the same political dilemmas. They have been coping with the issue of extreme heterogeneity in ethnic composition in an effort to gain political integration and national unity. They have been experiencing conflicting choices between pluralist and authoritarian political systems. They have, above all, seen a wide spectrum of ideology that has resulted in prolonged political disruption and social disintegration. The countries are different, but the problem they face is the same: the political consequences of modernization.

Analytical Framework

One part of my analysis is the link between democratization and the immediate protection of human rights. As noted earlier, the transition toward democratization, without well-established supporting institutions, is bound to exacerbate both socioeconomic and political problems. This study's analytical framework reinforces two widely shared propositions in the democratization literature: (1) While it is necessary to encourage the process of liberalization by implementing economic restructuring and expanding civil society, we should not equate democratization with the adoption of strictly Western values and structures; and (2) different types of democracy may surface in the process of a regime's transition. Given these propositions, I argue that liberalization plans, if properly designed and executed, are likely to lead to favorable conditions necessary for the effective functioning of a democratic system.

Consistent with the thrust of Robert Dahl's contention that "the most comprehensive systems of political rights and liberties exist in democratic countries," I support the premise that democratization and safeguarding human rights in the long run are mutually reinforcing practices.[48] While such a linkage appears valid prima facie, the evidence from the Third World does not substantiate the connection between "quick-fix" democratization and universal human rights. The ousting of the interim civilian government, the dissolution of the federal legislature, and the annulment of election results by General Sani Abacha in Nigeria on November 17, 1993, is but one example of an abrupt transition toward democracy that turned out to be counterproductive to human rights. Since 1993, with the election of Moshood Kashimawo Abiola as president and the annulment of the elections results by General Sani Abacha, Nigeria has experienced widespread human rights abuses and people have been striking to force the release of Abiola from prison. In August 1994, Nigeria's biggest union confederation called for a general strike to pressure the Abacha regime to release Abiola. Such strikes continue to have a destabilizing impact on the economy. It might be argued that liberalization provides a "golden mean" between democratization and basic rights protection. Liberalization is often more compatible with enhanced civil rights than a precarious, perilous, and sudden push for simple majority rule in Third World countries that have little or no historical preparation for democratic governance. This argument is not an apologetic exercise for the authoritarian policies or directions of Third World regimes. Rather, my intent is to illustrate how vital a role consensus building and/or national accommodation can play in the predemocratization process.

Historically, elections without broad consensus and tolerance have led to colossal difficulties. In the Third World, democratization, defined solely in terms of the "procedural minimum," falls well short of becoming coterminous with a greater recognition of human rights. Some writers assert that the burgeoning practice of competitive elections in the Third World (in Africa especially) alone will not rectify the widespread violation of human rights. An abrupt democratization may enhance unrealistic popular expectations at a time when governmental capabilities are declining. Moreover, ethnic and religious animosities can be inflamed in the process of electoral mobilization. To make a simple equation between sudden democratization and greater realization and protection of human rights is to make a fundamental error.[49]

One scholar has written that "human rights are not the equivalent of justice, or 'the good society,' or, as some think, democracy, although the human rights idea is related to all these."[50] The protection of basic human rights, not the promotion of swift democratization, should be the policy goal of the United States in the post–Cold War era. J. Bryan Hehir writes that, in much of the world, protecting human rights is a more precise, manageable, and direct objective than an over-the-horizon institutionalization of democracy and its ideal structures.[51] Donald Rothchild and John Ravenhill, in a critical assessment of U.S. policy toward Africa in the 1990s, argue that encouraging market-oriented economic reform might seem simultaneously compatible with promoting human rights and democratization on the continent. But there is a potential conflict—at least in the short and medium term—between economic liberalization and democratization. Structural adjustment involves the making of painful decisions, such as bringing about a reduction in budget deficits and expenditures on social programs and terminating government subsidies. These measures add to a popular discontent already provoked by a long period of economic decline. Democratization is certain to complicate governments' tasks as they face burgeoning demands for protection from the costs of adjustment. Thus, Rothchild and Ravenhill conclude:

> It may well be that full democratization will have to await the construction of a strong economic base, and it is to the latter that priority should be given. But if the United States chooses this alternative, it should not prevent the promotion of other dimensions of basic human rights throughout Africa.[52]

David Cingranelli has persuasively argued, albeit in a different context, that by emphasizing so emphatically the presence or absence of formal democratic institutions (for example, national elections) in places like El Salvador, Nicaragua, and Haiti, U.S. foreign policy has in the 1980s "appeared to be unconcerned about other kinds of human rights abuses by 'democratic' regimes."[53] Many have contended, appropriately, that the United States used elections in Central America as an anti–human rights device—promoting elections in El Salvador so that Congress would relinquish its pressures on the executive branch regarding summary executions, torture, and other egregious human rights abuses in that country. Additionally, elections by themselves are not a reliable indicator of improvements in the standard of living and have in numerous cases failed properly to address the living conditions of large segments of the populace (witness El Salvador since 1984).[54] In countries such as Angola, Ethiopia, and Ghana, democracy has not advanced beyond the holding of elections to validate the legitimacy of a dominant party already controlling the main government institutions.[55]

Notes

1. Lipset, "Some Social Requisites."
2. O'Donnell, Schmitter, and Whitehead, *Transition*.
3. Forsythe, *Human Rights and Development*.
4. Diamond, Linz, and Lipset, *Democracy*.
5. Huntington, *The Third Wave*.
6. Haggard and Kaufman, *Politics of Adjustment*.
7. Ibid., p. 348.
8. For an illuminating discussion on this subject, see Crystal, "Authoritarianism."
9. *Washington Post*, January 30, 1994, pp. H1, H5.
10. Quoted in *Washington Post*, January 30, 1994, pp. H1, H5.
11. George T. Kurian, ed., *The New Book of World Rankings*, New York: Facts On File, 1991. See p. 70.
12. Ibid., pp. 43–44.
13. Ibid., p. 46.
14. Ibid., pp. 232–233.
15. Weiner, "Empirical Democratic Theory." See p. 863.
16. Adam Przeworski, *Democracy and Market*. See p. 77.
17. Alfred Stepan, "Paths Toward Redemocratization: Theoretical and Comparative Considerations," in O'Donnell, Schmitter, and Whitehead, pp. 64–84. See pp. 73–75.
18. See Joan M. Nelson, "Poverty, Equity, and the Politics of Adjustment," in Haggard and Kaufman, *Politics of Adjustment*, pp. 221–269.
19. Focusing on a sample of twenty-three developing and middle-income countries outside of the Middle East, Haggard and Kaufman find that the economic structural adjustments of the 1980s led to regime changes only in countries that had a lower level of institutionalization and elite cohesion, irrespective of whether the regime was democratic or authoritarian. Haggard and Kaufman, *Politics of Adjustment*, pp. 324–328.
20. Rod Hague, Martin Harrop, and Shaun Breslin, *Political Science: A Comparative Introduction*, New York: St. Martin's Press, 1992. See pp. 39–40.
21. Huntington, *The Third Wave*, p. 9.
22. Przeworski, *Democracy and Market*, pp. 57–58.
23. Haggard and Kaufman, *Politics of Adjustment*, p. 332.
24. David Pool, "The Links." See pp. 47–51.
25. Ibid., p. 49.
26. Ibid., pp. 53–54.
27. Arat, *Democracy and Human Rights*.
28. Adam Przeworski, "Some Problems in the Study of the Transition to Democracy," in O'Donnell, Schmitter, and Whitehead, *Transition*, pp. 47–63. See p. 58.
29. J. A. Schumpeter, *Capitalism, Socialism, and Democracy*, London: Geo. Allen and Unwin, 1943; and Dahl, *Polyarchy*.
30. Terry Lynn Karl, "Dilemmas." See pp. 1–2.
31. Georg Sørensen, *Democracy and Democratization*, p. 43.

32. Ibid., p. 45.

33. Przeworski, 1991, *Democracy and Market,* p. 14.

34. Robert R. Kaufman, "Liberalization and Democratization in South America: Perspectives from the 1970s," in O'Donnell, Schmitter, and Whitehead, *Transition,* Vol. 3, pp. 85–107. See p. 106.

35. See Maurice Cranston, *What Are Human Rights?* London: The Bodley Head, 1973.

36. See, for example, Kothari, "North-South Issue."

37. See, for example, Shue, *Basic Rights.*

38. See, for example, Howard, "Cultural Absolutism."

39. *Facts on File*, Vol. 53, No. 2746, July 15, 1993, p. 516.

40. Ibid.

41. For further information on this topic, see *The Nation*, Vol. 257, No. 5, August 9, 1993, p. 161, where Gerald Piel defends the right to development, arguing that "history commends a first-things-first approach to the promotion of human rights. An examination of history that goes deep enough affirms the right to development as the original and truly universal human rights. . . . A right to development affirms the claim on that heritage of all to whom its denial precludes the practicability of purpose, even such as belongs to the very definition of their species."

42. Antonio Cassese, *Human Rights in a Changing World*, Philadelphia: Temple University Press, 1990.

43. For an excellent collection of articles on this subject, see Abdullahi Ahmed An-Na'im, ed., *Human Rights in Cross-Cultural Perspectives: A Quest For Consensus*, Philadelphia: University of Pennsylvania Press, 1991.

44. Donnelly and Howard, "Human Dignity, Human Rights."

45. Ibid., pp. 64–65.

46. Antonio Cassese, ed., *The International Fight Against Torture, La Lutte Internationale Contre La Torture*, Baden-Baden: Nomos, 1991. See also Karel Vasak and Philip Alston, *The International Dimensions of Human Rights*, Westport, CT: Greenwood Press, 1982. Two volumes.

47. In this book, Third World refers to non-Communist developing countries. Further, the terms *Third World countries, less developed countries (LDCs),* and *transitional societies* are used synonymously throughout.

48. Dahl, "Democracy and Human Rights."

49. Welch, "African Commission."

50. Henkin, "Universality." See p. 11.

51. Hehir, "United States and Human Rights." See pp. 252–253.

52. Rothchild and Ravenhill, "Retreat from Globalism." See pp. 412–413.

53. Cingranelli, *Ethics,* p. 214.

54. Tulchin and Bland, *Is There a Transition?* See p. 182.

55. See McColm, "Comparative Survey," p. 5.

CHAPTER 2

Human Rights Conditions and Democratization: Realities and Constraints

The obstacles to the realization of human rights and democratization in the Third World seem inexhaustible. Barriers that have long stood in the way of the effective implementation of human rights and the promotion of democratization continue to stand. Some of these constraints appear to be permanent, others do not. The end of the Cold War and the rising tides of democratization in the world since the 1980s have brought wide-ranging opportunities: political openings, electoral mobilizations, constitutional guarantees of fundamental human rights, and civil rights reforms. These opportunities, principally aimed at the renewal of civil society, have in several instances unleashed nostalgia for authoritarian order. Both the *obstacles* and the *opportunities* with respect to democratization and human rights need close scrutiny. This chapter addresses two themes: first, an identification of the various constraints on the protection of human rights in the Third World; and second, the limited prospects for the realization of human rights and democratization in the 1990s.

The major purpose of this chapter is to identify the sources of the restrictions. I do not attempt to analyze constraints using a developmental model or the dependency perspective. Given the diversity of the Third World countries, generalizations must be eclectic.

I demonstrate five types of constraints; namely, physical, structural, institutional-operational, cultural, and situational.[1] These categories are analytically different and distinct, although in both theory and practice they intersect at many points. Most of the constraints reflect politicoeconomic underdevelopment. It is necessary to acknowledge three limitations on identifying the constraints: (1) There are a great many curbs on human rights in the developing countries; (2) The temporal and spatial locations of these limits are hard to identify; and (3) Some of the generalizations regarding these constraints are made only after empirical investigation. In most developing countries, the combined characteristics of two or more of these categories of constraints are present at all times.

Physical Constraints

Physical constraints are the environmental, ecological, and geographical limitations of a given area. These constraints precede the human rights situation; they also develop from the exacerbation of human rights conditions. Poor soil, climate, and geography have made some Third World countries extremely vulnerable. These physical constraints restrict, to a large measure, the range of individual choice. Furthermore, internal sources of poverty (e.g., population pressure, low agricultural production, underutilization of labor, land, and capital, and structure of the economy) combined with a lack of infrastructure add to the difficulty of overcoming the forces of nature in these societies. The external sources of poverty are many and they are considered more fully later in this chapter.

The indigenous roots of poverty are often local physical conditions. Nature and poverty so pervasively dominate some societies that individuals can exert little control over their lives. Endemic poverty and uncertainty make change virtually impossible without some form of outside intervention—a scenario that was dramatically presented in the U.S. intervention in Somalia (Operation Restore Hope) in December 1992. The operation—morally defensible despite its shortcomings—was an effort to save the poor from starvation and clearly not to disarm the Somali gangs. Although little has been done to prevent the return of Somalia's warring factions, and although little if anything will be achieved in the long run as a result of the U.S. actions, the U.S. military presence achieved its limited goal of restoring some semblance of order prior to turning matters over to United Nations forces.[2] With no political settlement in sight, the United States finally pulled all remaining personnel out of Somalia in mid-September 1994. This will most likely expedite further international disengagement from Somalia. The United Nations Operations in Somalia (UNOSOM) is likely to speed up their withdrawal as the UN mandate expired on September 30, 1994.

While in the First and Second Worlds technology and cultural evolution have contained the cruelties of nature and poverty, this is not so in much of the Third World. Where poverty and nature have stubbornly prevailed, basic human needs are sometimes completely unsatisfied, and at best are satisfied only minimally. And this natural course of things in many parts of the Third World has facilitated the formation of coercive states. (The mechanisms involved in the emergence of these states can be discussed without elaborating on the origins of the states and the inevitability of political coercion.)[3]

In the poor and traditional countries of the developing world, sometimes called the Fourth World, the issue of political coercion is integrally related to mass poverty and the objective condition of life. (Before I pursue this point further, it should be noted that there are a few exceptions to this argument. Botswana and India are two such exceptions. Botswana, a landlocked and thinly populated southern African country, is one of the rare working democracies on the poor continent of Africa.) Theoretically, it seems plausible to espouse the view, as do Huntington and Nelson, that objective circumstances rather than placid acceptance of fate by the poor pave the way for, or even provoke, authoritarianism:

> In some nations widely dispersed settlement patterns and poor communications hamper political organization. In many areas laborers, tenants, sharecroppers, and smallholders alike depend on one or a few landlords, who are the sole source of wage employment, assistance in emergencies, brokerage with government officials, and other benefits. Thus, the rural poor are often more vulnerable to informal sanctions for maverick political behavior than are their urban counterparts, who have a wider range of alternative sources of employment, credit, emergency assistance, and brokerage . . . [thus] for most of the poor . . . political participation was and is, objectively, a difficult and probably ineffective means of coping with their problems or advancing their interests.[4]

There is a certain logic in the process. These conditions, in which people experience insecurity in terms of physical survival, lead to authoritarianism since satisfaction of basic needs is of disproportionate concern. Under such circumstances, the government draws preponderant support from the populace only if it does what it takes to guarantee survival. Doing so, the government gains legitimacy and authority. At this stage, legitimacy has no connection to ideology. As one observer has aptly remarked, "A bowl of rice is a bowl of rice to a hungry stomach irrespective of whether it is from a collective farm or the black market."[5]

Miserable living conditions have a discernible impact on tolerance for authoritarian politics. Lack of opposition to authoritarianism reflects to a large extent physical (as well as social) insecurity. In short, high risks discourage a person from taking chances, and paternalism precedes repression. The elite in a paternalistic society feel relatively secure and attempt to act efficiently. Often the elite do not intend to be repressive. It has been argued that in some societies, both traditional and modern, there exists a genuinely cooperative paternalism that operates on nonexploitative and reciprocal moral ground. An extension of this view argues that life in premodern societies was stable, consistent, and, more importantly, secure for both a majority of poor peasants and a wealthy elite: "Aristocracy cared for and looked after the peasants or serfs and managed their lives in a remarkably efficient manner, given the overall scarcity of goods for society generally."[6] Jack D. Douglas writes that this brand of paternalism "works as an insurance system in a very poor society beset by high risks, a society in which experience (of failure in revolution, to give one important example) has taught a fatalistic acceptance of dependent submission."[7] Some argue that benevolent paternalism may prove to be an appropriate remedy in some cases.[8] Conflictual paternalism, however, is authoritarian in nature, as evidenced through the emergence of the centristic-authoritarian forms of government; that is, the institutionalization of the coercive power in the poorest of the developing countries, a point to which I will return.

In those developing countries where government assistance is minimal, where people are not living at the so-called bare-subsistence level, the ability to survive without perpetual government aid leads people to adopt challenging and defiant attitudes. Government responses to such challenges may lead to the suspension of civil-political rights. The Afghanis' reactions to the Soviet invasion and open and violent disagreements with the regime in Haiti have illustrated such attitudes of challenge in countries suffering from a hostile environment and abject poverty. The poor in Haiti became more vocal and organized in pressing their demands and priorities.

In the developing countries, the living conditions noted above are different. But the fact cannot be denied that political repression is, among other things, a result of, as well as a cause of, the prevailing poverty and lack of development in these countries. Improved living conditions correlate inversely with levels of repression under these conditions. Hopkins's findings that poor countries are prone to military intervention[9] and Huntington's findings that "poverty is a principal—probably the principal—obstacle to democratic development"[10] are consistent with my thesis here. These causes of repression are related and are important even though there may also be other unidentified potential explanatory variables. There are still some Third World countries (e.g., Botswana and India) that, though they are among the low-income countries, have unusually good human rights records (civil-political rights), relative to other low-income developing countries.

Structural Constraints

Structural constraints are fabricated or induced by a complex and interrelated network of socioeconomic and political systems, both global and local. Some structural obstacles are internally induced; some are externally fabricated. They operate interactively in all Third World countries, in varying combinations. How to ascertain (1) the patterns of interaction between internal/external and (2) the cycles of constraints depends largely on how far back those patterns and sequences are extended. The validity of the arguments presented here rests on the distinction between internal and external sources of the structural constraints and their history. However, I do not attempt a lengthy history in this chapter; nor do I analyze the multiplicity of causes along fine lines. Rather, I *identify* those fetters that inhibit the realization of human rights.

Internal Structural Constraints

A brief and systematic review of many internal obstacles to human rights considerations in the Third World reveals recurring barriers that cut across most or all of the Third World and relate directly to social stratification and to inequality. Although it seems that some degree of social stratification and inequality is part of all human societies, high degrees of stratification place particularly heavy strains on human rights conditions in many developing countries. Many forces determine social structures in these countries. Social and class rigidity; dualism in society (as manifested in uneven geographical development); and patron-client networks—all these are important,[11] as are a complex array of rural development problems including difficulties related to land reforms and farming systems. For instance, whether farms are operated communally or as plantations is important. Many forces generate inequality: demographic pressures, material and labor scarcities, value-systems, patriarchal sociopolitical lifestyles, social and racial discriminations, and the distribution of social goods. Typical systems of stratification in the developing countries are based on ascribed and hierarchical substructures, such as tribe or social status—quite different from the situation in most developed countries, where stratification usually depends on merit, skill, and erudition. And this stratification is an important source of inequality and constraint on change.[12] Analysis of all the variables, though relevant, lies beyond the scope of this chapter. For present purposes, I focus on ascribed features of stratification systems, such as caste.

Social discrimination manifests itself structurally in the hierarchical caste system in India, in the legacy of apartheid in South Africa, in the tribalism that predominates in black Africa, and in the sexist, patriarchal, sociopolitical life of most Third World countries. These social discriminations have had the sanction of law until recently and they continue to be enforced by de facto, if not de jure, sanctions. S. M. Greenwold (1981), in a discussion of ascribed stratification in Nepal, writes that:

> Caste in Nepal was based upon the use of a ritually determined language, but this language was used for specific political purposes, to validate and reinforce the state's own political authority and to ensure the political stability of what was an initially fragile nation. Thus, caste became a matter of governmental concern. It was actual Nepalese law which determined the general outline of the caste hierarchy, and it was enacted Nepalese law which regulated the relations between castes. Moreover, not only was a caste hierarchy enforced by law, but the civil courts of the land were used to uphold and enforce such a law.[13]

Such a use of law to reinforce caste is typical in India and Nepal and continues to serve as a powerful source of social status alongside the current class structure. In India, the significance of the caste, which was the basic institution of traditional society, continues in the social spheres of life: caste affects marriage and the practice of dowry. Hence, it perpetuates indigenous structural curbs on women's rights. While acknowledging the social, economic, and political relevance of the caste system, especially for rural people, some human rights observers contend that (in the words of one of them) "the traditional coincidence of caste, class, and power is increasingly under attack, both indirectly through the processes of economic modernization and political democracy, and directly through political action by and on behalf of untouchables and other 'backward' or 'depressed' communities."[14]

It has been argued that strategies of democratization are largely influenced by the *social* environments of the political systems involved. Differences between societies render impossible a single, uniform strategy of democratization across the globe. Extrapolating from a set of empirical links among several variables drawn from a sample of 145 countries during the period of 1980–1990, Tatu Vanhanen concludes that the dispersion or concentration of economic, intellectual, and organizational power resources is the key factor shaping the social constraints on democratization. Vanhanen argues that

> the adaptation of political systems to environmental conditions means that power structures become adapted to resource structures. The concentration of power resources leads to autocratic political structures, whereas the wide distribution of the same resources makes the sharing of power and democracy possible.[15]

External Structural Constraints

The contemporary structural constraints in many Third World countries must be seen against the backdrop of colonialism and external influences associated with economic adjustment policies of the World Bank and International Monetary Fund (IMF). The colonial period, from A.D. 1500 to roughly the mid-twentieth century, involved economic, political, military, and even cultural penetration and domination in both latent and manifest forms. It shaped the history of many Third World countries through the introduction of intrusive modern technology, which was unresponsive to the needs of indigenous populations, and through disruptive and unequal rates of innovation and diffusion of Western cultural patterns and values. The persistence of colonial influences is reflected in the hegemonic structure of the international politicoeconomic order.

Many scholars believe that the key explanation for political coercion and repression must be sought in global linkages among societies.[16] Political instability is most evident in the transitional societies undergoing rapid economic growth. This stands in marked contrast with traditional societies, where social change and instability seem less obvious. In the transitional societies, the dynamics of economic growth (or, more accurately, industrial growth) are based on primary exports and so-called import substitution. Imports are oriented more toward gratifying the needs of the ruling elite for luxury and less toward availing a large fraction of the populace of the tangible gains of economic growth. Economic growth is therefore highly asymmetrical.

Structural inequality fueled by foreign-induced growth blocks autocentric and autodynamic growth,[17] generates relative and absolute poverty,[18] establishes exclusionary productive processes,[19] and helps to bring about intersectoral shifts in the structure of production. These changes correlate significantly with income inequality, and one might say they cause it.[20]

When a government is unable to deal with the uneven distribution of economic gains, geographical differentiation of economic opportunities, and increasing technological unemployment, the basis is laid for sustained deprivation and state coercion. Any political stability maintained by such a structure is not logically consistent and sustainable in the long run. The resultant uncertainty and instability can best be understood in relation to the interaction of, on one hand, global structure and, on the other, the mechanism of state sovereignty. In light of these inequalities, the status quo in many Third World nations was made possible through state-sponsored repression and the strengthening of the state's supreme authority in international arenas.[21] In countries like Brazil, Taiwan, South Korea, and Iran during the 1960s and 1970s, the authoritarian approaches of government were reinforced by both the state's free hand in economic modernization and its unquestioned authority in the global sphere.

A compromise between statist and hegemonic logic, to use Falk's ordering scheme, seems to have been at work here.[22] State sovereignty has some built-in features that ultimately lead to both stability and instability. State sovereignty advocates seek rational ideology, political legitimacy, and self-determination. A shield of sovereignty protects the ruling elites in many developing countries from exogenous penetration, however justifiable and humanitarian the intervention might be.

In recent years, as Pease and Forsythe note, while there has been a revolution regarding human rights in terms of legal theory and diplomatic practice, this revolution has yet to change the fact that state sovereignty has primacy in cases demanding forcible interference to safeguard individual rights.[23] Indigenous problems in the human rights area, shielded by state autonomy, remain stagnant unless configurations of internal forces create change. This feature of state sovereignty, along with the hegemonic world order, determines to a large extent the outcome of human rights issues in many developing countries. "In essence," writes Falk, "national political institutions both *reflect* and *shape* the international context."[24] This is paradoxical, yet understandable, given the problems of national unification, integration, and economic modernization in the developing nations.

The strength of the state machinery in newly emerged Third World countries creates an obvious problem: some of the virtues of national autonomy are also some of its vices. A case in point is the emergence of military or economic populism in Latin America as a response to economic underdevelopment and distorted economic systems. Populism refuted classical liberal political economy and attributed the lack of broad-based economic development to the inability of the states of Latin America to contain the impact of external forces. This inability caused populist advocates to contemplate ways of controlling the state, the local oligarchy, and external economic actors. "The real problem," writes James M. Malloy in behalf of the defenders of populism, "was to seize the state and create a base so as to render it capable of acting as an autonomous factor shaping both its internal and external environment rather than as a more or less passive instrumentality reflecting the push and pull of environment stimuli and pressures."[25] Nevertheless, the conflict between statist and populist forces persisted and eventually (as in Peru and Brazil) led to the formation of other types of populist governments, ranging from an implicitly democratic corporatism to explicit authoritarian corporatism.[26] Irrespective of the forms an authoritarian government assumed, whether populist, corporatist, technocratic, or some combination of these, the statist model seemed to be its prevailing feature.

The shocks of economic structural adjustment, along with the political influence of international creditors and multilateral financial agencies, have narrowed the range of sustainable policy choices available to many debtor nations in the Third World. These actors have adopted many measures that have considerably contained the domestic policy choices of Third World countries. These include high interest rates associated with the cost of servicing external debt, the withdrawal of foreign lending, the conditionality norm, and a wide-ranging leverage exercised by creditors through the financial, political, and ideological powers.[27] Although domestic characteristics of countries (such as government, ideology, regime type, interest-group organization and mobilization, and state capacity) help to mediate the impact of the international environment, the latter plays a crucial role in domestic transformation.[28]

Institutional-Operational Constraints

Although institutions are reflective of social structures, once implanted they generate their own, if not always independent, influences on societal values. According to Lucian W. Pye, the linkage between institutions and social settings is a circularity of relationships.[29] Institutional constraints are difficult to define precisely, insofar as they relate to or rest upon the structural constraints. I define institutional constraints as those restrictions affecting the major institutions within which behavioral patterns, interactions, customs, and traditions are being established and practiced. Operational constraints are closely related to institutional constraints. Operational constraints are those pressures that impede the normal functioning of institutions. Operational constraints prevent institutions from performing their functions. The sources of these obstacles can be sought in operations of the state, the military, the church, the party systems, or a prevailing religion. Sometimes semifeudal oligarchical institutions (e.g., land tenure; patron-client networks) generate operational restraints. I will not attempt here to rehearse at great length all of these factors, but a brief note on some may help.

The State

The developing countries can be characterized as traditional, modern authoritarian, and transitional systems. Whatever form they assume (whether praetorian, personalized, corporatist, populist, technocratic, or democratic), all operate under institutional limits. Some suffer from lack of effective institutions, others from a low level of institutionalization, still others from the absence of legitimate institutions capable of supporting political structures. In the absence of political establishments capable of regulating legal codes, rules, and behaviors, *authoritarian* regimes in the developing countries rely on the spoils, or on personalized and syncratic systems of relationships.[30] Under these circumstances, the authoritarian state grows out of (and despite) a lack of legitimacy and of the authority to carry on the task of national unification. The absence of law and of the legitimate and authoritative methods of resolving conflicts in politically underdeveloped and traditional societies results in praetorian politics.[31] In some Central American and African nations, such political arrangements are embedded in the culture of the society.[32] In those developing countries lacking orderly bargaining and consensus, which Chalmers refers to as "politicized societies,"[33] the reliance on a dominant executive system becomes a modus operandi. A wide range of social forces (including the military) determine the patterns of political participation in these societies.

An absence or paucity of institutionalization generates political instability, a distinguishing characteristic of *transitional* societies. Modernization studies have demonstrated that, as nations become more socially mobilized, mass political participation increases.[34] Mass communication, urbanization, secularization, and modern education increase political participation and mass involvement in politics. Social mobilization generates increasing demands upon the government by newly mobilized and politically relevant strata of society. Failure to respond to the increasing burdens put upon government by the process of social mobilization is, in Deutsch's words, likely to result in a situation in which the regime's subjects "will cease to identify themselves with it psychologically."[35] The government, writes Deutsch, "will be reduced to ruling by force where it can no longer rule by display, example, and persuasion."[36]

The growth in the size of modern states is a function of social mobilization. The increase in the size of transitional societies, however, has yet to enhance their ability to respond effectively to the needs and expectations of large segments of their populaces. Utilizing Huntington's hypothesis, Hibbs writes that increases in the ratio of social mobilization to institutionalization generate burdens that may surpass the capabilities of institutions. Thus elites may perceive the situation as threatening.[37] Consequently, governmental repression and liberalization may be perceived not as moral opposites but as equally viable alternative modes of social control and adjustment. If the latter mode is adopted, through either grudging concessions by or the wilful acts of leaders, drastic political openings and economic liberalization can lead to spiraling demands and unsettling impacts on the very government responsible for initiating those measures. The upshot might very well be a series of swings of the pendulum of policy between liberalization and repression.

Another factor is the development of military technologies. Extensive coercive forces are now available to ruling elites and repressive social control has grown dramatically. Clearly, the availability of military hardware to security forces has facilitated repression in the Third World. The supply of police weapons through commercial sales programs and military assistance to authoritarian regimes has inclined ruling elites toward policies of repression.[38]

To be sure, some have viewed government repression as an inevitable response to, or a precaution against, internal instability. In the words of one observer, "maintaining a strong coercive capability is one way regimes in transitional societies undergoing rapid social mobilization are able to neutralize the accompanying instabilities."[39] Nonetheless, the application of repressive measures in response to political instability and the elite's insecurity tends to breed more instability in the long run, blocking effective operations within the state.[40]

The Military

Effective autonomous political institutions reflect the popular will; constitutional laws display the foundation of civil society. Civility also requires a supportive political orientation, especially a society's belief in its government structures. In the absence of such conditions, distrust and alienation are institutionalized and force becomes the source of conformity. Government coercion, as manifest in the role of the military in domestic politics, seeks legitimation in many ways. Some have defended the role of the military because it is a modernizing agent.[41] Others argue that the military lacks legal authority, and that military rule prevents legitimacy from evolving.[42]

Gavin Kennedy, having examined the distribution of coups and attempted coups in Asia, Africa and the Middle East between 1945 and 1972, concludes that military intervention exacerbates crises of legitimacy.[43] Miles D. Wolpin, while not justifying the role of military on the grounds that they are modernizers, points out that military regimes of different kinds "have in most cases failed to acquire legitimacy because of their incapacity to fulfill either . . . democratic procedural or substantive goals."[44] The evidence suggests that military institutions regularly become constraints on the promotion of human rights conditions if the military's policies do not lead to the fulfillment of popular expectations or to the generation of popular support.

Recently, sweeping democratic reforms in many transitional Third World countries have spawned a daunting array of challenges for the governments involved. The difficulties of managing political and economic reforms resurrect the familiar dilemma: What role will there be for the military in the transition process? Government inevitably seeks peaceful reconciliation with the armed forces. This presumes that the armed forces are a potent political actor. In some cases, the military has, however irregularly, promoted civil society. This has been the case in Brazil, Chile, Guatemala, Côte d' Ivoire, Peru, and Sierra Leone. In other cases (Kenya and Ghana) the military is showing signs of flexibility. Algeria, Haiti, Madagascar, and Sudan have reverted to authoritarianism. In these countries, the armed forces have a sustained role in politics.

The continuing poverty and inequality in many Third World countries undermines the regimes in both the short and long terms and paves the way for an active role for the armed forces in national politics. That Central Americans have turned to their armies many times since the democratic reforms of the mid-1980s suggests that the existing structural problems such as poverty and economic inequality are unabated. There is ample room for the military to maneuver its way back into politics.

Religion

Religion is normally an integrating force in society. How and under what conditions it is a disruptive force and when it may impede cultural change and the betterment of life are questions worth studying. Such investigations, however, exceed the scope of this chapter.

The evidence connecting religion to social change is mixed and nebulous. William C. Shepherd offers a typical view. He writes that religions, by making tribal folkways sacred, limit social change and provoke ethnocentrism, adding however, that "religions also function to dull the hard edges of individual egocentrism and to encourage the social cooperation vital to civilization at all."[45] It appears that religions in the Third World, while having very different histories, have been influential in promoting mass mobilization and politicization. These religions have had a role in secular politics and have influenced the process of social change.[46] But the nature of this role is immensely varied and inconsistent.

Donald Eugene Smith writes that "the religious factor has been relatively more important in the mass politicization of Hindu, Buddhist, and Muslim societies. . . . For four and a half centuries, Latin American rulers and ruled have shared a common Catholic faith. By contrast, nationalist struggles in Asia and Africa took the form of Hindu, Buddhist, and Muslim mass movements in opposition to Christian colonial governments."[47] Religion has typically upheld the status quo, but the evolution of "liberation theology" in the Third World[48] and the mobilizing role of religious bodies to challenge injustice in the Middle

East and Latin America point to a radical role for religion.[49]

Ted R. Gurr, who documents 233 politically active communal groups in ninety-three countries, explores the link between religion and ethnic strife. He poses a key question: "How serious is religiously based communal conflict?" Gurr's findings indicate that religious rifts are at most a contributing factor in communal conflict; hardly, if ever, are they the root cause:

> Only eight of the forty-nine militant sects in the study are defined solely or mainly by their religious beliefs. Examples are the politically mobilized Shi'i communities in Iraq and Lebanon, whose goals are political rights and recognition, not propagation of their faith. The other sectarian minorities also have class identifications, such as the Catholics of Northern Ireland and Turkish immigrants in Germany, or nationalist objectives, such as the Palestinians in Israel's Occupied Territories and the Moros in the Philippines. The driving force of the most serious and protracted communal conflicts in the Middle East is not militant Islam but the unsatisfied nationalist aspirations of the Kurds and Palestinians.[50]

Gurr's overall findings suggest that "groups defined wholly or in part along lines of religious cleavage accounted for one-quarter of the magnitude of rebellions in the 1980s by all groups in the study."[51] Gurr's analysis does not bode well for arguments made by Huntington, who gives religion the central role in his so-called "Clash of Civilizations" paradigm. Huntington argues that world politics is entering a new phase, in which the fundamental source of conflict in the post–Cold War world will be, not primarily ideological or economic, but cultural. Future conflicts, he stresses, will occur between nations and groups of different civilizations and the fault lines between civilizations will be the battle lines of the future.[52]

Deeper probing into the world's religions makes it evident that some religious values can mesh with universal human rights and democratic values. In a broad sense, all religions of the world have some precepts that are compatible with democracy and individual rights and some that are not. Egalitarianism, charitable obligations, personal responsibility, and collective moral standards are elements that are consistent with the realization of human rights and the enhancement of democratic infrastructures. By contrast, many religious doctrines inhibit the exercise of certain human rights and the effective functioning of democracy; for example, the acceptance of the social hierarchy in both orthodox Christianity and Judaism; limits on apostasy and gender inequality in orthodox Islam; the consensual—not adversarial—governing patterns in Confucianist societies, the perceived social roles and expectations based on gender distinctions in Southeast Asian traditions of Buddhism; and the submissive attitudes required of women under Hinduism. All of these bear witness to the incongruities at play.

The essential question, therefore, concerns the reconciliation of religious precepts with the upsurge in demands for modern protection of human rights. How does one attempt to harmonize religious morals with the dicta of modern society? Some common grounds seem to be both logical and possible. In reality, writes Ann Elizabeth Mayer, an expert in Islamic and comparative law, one cannot foretell the position that a person will adopt concerning a human rights problem solely on the basis of the person's religious affiliation—and this is true of members of all faiths.[53] The relationship of religion to the protection of human rights and the adoption of democratic reforms is complicated. Scholarly reflection is mixed. The topic needs further, more detailed, investigation.

The Bureaucracy

In many transitional Third World regimes, bureaucracy occupies an important position in the process of socioeconomic modernization and nation-building, providing an instrument for building consensus. It is not clear to what extent corruption and inefficiency in bureaucracies is a legacy of colonialism, but they clearly have created a subculture. S. C. Dube suggests that bureaucracy "had a class bias and it tended to have a stratification of its own; its upper crust functioned as a privileged class."[54] Fred W. Riggs rightly contends that rapid growth of the bureaucracy does not correlate to growth in popular control over government.[55] Dominant bureaucracies are capable of stifling the growth of democratic infrastructure.[56] There is a great deal of evidence that bureaucratic systems do not guarantee reasonable access to the political process. In some cases, bureaucracy (military or civil) has led to the strengthening of central bureaucratic administration at the expense of local self-government, culminating in further control of the political system by bureaucrats (consider, for example, the strong bureaucracies in Egypt, Sudan, and Pakistan). Further, bureaucracies of assorted kinds in the Third World have assisted the expansion and intrusion of state influence in socioeconomic life but have not produced appropriate institutional arrangements to improve living conditions.

Cultural Constraints

Cultural constraints are obstacles to cultural cohesion and integration and to the process of social change. They are associated with ethnicity and nationality. Cultural constraints, elusive and difficult to study, are nevertheless important influences on human rights conditions. Rightly or wrongly, they have received little treatment in the theoretical literature.

In seeking to determine the cultural origins of economic growth and development, social scientists have emphasized several features. Among the preconditions for industrialization, democratization, and development are listed achievement motivation, the right orientations and attitudes, specific ethics, and suitable legal traditions. Other scholars have strongly criticized these positions, explicitly emphasizing the role of structural conditions. I emphasize cultural and subcultural cleavages based on ethnicity and nationality because these features affect political stability and the presence (or absence) of democratization. Third World countries generally are heterogeneous. In many states, ethnic discord impedes national unity and societal and cultural integration and, in most of these societies, this contributes to political instability.[57]

Instead of stressing cultural and ethnic differences, some analysts identify the causes of political tensions as inequality of benefit from and access to economic modernization.[58] While analyzing primordialist and instrumentalist interpretations of ethnicity, Ted R. Gurr argues that economic differentials are more important than political ones. Access to political rights for disadvantaged minority and ethnic groups has failed to eliminate economic inequalities.[59] Economic discrimination weighs most heavily on indigenous peoples and ethnoclasses.[60] Here Gurr stresses that, whereas in advanced industrial democracies as well as in strong states the opportunity structure for communal groups provides incentives for political protests and disincentives for rebellion, in the Third World the success of democratization in general (and its impact in the sense of diminishing communal conflicts) is problematic. Gurr writes: "The most dubious expectation of all is that authoritarian states such as Sudan, Iraq, and Burma might be able to defuse ethnopolitical wars by moving toward democracy."[61] This is so simply because these countries lack the resources and industrial means needed to facilitate the accommodations found in established democracies. In such circumstances, Gurr notes, democratization is likely to precipitate both protest and rebellion, leading, in some cases to civil war and the reimposition of autocratic rule.[62]

Another observer is concerned that "social heterogeneity and social inequality constitute strains that are likely to influence the process and condition of institutionalization."[63] Given the linkage between political instability and low levels of institutionalization, it seems to follow that social heterogeneity and inequality will adversely affect democratic institutions and values. Whatever the connection between ethnic diversity and instability, ethnic loyalty is a factor in authoritarian rule in developing countries and one can ill-afford to underrate its influence. In some cases, the contribution of ethnic bigotry to societal disintegration and political instability is ostensible, for example, Hindu extremism in India, the Serbs' outrageous "ethnic cleansing" in Bosnia, and the ethnic massacres in Rwanda.

Here, a caveat: Although disintegrative ethnic policies often cause instability and, consequently, governmental repression, the absence of ethnic tension is not a sign of democratization. Ethnic diversity does not account for all repression. Nation-building in South Korea is presently immune from the issue of ethnic diversity, South Korea being among the most ethnically homogeneous nations of the world. At the same time, its regimes have been repressive. No causal link between ethnic diversity and governmental repression has ever been established. Tensions among ethnic groups contending for political power, when temperate and controlled, are not of themselves unhealthy and need not produce fractures in the body politic.

Ethnic parochialism, however, is dangerous and its link to human rights abuse is clear from the evidence. One must go beyond the internal approach to ethnic diversity since ethnic agitation cannot strictly be divorced from the colonial legacy. It can be adequately analyzed only within a wider context of social change. Its political consequences are manifested in the nationalism and the aspirations for self-determination of modernizing developing countries.[64] With the rise of nationalism and self-determination, ethnicity has become politically relevant in ways that it was not under colonialism.[65]

Separatist aspirations for self-determination, often given impetus by modernization and/or industrialization, are invariably taken by those in authority as an antiestablishment menace and as a threat to the integrity of the multiethnic state.[66] This is evidenced by the secessionist aspirations of the Kurds in Iraq, the Sikhs in India, the Ibos in Nigeria, and the Bengalis in Pakistan (who separated from East Pakistan in 1971 to form what is known today as Bangladesh).[67] Cruel interethnic conflicts in Burma, Bangladesh, Biafra, Sudan, Rwanda, Burundi, Iraq, Sri Lanka, Pakistan, and India have posed and still pose threats to the stability, and in some cases the viability, of these states.[68] Ethnic conflict threatens any heterogeneous state that is susceptible to riot and rebellion.[69]

The dangers of ethnic cleavages and the resultant social tension, violence, conflict, and dismemberment loom especially large in the minds of ruling elites. The instability aroused by such tensions leads to repressive sanctions. Interethnic struggles often revolve around politicoeconomic sources of power and autonomy, and ethnic cleavages linked to ideological and political divisions are profoundly unsettling. To the extent that ethnic diversity culminates in ethnic separatism, ethnic diversity is linked to government intolerance.

Further, the role of religion, language, and nationalism in exacerbating ethnic and other conflicts should not be underestimated. These, too, are an integral part of any analysis of cultural constraints. India, which has a very complex ethnic configuration, is a relatively stable country with lower degrees of government repression than much of the Third World. The common adherence to Hinduism by the overwhelming majority of the Indian population is held to have had a moderating influence on the divisive tendencies of ethnic groups in India.[70] The communal strife that broke out in the aftermath of the demolition of the Babri Mosque (December 6, 1992) by Hindu fanatics in the northern city of Ayodhya, sent unsettling waves throughout urban India. This strife has the potential dreadfully to undermine the secular democracy practiced in India since partition in 1947. India's attention in recent years has shifted from the Ayodhya destruction to regional security problems, such as the crisis in Kashmir, which is also a function of ethnic, territorial, and irredentist conflicts. The June 19, 1994, assassination of the influential Muslim cleric Qazi Nissar Ahmed in Kashmir has prompted a series of assassination attempts in the country. Delhi has become preoccupied with the prospect of further ethnic turmoil aimed at seeking self-rule from the federal government. In West Africa, Islam and Christianity have subdued centrifugal tendencies among ethnic groups, as have linguistic integration and nationalistic aspirations and unity.[71]

In this context of identifying cultural constraints, the specific features of each religion also merit consideration. Religious dogma, it is argued, explicitly circumscribe the extent to which individuals can exercise autonomous choice. As noted earlier, Islamic orthodoxy restricts apostasy and generates harsh jurisprudence in traditional Islamic societies.[72] The strict abortion and divorce laws of the Roman Catholic Church affect Latin American societies. Many traditional African countries accept polygyny and other customs that have political ramifications. In an obviously slanted view of Islam, Max Weber attempts to draw a linkage between religion and political coercion:

> Religion makes obligatory the violent propagandizing of a true prophecy which consciously eschews universal conversion and enjoys the subjugation of unbelievers under the dominion of a ruling class dedicated to the religious war as one of the basic postulates of its faith, without however recognizing the salvation of the subjugated. The practice of coercion poses no problem, since God is pleased by the forcible dominion of the faithful over the infidels, who are tolerated once they have been subjugated.[73]

Failing to make a distinction between orthodox and modern thinking in Islam, Weber's one-sided views are woefully inadequate. Further, the logic of such a statement is hampered by cultural relativism and the difficulties inherent in the related moral and value judgments.[74] In all religious schools, there are teachings on the connection between morality and culture.[75] We need more study of and debate about religion as a source of cultural constraints and commonalities in the observation of human rights in the Third World.

Situational Constraints

Situational constraints are specific sets of social or interpersonal conditions that limit the range of choices available to individuals and to society at large. Situational constraints sometimes reflect specific domestic problems: internal economic crisis; an elite's idiosyncratic style of leadership; elite fragmentation; factional strife within the military or the political elite; and the intelligence operations—all these factors affect human rights and democratization.

External situations also can become constraints. War, border disputes, market fluctuations, military coups in neighboring countries, and external intervention may trigger repressive reactions. The coercive measures adopted by the local power elite in these circumstances are, of course, considered to be the sine qua non for the elite's political survival, but they usually fail to resolve the situational crises. Examples are the emergency rule in India (1975–1976) and in South Korea (1977), and the declaring of martial law in the Philippines (1973), Chile (1973), and Iran (1978–1979).

David Scott Palmer, in searching for explanations of authoritarianism in Spanish America, writes that "it is also possible that there may be idiosyncratic forces at work within particular Spanish American countries, such as economic crises, immigration, political movements, wars, regional variations, or individual caudillos."[76] To what extent the prevalence of authoritarian regimes is related to these factors and what impact these constraints exert on human rights and democratization in the Third World countries is by no means obvious.

Huntington and Nelson appear to have given due weight to situational constraints when accounting for political participation in some Third World countries:

> The level and forms of participation in a society during any period are affected by communal tensions that may be unrelated or only peripherally related to modernization, by the attitudes and policies of political elites, and by contingencies such as droughts or border disputes. These and many other factors may produce far greater or far less participation than the country's degree of social and economic modernization would lead one to expect.[77]

No matter what approach is adopted toward the social change, it is evident that the decisions of elites are important in shaping local conditions. Huntington and Nelson believe that the choices and attitudes of elites toward political participation and other goals are indeed the most powerful determinants of the extent and nature of political participation in a society at any given time.[78] Although the trade-off between economic and political conditions in the Third World complicates evaluation of the state of human rights,[79] it should be noted that in some cases, (e.g., Colombia, Costa Rica, and Mexico) the ability to avoid extreme repression has not prevented them from achieving good rates of economic growth.[80] This indicates that the adoption of highly repressive measures by some Third World leaders cannot be vindicated in the name of economic growth.

Huntington identifies the absence or weakness of real commitment to democratic values among political leaders of the Third World countries as a major impediment to democratization:

> Political leaders out of office have good reason to advocate democracy. The test of their democratic commitment comes when they are in office. In Latin America democratic regimes were normally overthrown by military coup d'etat. This also, of course, happened in Asia and the Middle East. In those regions, however, elected leaders themselves were also responsible for ending democracy: Syngman Rhee and Park Chung Hee in Korea; Adnan Menderes in Turkey; Ferdinand Marcos in the Philippines; Lee Kwan Yew in Singapore; Indira Gandhi in India; Sukarno in Indonesia.[81]

It is hard to imagine any successful democratization without leaders firmly committed to democratic values and practices. Liberalization in some Third World countries has led to the promise of sustained political openings in the future. Jordan, Côte d'Ivoire, Zambia, and Mexico may see the emergence of restricted types of democracies in the not too distant future.

Prospects in the 1990s

The decade of the 1990s—now nearing midterm—still offers new opportunities for human rights improvement in many Third World countries; yet these opportunities may well be lost if constraints and realities are not carefully examined. New global paradigms have affected politics and the internationalization of human rights standards may have made improvement a legitimate and realistic expectation. Stephen P. Marks links the debate on the internationalization of human rights to the political texture of changing world politics: "East-West and North-South relations determine, in large measure, the limits of the possibilities in promoting human rights. The shifts and transformations of these two international conflict formations continue to affect the province and function of human rights in the 1990s."[82] I concur with this statement, but the results of the human rights battle in many Third World countries remain unclear.

The Soviet Union and the Socialist camp have dissolved. The end of the crusade against Communist subversion, the burgeoning rancor against authoritarianism of the right and left, the transformation of East-West ties, and the shifting global geopolitics and political economy will have enormous effects on Third World nations. The idea of structural reforms in the post–Cold War era is noble, but its implementation demands long-term strategic planning for which many Third World countries are ill-prepared. The response by some African leaders to internal and external pressures for democratization, in the words of Rothchild and Ravenhill, has been "cautiously positive: In Côte d'Ivoire, Gabon, Benin, Tanzania, Mozambique, Zambia, and Zaire governments have scheduled multiparty elections or indicated a willingness to consider the legalization of opposition parties."[83]

Nonetheless, to promote a democratic agenda of any sort in the Third World is to encounter inherent and contextual difficulties surrounding the human rights conditions of these societies. The end of the Cold War may have opened up new opportunities for a better understanding of human rights obstacles, but the unreasonable proclivity for programs with drastic alterations may bring about unexpected degrees of resistance and political opposition. It is clear that there is potential tension—at least in the short and medium terms—between economic liberalization and democratization.[84]

In the Third World, priority should be given to building up and reforming the infrastructure, a vital condition if democratization is to be maintained.

Basic structures that limit human rights must effectively be dealt with throughout the Third World prior to transitions to democracy. Any initiative for the improvement of human rights should thus begin with small, measured adjustments. Many countries lack the economic, political, cultural, and military capacities to endure large scale and wide-ranging changes. For small adjustments to take root and succeed, the countries need to address an array of constraints symptomatic of underdevelopment, poverty, inequality, and in-competent, vacillating leadership. Democracy does not run on empty bellies: some degree of economic reform and liberalization precedes democratization. Economic reforms and development promote the possibility of democratiza-tion through widespread education, communication, sense of national unity and identity, and political participation. Economic reform and development are a foundation for the protection of human rights and fundamental freedom. Arguing that cultures historically are dynamic, Huntington concludes that economic development is a primary force for cultural and religious evolution. This has been the key to Roman Catholicism's evolution in the 1970s and 1980s. Islam and Confucianism will have to cede comparable changes.[85]

There are no easy or simple solutions nor cost-free ways to handle these constraints, and it may well be that some constraints will not weaken in the short run. Some have pointed to the artificial distinction between civil-political rights and socioeconomic and cultural rights, arguing for an integrated ap-proach. This has appeal, but such an approach must be sensitive to the existence of constraints. Since a comprehensive set of human rights reforms has not been accomplished even in most developed nations, we are justified in separating *desirability* from *feasibility*.

This is not to imply that civil-political rights come after development is fully achieved or that economic development is the sole guarantor of human rights.[86] Rather, I would argue that, in the absence of economic reforms, political reforms carry little weight. Recent human rights literature agrees that some kind of institutional reform in state apparatus and political process is crucial for the improvement of human rights conditions. In a transition to democracy, basic developmental achievements and balanced liberalization are needed too.

Conclusion

It is clear that the capacity of the Third World governments to protect human rights depends largely on how the various constraints interact with one another and on how they can be dealt with by policy, strategy, and leaders. Structural obstacles in many of these societies limit the choices available to local policymakers. A structural setting that promotes an arms race, local and regional militarism, and civil disorder and strife imposes a huge barrier on Third World human rights conditions. Institutional-operational constraints are inevitable, given the fact that economic liberalization appears, at early or even intermediate stages, to be inconsistent with democratization. At later stages of economic reform, development and modernization, my argument corresponds to the conventional proposition that economic liberalization increases over time the possibility of transition toward democracy.[87]

Cultural constraints can be eliminated over time through the political management of cultural and subcultural cleavages, mostly by implementing effective distribution of power, wealth, and status among different ethnic groups. Situational constraints are also connected to the structural, operational, and cultural constraints. Hence, the susceptibility of the developing nations to global, regional, and local crises can be drastically curtailed if other obstacles can be held in check. A Third World country that is economically strong and politically unified deters external intervention and enjoys a higher degree of political stability. The case of ministates (e.g., tiny states in the Gulf, such as Kuwait, Qatar, and Bahrain) is an exception.

Structural change does not in itself guarantee improvement in human rights conditions. Similarly, structural stasis precludes political change. I support Miles Wolpin's view that rapid progress in socioeconomic conditions may "enhance the feasibility, if not certainty, of long-term tolerance and respect for political dissent."[88] Finally, the clear policy implication to be derived from the arguments offered above is that, in the post–Cold War era, human rights will assume more prominence than they have done previously. Today, human rights–derived considerations seem to have a better chance of moving up the international political ladder of priority and of injecting themselves into foreign policy agendas. Nonetheless, the realities of Third World societies suggest that the rhetoric of the "new world order" and the actual outcome of so-called economic interdependence may not necessarily optimize human right conditions in the 1990s unless Third World leaders make their structural and monetary reforms overlap. To this subject we turn in Chapter 3.

Notes

1. For the purposes of this book, a constraint on human rights may be defined as the existence of conditions (underdevelopment, repression, dependency, etc.) or the absence of conditions (democratic institutions, rules, equitable distribution of resources, national unification, etc.) that deprive an individual from fulfilling his or her objectives. Caution must be exercised in not defining these constraints along a particular line. As Hirschman (1965) demonstrates, an alleged obstacle (i.e., the extended family) in one situation may turn into an asset in another. See Albert O. Hirschman, "Obstacles to Development: A Classification and a Quasi-Vanishing Act," *Economic Development and Cultural Change,* July 1965, pp. 385–389.

2. For a critical view on the nature of Operation Restore Hope in Somalia, see Edward Luttwak, "Unconventional Force," *New Republic,* Vol. 208, No. 4, January 25, 1993, pp. 22–23.

3. An interesting and stimulating look at the theory of the origin of the state, albeit

from a substantially different perspective, has been provided by Robert L. Carneiro, "A Theory of the Origin of the State." He argues that warfare has played a decisive role in the rise of the state. "Historical or archeological evidence of war is found in the early stages of state formation in Mesopotamia, Egypt, India, China, Japan, Greece, Rome, Northern Europe, Central Africa, Polynesia, Middle America, Peru, and Colombia, to name only the most prominent examples"; in Peter J. Richardson and James McEvoy III, eds., *Human Ecology: An Environmental Approach,* Belmont, CA.: Wadsworth, 1976: 239–249; esp. 241.

4. Huntington and Nelson, *No Easy Choice,* p. 119.

5. Park, *Human Needs,* p. 138.

6. Robert P. Clark, *Power and Policy,* p. 4.

7. Douglas, "Cooperative versus Conflictual." See p. 188.

8. Donald H. Regan, "Paternalism, Freedom, Identity, and Commitment," in Rolf Sartorious, ed., pp. 113–138.

9. K. Hopkins, "Civil-Military Relations in Developing Countries," *British Journal of Sociology.* Vol. 17, No. 2, June 1966; see p. 175.

10. Samuel P. Huntington, "A New Era in Democracy: Democracy's Third Wave," in Soe, *Comparative Politics,* 1993.

11. On the relevance of clientelist politics to urban life see Huntington and Nelson, *No Easy Choice,* 1976, especially p. 128. Also on the relevance of clientelist politics to the peasant-based societies see John Duncan Powell, "Peasant Society and Clientelist Politics" *American Political Science Review,* Vol. 64, June 1970, pp. 411–425.

12. Eckstein and Gurr, *Patterns of Authority,* 1975, see p. 416.

13. See S. M. Greenwold "Caste: Moral Structure and Social System of Control," in Mayer, *Culture and Morality,* 1981, p. 102.

14. Donnelly, *Universal Human Rights,* 1989, pp. 125–142, see p. 137.

15. Tatu Vanhanen, "Social Constraints of Democratization," in Vanhanen, ed., *Strategies of Democratization,* 1992, p. 21.

16. See the following sources; O'Donnell, *Modernization and Bureaucratic-Authoritarianism,* 1973. Klare and Arnson, *Supplying Repression,* 1981. Wai, "Human Rights in Sub-Saharan Africa," in Pollis and Schwab, *Human Rights,* 1979. Andre Gunder Frank, "Unequal Accumulation: Intermediate, Semi-Peripheral, and Sub-Imperialist Economies," *Review,* 1979, Vol. 11, No. 3, winter, pp. 281–350. Amin, *Unequal Development,* 1976. Frank, *Crises,* 1981. Richard A. Falk, "Militarization and Human Rights in the Third World," *Bulletin of Peace Proposals,* 1977, Vol. 8, No. 3, pp. 220–232. Celso Furtado, "The Post–1964 Brazilian 'Model' of Development." *Studies in Comparative International Development,* 1973, Vol. 8, No. 2, summer, pp. 115–127. Richard A. Falk, "Comparative Protection of Human Rights in Capitalist and Socialist Third World Countries," in Falk, *Human Rights.* Galtung, *The True Worlds,* 1980. Kenneth Bollen, 1983, "World System Position, Dependency, and Democracy: The Cross-National Evidence," *American Sociological Review,* Vol. 48, August, 1983, pp. 468–479. Michael Timberlake and Kirk R. Williams, "Dependence, Political Exclusion, and Government Repression: Some Cross-National Evidence," in *American Sociological Review,* Vol. 49, No. 1, February 1984, pp. 141–146. Immanuel Wallerstein "The Present State of Debate on World Inequality," in Wallerstein, *World Inequality,* 1975. Girling, *America and the Third World,* 1980.

17. Amin, *Unequal Development,* op. cit., 1976.

18. Adelman and Morris, *Economic Growth.*

19. Frank, op. cit., 1979.

20. Ahlluwalia, "Inequality."

21. See Ted C. Lewellen, "Structures of Terror: A Systems Analysis of Repression in El Salvador," in George W. Shepherd, Jr., and Ved P. Nanda, eds., *Human Rights and Third World Development,* Westport, CT: Greenwood Press, 1985, pp. 59–81. Also

Gordon L. Bowen, "The Political Economy of State Terrorism: Barrier to Human Rights in Guatemala," in Shepherd and Nanda, op. cit., pp. 83–124.

22. Falk, *Human Rights*, p. 47.

23. Kelly Kate Pease and David P. Forsythe, "Human Rights, Humanitarian Intervention, and World Politics," *Human Rights Quarterly*, Vol. 15, No. 2, May 1993, pp. 290–314; see p. 314.

24. Falk, *Human Rights*, p. 63.

25. James M. Malloy, "Authoritarianism and Corporatism in Latin America: The Modal Pattern," in J. M. Malloy, ed., *Authoritarianism and Corporatism in Latin America*, Pennsylvania: University of Pittsburgh Press, 1977, p. 13.

26. Ibid., p. 17.

27. See Barbara Stallings, "International Influence on Economic Policy: Debt, Stabilization, and Structural Reform," in Haggard and Kaufman, eds., *Politics of Adjustment*, pp. 41–88.

28. Ibid., pp. 87–88.

29. Pye, "Armies."

30. Organski, *Stages of Political Development*.

31. Weiner and La Palombara, by highlighting the two cases of India and Indonesia, exemplify this point. They write that "in India for example the presence of a decentralized broad-based Congress Party functioning in a federal system has meant that disputes could be fought out at local and state level without endangering the stability of the central government. In contrast, the absence of an acceptable procedure for the settlement of inter-island conflict within Indonesia culminated in the eruption of a civil struggle." See Myron Weiner and Joseph La Palombara, "The Impact of Parties on Political Development," in Finkle and Gable, eds. *Political Development and Social Change*, New York: John Wiley, 1971, pp. 485–502. See p. 499.

32. Huntington, *Political Order*. See pp. 196–237.

33. Chalmers, "The Politicized State."

34. Deutch, *Tides Among Nations*, p. 282.

35. Karl W. Deutsch, "Social Mobilization and Political Development." *American Political Science Review*, Vol. 55, 1979, pp. 493–514. See p. 502.

36. Ibid., p. 502.

37. Douglas A. Hibbs, *Mass Political Violence: A Cross-National Causal Analysis*, New York: John Wiley, 1973, p. 11.

38. See esp. Michael T. Klare and Cynthia Arnson, *Supplying Repression: U.S. Support for Authoritarian Regimes Abroad*, Washington, D.C.: Institute for Foreign Policy Studies, 1981.

39. Ake Claude, quoted in Hibbs, op. cit., p. 82.

40. For empirical evidence on the relationship between coerciveness level and political instability, see I. K. Feierabend, B. Nesvold, and R. L. Feierabend, "Political Coerciveness and Turmoil: A Cross-National Inquiry," *Law and Society Review*, Vol. 5, No. 1, August 1970, pp. 93–134; and I. K. Feierabend and R. L. Feierabend, "Coerciveness and Change: Cross-National Trends," *American Behavioral Scientist*, Vol. 15, No. 6, July–August 1972, pp. 911–928; and G. B. Markus and B. A. Nesvold, "Governmental Coerciveness and Political Instability: An Exploratory Study of Cross-National Patterns," *Comparative Political Studies*, Vol. 5, No. 2, July 1972, pp. 231–244.

41. For instance, see Pye, "Armies," p. 277–283; and Huntington, *Political Order*.

42. See Horowitz, "Political Legitimacy," p. 46.

43. Kennedy, *Military in the Third World*. See p. 26.

44. Miles D. Wolpin, *Militarism and Social Revolution*, pp. 222–224.

45. William C. Shepherd, "Cultural Relativism, Physical Anthropology and Religion," *Journal of the Scientific Study of Religion*, Vol. 19, No. 2, 1980, pp. 159–172.

See p. 169.

46. J. K. Hadden, "Religion and Construction of Social Problems," *Sociological Analysis,* Vol. 41, No. 2, summer, 1980.

47. Donald Eugene Smith, *Religion and Political Modernization,* New Haven: Yale Univ. Press, 1974, p. 23.

48. Walter B. Reymond, "Recent Themes in Catholic Social Thought in Latin America," in Lyle C. Brown and William F. Cooper, eds., *Religion in Latin American Life and Literature,* Waco, Texas: Markham Press Fund, 1980, pp. 29–51.

49. Kenneth Westhues, "The Church in Opposition," *Sociological Analysis,* Vol. 37, winter 1976.

50. Gurr, *Minorities at Risk,* p. 317.

51. Ibid., p. 318.

52. Huntington, "Clash of Civilizations?" See p. 22.

53. Mayer, *Islam and Human Rights.*

54. S. C. Dube, "Bureaucracy and Nation Building in Transitional Societies," in J. L. Finkle and Richard W. Gable, eds., 1971, pp. 325–330. See p. 327.

55. Fred W. Riggs, "Bureaucrats and Political Development: A Paradoxical View," in Finkle and Gable, op. cit., pp. 331–351.

56. See Myron Weiner and Joseph La Palombara, "The Impact of Parties on Political Development," in Finkle and Gable, op. cit., 1973, p. 501.

57. Ethnicity is used here to refer to both tribal and racial identities and affiliations.

58. Michael F. Lofchie, "Observations on Social and Institutional Change in Independent Africa," in M. F. Lofchie, ed., *The State of the Nations: Constraints on Development in Independent Africa,* Berkeley: Univ. of California Press, 1971, pp. 261–283. See p. 274. See also the seminal survey conducted by Gurr, *Minorities at Risk.*

59. Gurr, *Minorities at Risk,* pp. 41–42.

60. Ibid., p. 45.

61. Ibid., p. 138.

62. Ibid.

63. Mary B. Welfling, *Political Institutionalization: Comparative Analysis of African Party Systems,* Beverly Hills: Sage Publications, 1973, Series No. 01-041, *Comparative Politics Series,* Vol. 4, 1973. See p. 56.

64. For illuminating discussions in this regard, see especially W. Connor, "The Politics of Ethnonationalism," *Journal of International Affairs,* Vol. 27, No. 1, 1973, pp. 1–21; and A. A. Mazrui, "Ethnic Tensions and Political Stratification in Uganda," in Brian M. du Toit ed., *Ethnicity in Modern Africa,* Boulder, CO: Westview Press, 1978, pp. 47–68 and Peter Worsley, *The Three Worlds: Culture and World Development,* Chicago: University of Chicago Press, 1984.

65. See Connor, op. cit., 1973, p. 2.

66. Clark, *Power and Policy,* p. 45.

67. Ibid., pp. 46–47.

68. Connor, op cit., 1973, p. 12.

69. For further details see Enloe, *Ethnic Conflict,* p. 223.

70. George Thomas Kurian, *The Book of World Rankings,* New York: Facts on File, 1979, p. 45.

71. Wallerstein, op cit., 1971, p. 676.

72. Donnelly, "Cultural Relativism," p. 419.

73. Weber, *Sociology of Religion,* p. 227.

74. Renteln, "Unanswered Challenge." For a general discussion also see Hugh LaFollette, "The Truth in Ethical Relativism," *Journal of Social Philosophy,* Vol. 22, No. 1, spring 1991, pp. 146–154.

75. Swidler, *Human Rights in Religious Traditions.*

76. David Scott Palmer, "The Politics of Authoritarianism in Spanish America," in James M. Malloy, ed., 1977, p. 377–412. See p. 389.

77. Huntington and Nelson, *No Easy Choice,* p. 167.

78. Ibid., p. 169.

79. See Hewlett, "Human Rights."

80. See John Sheahan, "Market-Oriented Economic Policies and Political Repression in Latin America," *Economic Development and Cultural Change,* Vol. 28, No. 2, January 1980, pp. 267–291. See p. 281–282.

81. Huntington, *The Third Wave,* p. 297.

82. Marks, "Promoting Human Rights," p. 299.

83. Rothchild and Ravenhill, "Retreat from Globalism," p. 409.

84. Ibid., p. 412.

85. Samuel P. Huntington, "Religion and Third Wave," *The National Interest,* No. 24, summer 1991, pp. 29–42. See p. 42.

86. For an excellent treatment of this subject see Rhoda E. Howard and Jack Donnelly, "Introduction," in Donnelly and Howard, *International Handbook,* esp. pp. 23–26.

87. See Seymour M. Lipset, *Political Man: The Social Bases of Politics,* Baltimore, MD: John Hopkins Univ. Press, 1981. See also Kenneth A. Bollen, "World System Position, Dependency and Democracy: The Cross-National Evidence," *American Sociological Review,* Vol. 48, August 1983, pp. 468–479. See Kenneth A. Bollen and Robert W. Jackman, "Political Democracy and Size Distribution of Income" *American Sociological Review,* Vol. 50, August, 1985, pp. 438–457. See also Miles Wolpin, "Third World Repression: Parameters and Prospects," *Peace and Change,* Vol. 11, No. 2, 1986, pp. 95–124. See p. 100.

88. Miles Wolpin, op. cit., 1986, p. 98.

CHAPTER 3

Human Rights Conditions and Democratization: Global Changes and Opportunities

Following the waves of democratization that swept Eastern Europe and Latin America in the mid- and late 1980s, Third World countries of Africa, Asia, and the Middle East began to show signs of political and economic reforms. These reforms were initiated at times primarily from above, under so-called liberalization programs, and at other periods largely in response to grassroots pressures. The reforms led to the emergence of a new political climate, culminating in many political openings in these societies. The end of the Cold War (dissolution of the former Soviet Union; demise of the threat of United States–Soviet confrontation; and global democratic revolution) has created many opportunities for the advancement of human rights in the Third World. Opportunities exist in two areas: the construction and renewal of civil societies; and the promotion of collective and bilateral actions against human rights abusers. Realistically, such opportunities must be viewed with caution in light of the fact that civil society is almost nonexistent in many parts of the Third World and that international collective action has failed miserably to deter aggression and abuse of human rights in Bosnia. Nevertheless, there exists a wide range of new opportunities. If exploited, they could have inhibiting effects on the repressive acts and policies of Third World governments. Having dealt with constraints and uncertainties in the preceding chapter, I devote this chapter to these new opportunities.

The first part of the chapter explores the fate of armies in the politics of accommodation, transition, and liberalization. It also looks at the perennial question of whether the evolution of civil society is at odds with the interests of the state. The second part is organized in five sections, dealing with structural adjustment, foreign aid, funding for democratic assistance, promotion of human rights vis-à-vis sovereign rights, and the rising prominence of nongovernmental human rights organizations (NGOs).

The Renewal of Civil Society

It has generally been argued that the renewal of a civil society and the building of a democratic polity depend ultimately on civilian rule and politics. The quest for civilian rule in the post–Cold War era has been precipitated by new opportunities and hindered by formidable—and sometimes unforeseen—challenges. Defiance has come mainly from armed forces, whose role in the post–Cold War world has been transformed. They have been turned into a base of support for elected civilian governments. Transition from military to civilian rule, which I consider crucial to the reconstruction of a democratic polity, will be treated at some length in the following sections.

The turbulent nature of transition and the growing threat of regional and intrastate violence in the Third World have continued the military's pervasive role in politics. Modern armies enjoy a functional capacity based on elaborate support systems that overlap with almost all other areas of governmental policy, including foreign relations, international trade, and domestic economics. The military plays a major role in determining whether nations are democratic, totalitarian, or authoritarian.[1] Caught between the dilemmas of security and development, many Third World elites regard the role of the armed forces in the process of transition as crucial. Some analysts tend to gloss over the fact that transitions from authoritarianism to democracy in these countries are made possible only with either the active participation or the acquiescence of the military.

The end of the Cold War threatens to render the Third World a dumping ground for military exports.[2] As superpower war becomes less likely, considerable increases in the military productive capacity of the newly industrialized countries (NICs) complicate arms transfers to the Third World. These countries themselves seek to expand their export markets. All this indicates that the military will continue to play a part, however constrained, in the politics of many Third World nations.

The Politics of Accommodation

Continuing military influence renders the renewal of civil society a highly complex task in many Third World countries. Despite the shifting nature of civil-military relations in much of Latin America, some form of military antipolitics seems to have persisted, directly or indirectly. Loveman and Davies argue that in Latin America, the military antipolitics can "even use 'elections,' pseudopolitical parties, and plebiscites in order to give a veneer of 'democratic' legitimacy to authoritarian direction of the state and society."[3] This has hardly been called into question in the wake of democratic transitions in Latin America. The army's support for the executive coup of President Alberto Fujimori of Peru and for the subsequent formation of a new assembly displays, to some extent, a different form of military antipolitics. Although Peru's government is described as civilian, it typically falls into the category of civilian-led regimes where "nominal civilian supremacy does not necessarily mean military subordination, and acceptance of the rule of law and the principles of the hierarchy of command."[4]

Likewise, the army's initial support for Guatemalan President Jorge Serrano Elias's "self coup" (leading to the suspension of constitutional courts and congress) on May 25, 1993, and its subsequent withdrawal of this support (leading to his dismissal on June 1, 1993) is a case of civilian leadership and military dominance. In such military-bolstered regimes, the transition to genuine civilian rule is a long-term process. Overthrowing a military regime is quite different from overthrowing an absolute monarchy. Weiner's exploration is apt:

> A monarchy that is overthrown can be removed from the scene, but the military remains even after its political domination has ended. For this reason, popular mobilization against a military regime is not sufficient. . . . While power almost never reverts back to a monarchy after it has been deposed, there are numerous instances of alternations in power between the military and civilians.[5]

The difficulties inherent in renewing civil societies are also compounded by the fact that Third World ruling elites seek to unify the various phases of state- and nation-building into one all-encompassing effort in a brief period of time. The result is the enhancement of the coercive functions of the state, and hence of agencies like the military that perform such functions.[6] Although experiments with praetorianism have failed and praetorian regimes with few exceptions are now in full retreat, it is no surprise that the military continues to be a significant part of the power structure in a considerable number of Third World countries.

Liberalization: An Inevitable Step

Notwithstanding recent evidence that military supremacy over civilian government has ended in all but a few Third World countries, the transitional phases that these countries are undergoing are interesting. In some instances, the transition has faced few difficulties. Chile, Thailand, Mexico, South Korea, and Argentina are the salient examples. Yet in a multitude of Third World countries—including Algeria, El Salvador, Guatemala, Haiti, Côte d'Ivoire, Nigeria, Pakistan, Peru, Togo, and many others—transition has been beset by structural and institutional problems that have long plagued their political systems. Furthermore, although some military officers at present may have no political aspirations, the long-term nature of their ambitions is not clear. Some analysts warn of trends and developments that might create future military involvement in domestic politics. In an effort to build a sense of national identity, the Singapore Armed Forces (SAF) appear to be gradually moving away from their British traditions and developing a more indigenous military ethic. The SAF trains officers at local military institutes and emphasizes an aggressive and self-confident ideology that is less Western-oriented and less politically tolerant than in earlier times. Military commanders thus trained could exercise a sizable influence in the future: "A confident and aggressive military establishment that does not necessarily subscribe to Western notions of an apolitical military institution could play a role in defending the nation from national instability as well as external threats."[7]

More generally, however, over the past decade liberalization has been on the rise. Third World governments, constrained by problems of inequality, poverty, debt, inflation, unemployment, ethnicity, insurgency, terrorism, and bloated bureaucracies are under great public pressure to renew civil society. In much of the Third World, governments are wrestling with crises of legitimacy. Even in the Middle East, where many observers have long insisted that the long-term prospects for democratization are bleak, events point to a renewal of civil society. Trade and professional unions, organized labor, and an array of professional organizations have emerged in several socioeconomic spheres in Egypt, Iran, Jordan, Lebanon, and Turkey. Governments have also learned that suppression of these professional organizations has only helped to broaden the appeal of the populist Islamist movements.[8]

Civil Society and the State

Government tolerance of private associations raises the question of whether or not civil society is inherently at variance with the authoritarian state—of whether the rise of civil society is equivalent to the decline of the government. I submit that it is not. Civil society is no surrogate for the state. The state plays the essential roles of referee, rulemaker, and regulator of civil society. Some elements of civil society are likely to be a source of opposition to the government, but it is naive to expect civil society to supplant the state.[9] Political transactions between government and civil society can be governed by law rather than arbitrary force.

In Africa, while many precolonial cultures may have lacked states, according to Michael Bratton, they surely were civil societies with a multitude of institutions protecting collective interests. In the postcolonial period, writes Bratton, associational life took different forms in different countries, providing ordinary Africans with an outlet for the pursuit of common goals. These associations included "the Christian Churches in Kenya and Burundi; Islamic brotherhoods in Senegal and Sudan; lawyers' and journalists' associations in Ghana and Nigeria; farmers' organizations in Zimbabwe and Kenya; and the mineworkers' unions in Zambia and South Africa."[10] In general, state control of society in Africa has been tentative at best and its retreat is bound to create an enlarged political space for associational life.[11]

Bratton asserts that associational life is most likely to thrive in the presence of an effective state[12] and that "weak states can sometimes become stronger—meaning more effective at accumulation and distribution, and more legitimate—by permitting a measure of pluralism in associational life."[13] His view supports the general notion that civil society need not be of necessity antistatist. On balance, a civil society is most likely to expand its political significance in the wake of a gradual change by the state.

This discussion, however, leaves us with a paradox. Pace is a major issue in political change. In some cases, a fast-paced liberalization process can and will destabilize rather than consolidate the advance of political change. Ruling elites are not inclined to mark their calendar with the date of their voluntary surrender of power. While not denying the political and economic necessity of change, as well as the ramifications of political suppression of it, most elites view hastened and drastic reform as detrimental to their rule and to the stability of the country. They also realize that it is difficult to avoid the consequences of greater integration into the international economy. Integration enlarges the role of the private sector, promotes a stable legal environment, and restructures the state's relations with its citizens. International economic participation widens political participation.[14] Alan Richards aptly sums up the economic elements driving change in the majority of Middle Eastern countries: "The old Nasirist social contract, the exchange of welfare for political quiescence, is dead because the state can no longer fulfill its side of the bargain."[15] In the following section, I argue that for long-term political change to go beyond the "facade of democracy," it needs to be premised on a balanced process of liberalization—balanced in the sense of both economic and political. For improvements to occur, both bilateral and multilateral transactions between developed and developing countries need to reflect such a balance. The extent to which such a change is valued is in part the subject of the next section.

Multilateral and Bilateral Actions

The newly formed and fragile democratic governments of the Third World face a wide range of difficulties. The trend toward increasing bilateral and collective leverage on these countries has raised legitimate concerns. A shift appears inevitable in the way international financial institutions—e.g., the International Monetary Fund (IMF), the World Bank, the European Bank for Reconstruction and Development (EBRD), and the UN; and regional organizations such as the Organization of American States (OAS)—treat the developing countries. The idea behind the shift is that international and bilateral policies and actions should be linked, however tenuously, to the realization of human rights. Instruments of such policies run the gamut from structural adjustment, humanitarian intervention, foreign aid, and funding for democratic assistance to collective punitive actions such as sanctions, blockades, and force. These policies have risks but offer major opportunities for the improvement of human rights and the enhancement of democratization in the long run.

Structural Adjustment

Adjustment programs include stabilization measures as well as structural reforms. The benefits associated with both stabilization and structural reforms take a long time to appear. In the short run, stabilization may lower the growth of economic output. Although some studies have found a strong relationship between adjustment programs and improvements in the balance of payments, the evidence on growth and inflation seems to be inconclusive.[16] The short-term adverse effects of austerity measures associated with stabilization programs include currency devaluation, reduction in government spending on social services and subsidies, and wage freezes.

The most important problem with structural adjustment is its immediate impact on the well-being of the poorest segment of the population. The poor and the most powerless—that is, women and children—must initially bear the brunt of the prescribed austerity measures. To force Third World countries to pay interest due on past loans, the World Bank and the IMF impose harsh economic measures on these countries at enormous human costs. Agricultural laborers on commercial farms and city dwellers, especially the working classes and the urban middle sectors, are others likely to bear a large share of the social costs of adjustment. These groups are strongly affected by price fluctuations, unemployment, and removal of price controls.[17] Real wages earned in the public sector and by organized labor are highly exposed to the effects of economic adjustment and, as Joan Nelson finds, the most exposed group, and those who have suffered the greatest losses in income relative to precrisis levels, may very well be public sector workers.[18]

Fran Hosken, who toured eastern and western Africa, visiting maternity hospitals in Somalia, Burkina Faso, and Mali, echoes a similar point. Expounding on the human costs of austerity measures forced on governments, she said:

> Not only do thousands of people lose their jobs (the government is the largest employer in most African countries), but often all services are drastically cut, especially those of the already underfunded health sector. Salaries of nurses, midwives, and health personnel are cut; at times the government runs out of cash altogether and cannot pay any of its employees.

Hoskin's account also substantiates the view that the poor are severely affected. She continues: "Hospital patients must buy their medicines from pharmacies in town, and families must bring their own food into the hospital. Huge lines of women, often accompanied by their small children, wait for hours in front of clinics in oppressive heat with flies everywhere."[19] Also in connection with the "intolerable" social costs of adjustment for the poor, John

P. Lewis advocates enhanced donor emphasis not just on the country's need but on its performance toward the poor. For pro-poor conditioning to be effective, he suggests, donors must be prepared to suspend aid to regimes that fail to implement policies for strengthening their poor.[20] Richard Jolly supports the deepening of adjustment's social dimensions, but by introducing a "human face" element into orthodox approaches. Jolly writes that the objectives of such an alternative approach must be to accelerate growth, with an emphasis on growth of production and incomes among low-income groups, and to restructure social expenditure toward low-cost, basic education, primary health care, and other basic, mass-coverage services. Poverty eradication, Jolly insists, must be part of the range of socioeconomic decisionmaking; i.e., part of adjustment, finance, debt, and development planning. Micro and sectoral policy and grassroots approaches alone will not, in the long run, cope adequately with the issue of poverty.[21]

Successful structural adjustment presupposes strong government action. Measures to neutralize some of the ill effects of privatization surely demand vigorous government intervention, at least in the short run. Haggard and Kaufman argue that the challenge is to find ways to extend social compensation without recourse to the large and inflationary state sectors that characterized developmentalism of the 1960s and 1970s.[22] The implementation of structural adjustment programs in countries under military rule (e.g., Nigeria and Ghana), which involved the imposition of politically unpopular programs, has been a little easier than in countries under a civilian regime (e.g., Zambia).[23] This may account for why the IMF and the World Bank have seldom, if ever, pushed for political reforms to match the economic reforms that they advocated.[24]

The strategists of structural adjustment must now find a way to deal with an expanded and more viable state as a major player in social welfare policy.[25] The main difficulty appears to be how to reconcile privatization programs with social welfare programs that require an expanded role for the government in the service sector. One solution is liberalization at a carefully balanced pace. Privatization that is too fast or too slow causes widespread public frustration and numerous socioeconomic and political difficulties.

Free from the geostrategic considerations of the Cold War, Western creditors and donors must now stress the relevance of liberalization to structural adjustment. They can be supported in this by the IMF and World Bank. The implementation of policies of structural adjustment such as market liberalization, deregulation, lower government budget deficits, and reformed parastatal organizations requires simultaneous political reform. Obviously, the government does not control all the levers of economic power. Although rhetoric linking aid to "good governance" has become more explicit, it remains to be seen whether the linkage endures. In the past, aid donors and investors gave "a nod and a wink" to authoritarian regimes that displayed high economic growth (e.g., Ghana, Pakistan, Singapore, South Korea, and Taiwan). This raised the classic question of whether democratization is indeed a prerequisite for economic growth.

Many popular protests in the Third World in general, and in Africa in particular, have been primarily related to economic grievances.[26] Reforms must be adjusted accordingly. Hence the conclusion that democratization in the Third World may be slowed, pending successful economic and political liberalization. If this is not done, the economic uncertainties that democratization is bound to cause may lead to the collapse of the state. One Zambian analyst has remarked that the future of democracy in Africa sometimes hinges on the price of bread or cornmeal. If the donors force an abrupt cutback on Zambia's costly subsidy for cornmeal, the government could face riots that would undermine the country's new democracy.[27]

The basic problem is a matter of pace—the pace of reform dictated by international financial institutions. Should reform be gradual or instantaneous ("shock therapy")? The case for gradualism made by some experts is that it renders the costs of adjustment bearable by spreading them out over time. Gradualism also allows for temporary adjustments and political fine-tuning in the case of unexpected economic conditions and market failures. Gradual trade liberalization has already been adopted by Indonesia, South Korea, Mauritius, Morocco, and Turkey. Gradualism may be the proper way to reform, given the existing institutional constraints in these countries.[28]

The case for shock treatment, on the other hand, can be made where rapid action generates quick gains in welfare, makes reforms politically sustainable, and deals effectively with a climate of crisis. Several countries have used shock therapy and rapid reforms to eliminate economic distortions. These include Bolivia, Ghana, Mexico, Poland, and Chile.[29] Democratization in the Third World remains at least for the near future a highly destabilizing process.[30] Further, some have argued that there is no real evidence that the introduction of democracy alone is likely to result in burgeoning economic growth.[31]

Debate continues about which type of regime makes the best case for reform. World Bank officials report that democratic governments are not necessarily more proficient at managing reform in comparison with authoritarian ones:

> Democratic governments have a better record than authoritarian governments in countries that are not politically polarized; the reverse seems to be true in polarized societies. On the whole, the evidence suggests that the democratic-authoritarian distinction itself fails to explain adequately whether or not countries initiate reform, implement it effectively, or survive its political fallout.[32]

Bienen and Waterbury[33] cite many cases where, with leaders shifting gears significantly, the adoption of a structural adjustment package has been possible. Tunisia did this (under Burguiba), as did Côte d'Ivoire (under Houphouet-Boigny), Ghana (under Rawlings), the Malagasy Republic (under

Didier Ratsiraka), Mexico (under Lopez Portillo), Nigeria (under Babangida), and Algeria (under Bendjedid). None of these states, note Bienen and Waterbury, have a truly democratic system, with the problematic exception of Mexico. Moreover, they conclude, reform from within may be easier in systems where votes do not count.[34]

The effects of different types of government on change do not show a consistent pattern. One empirical study of sub-Saharan Africa reveals no statistically significant link between the degree of democracy, autocracy, and concentration of power in political structures on the one hand and the establishment or acceptance of conditional IMF relationships on the other.[35] The complexities and uncertainties associated with the effective implementation of structural adjustment, coupled with the constraints and inadequacies of the Third World countries, call into question the relevance of structural adjustment to full-scale democratization. As the debate about internal structural adjustment continues, the impact of external parameters cannot be downplayed. Foreign aid also affects the prospect for change.

Foreign Aid

The relationship between foreign aid and human rights, although interesting, is underresearched. There are few scholarly studies of the attempts to link the two. One credible study has documented a weak connection between foreign aid and the promotion of human rights. It shows that the use of foreign aid on behalf of human rights, especially the political rights of democracy, has been a marginal consideration.[36] Another study has persuasively demonstrated that the distribution of aid and voting on development loans in multilateral development banks (MDBs) and bilateral frameworks has had very little to do with a systematic assessment of the degree of respect for human rights in recipient countries.[37] This is traditionally true of the international financial regimes associated with the IMF, the World Bank, and the U.S. Agency for International Development (AID).

Foreign aid policies presumably reflect in part the global changes transpiring in post–Cold War politics, and in part the internal economics of donor countries. New policies are expected to be reformulated and thus redirected toward new tasks, linking lending to human rights. This reinforces the process of democratization in the Third World. Over the past few years, the U.S. State Department has reviewed aid strategies and set new guidelines for the disbursement of funds. Rhetorically, the State Department has embraced the notion of linking foreign aid and debt relief policies to demonstrable progress toward democracy and market reforms in the Third World countries. However, the execution of U.S. aid toward human rights, democracy, environmental protection, and the empowerment of the poor of the Third World has clearly reflected U.S. political considerations. In 1993, the list of ten nations that receive the largest amounts of AID funds did not include a single country in Africa, the poorest region in the world. Most funds were earmarked for the so-called friendly regimes: Israel, Egypt, Peru, Nicaragua, Turkey, El Salvador, India, Bolivia, Bangladesh, and the Philippines.[38]

The European Union's insistence that human rights and environmental issues be incorporated into the new generation of economic agreements that is being negotiated with its trading partners has generated widespread objections from the Third World. Wary of any linkage between development aid and human rights, ASEAN officials have accused the European Union of a "tendentious application of Western norms and values in inter-state relations [aimed at] creating standards and criteria by which to judge people and condemn countries."[39] According to State Department reports, U.S. foreign aid, in whole or part, to countries that have committed grave violation of rights has been suspended. These include Indonesia, Togo, Cameroon, and Kenya. Sanctions have at times been imposed on human rights violators: Libya, South Africa, Serbia and Montenegro, and Somalia.[40] The State Department's track record shows no consistency across the board, however. Notwithstanding strong words of condemnation for the Mobutu dictatorship in Zaire, which could lead that country into civil war, strong action to remove the regime does not seem to be in the offing.[41]

The suspension of foreign aid appears to be based on more factors than the single criterion of human rights abuse. (It should be noted that the U.S. State Department has yet to declare any country a gross and consistent abuser of human rights: no such category exists in State Department's policy framework.) The variables that determine whether or not foreign aid continues or is suspended also include political and economic ties, economic performance, and progress toward structural adjustment. When asked whether U.S. aid to Turkey should be contingent on an improvement in that country's human rights record, U.S. Secretary of State Warren Christopher pointed out that human rights must be "factored against many other criteria."[42] Since political considerations weigh heavily in the aid equation, the use of foreign aid as a policy tool invariably reflects politics, even in the case of blatant abuse of human rights. Moreover, systemic changes, such as the creation of an independent judiciary or the rise of a sizable middle class or the development of broad-based economic growth, are conceived of as long-term goals; thus, policy need not be sensitive to the existing imperatives of political human rights in these countries.

It is too early to determine whether or not aid policies tied to the human rights policy of donor countries will fundamentally alter the human rights performance of recipient countries. The emphases of traditional diplomacy have yet to change dramatically. The UN agencies and Western donors, be they the government of the United States, or that of Canada, Norway, or the Netherlands, or intergovernmental institutions like the World Bank and the IMF, have adopted politicized, and sometimes over-politicized, lending policies. These do not promote human rights. As Tomasevski points out, the suspension of aid to developing countries because of their governments' violations of human rights is also a problem. It exacerbates the very lack of subsistence, health care, and primary education that it purports to cure, punishing people for the sins of their rulers.[43] On May 26, 1994, when U.S. President Bill Clinton renounced the linkage between China's most-favored-nation (MFN) trading status and its human rights record, the message became clear: liberal trade policies are more suitable to fostering human rights gains in China in the long run than swift political and social reforms. This was a reminder that abrupt democratization in Russia has, if anything, rendered liberal trade programs ineffectual. The bottom line is that bolstering the standard of living of China's citizens is the first step toward political liberalization and democratization.

In light of the basic structural and institutional constraints discussed in Chapter 2, the possibility of realizing greatly increased human rights in a majority of Third World countries is very small. Some African specialists have repeatedly argued that the injection of sudden democratization as a condition of further aid cannot succeed in a climate of extreme deprivation.[44] These specialists do not disdain democracy; nor are they nostalgic for authoritarianism. Their arguments are, rather, thoughtful efforts to be realistic: to advocate not doing harm while trying to do good. In the post–Cold War era, foreign aid policies must be reformulated effectively to address the essential issues of development and political liberalization. Tomasevski is right to argue that the major obstacles to tying development aid to human rights has been the preponderance of the economy in the design, planning, and evaluation of aid, and to the primacy of foreign policy exigencies in its use.[45]

There also appears to be a strong correlation between indigenous circumstances and the usefulness of foreign aid, a point underplayed by Tomasevski. One can argue that the transitions from military to civilian rule in Latin America in the 1980s were more caused by internal conditions and the failure of the military regimes to cope with economic problems and political instability than by the effectiveness of U.S. foreign assistance policies or diplomacy.[46] Whether new policies, linking foreign aid to human rights priorities, will replace older policies of marginal adjustment is an open question. Thus far, the latter have prevailed. Despite its limits, foreign aid has proven to be a critical element of economic growth in the poorest countries. Economic growth has indeed become, according to Joan Nelson, a necessary if not sufficient condition for the consolidation of democratic openings unfolding in these countries.[47] This is not to downplay the role of commercial and political concerns in bilateral relations. Nelson is quick to acknowledge such concerns:

> The wealthy nations' zeal for new, or newly elevated, goals on their agenda will be diluted by perennial diplomatic, commercial and residual security

considerations. Sanctions against blatant violations of international norms have already been eroded or abandoned—not only with regard to major countries such as China, but also in the case of far smaller ones like Haiti. However, more specific offers of assistance linked to requirements for policy reforms are likely to be increasingly common in areas such as environmental reform, arms reductions and pro-poor measures.[48]

A growing number of developing countries have disputed IMF and World Bank insistence on conditionality, contending that their emphasis, in addition to being selective and discretionary, infringes on national sovereignty.[49] From the recipient's perspective, some argue, conditionality implies that the donor's or lender's priorities and ideas regarding policy formation are superior to those of the recipient. Additionally, conditionality is a constant reminder of power disparities between donors and recipients, thus accounting for recipients' resentment toward such an external influence.[50] Having raised doubts concerning the actual leverage of the international financial institutions over wide realms of debtor-country policy choice and implementation, Miles Kahler argues that the creditors' multiple and conflicting goals vis-à-vis the debtors lead to inconsistent and poor implementation of the "conditionality leverage."[51] In some cases, Third World countries managed to do without "conditionality," opting for heterodox policies. Nevertheless, as Kahler cites, Indonesia and Turkey are cases where both international financial institutions and national governments collaborated successfully to produce improved economic prospects within the framework of conditionality bargains.[52]

Arguably, the strict application of conditionality accentuates internal difficulties at a time when the effective operation of economic reforms requires a strong government. Too often, the costs associated with the fiscal austerity measures are intolerably heavy. They include both serious impacts on employment and the loss of social safety networks. Needless to say, these costs have on many occasions been responsible for riots and political instability. Despite these criticisms and doubts about the efficacy of the effective use of conditional financing, either in the form of lending policies or foreign assistance, its use as a policy instrument is likely to grow.[53] Perhaps the most controversial form of foreign aid is funding for democratic assistance. Initiated under the Reagan administration, this funding and its underlying premises have raised serious concerns.

Funding for Democratic Aid

The phrase "political foreign aid" has become fairly common in the jargon of the last decade. The term refers to money funneled to foreign political parties, labor unions, and similar organizations to foster democratic reforms. This type of aid, which was regarded as a legitimate tool of modern diplomacy by the Reagan administration, involves helping a target country to endure a transition of government, maintain electoral rules and processes, enhance private associations, and promote contacts between the elites and opposition parties.

Germany, according to Michael Pinto-Duschinsky, has a long tradition of political payments to foreign groups. Four German foundations (the Ebert, Adenauer, Naumann, and Seidel) have sent money overseas. In 1988, the Ebert and Adenauer foundations devoted nearly 30 million DM to trade union projects outside Germany and about 20 million DM to foreign mass media.[54] Funding for democratic assistance was aimed at encouraging certain civil and cultural groups as well as the independent media pivotal to democratic transition. Germany's involvement is exemplified by Ebert's support for African trade unionists, by Adenauer's for Christian professional groups in Tanzania and Zaire, and by Naumann's for human rights groups in Paraguay.[55]

In the United States, the system of distributing political aid is more elaborate and complicated than in Germany. In 1989, the amount of political foreign aid in the United States totalled nearly $100 million.[56] Many organizations raise funds for political aid abroad: the National Endowment for Democracy, the Agency for International Development, the Special Democracy Program for Latin America, the U.S. Congress, and the AFL-CIO, to name only a few. Supporting the cause of the National Endowment for Democracy in 1992, President Clinton—then president-elect—maintained that the United States "should regard increasing funding for democratic assistance as a legitimate part of [its] national security budget."[57] The European Union, Japan, and Sweden had similar views.[58]

The goals of giving democratic assistance, like those of conventional development aid, may at times be compromised to promote the national interests of the donors. The case of Nicaragua, where U.S. intervention in 1990 led to the rise to power of Violeta Chamorro, is typical.

Most Third World countries view funding for democratic assistance with skepticism, regarding this form of aid as meddling in their internal politics. Nor are doubts limited to people outside the United States. U.S. intervention into the domestic politics of others has been widely debated in the U.S. Congress. The doubts usually have stemmed from the claim that such interventions have been orchestrated to muster support for pro-Western right-wing regimes;[59] hence, Congress in mid-June 1993 terminated funding for the National Endowment for Democracy, whose establishment was said to have been nurtured by Cold War premises.

Democratic aid may be put to legitimate uses but often it is not. In the past, such funding has propped up regimes that have, behind the mask of pro-Western political proclamations, widely abused the human rights of their people. In the so-called new world order, the facilitation of gradual political liberalization and respect for civil liberties constitutes a tenable logic for such funding. The end of the Cold War and the burgeoning demand for the realization of human rights offer another opportunity to reassess the limits of state sovereignty and the norm of nonintervention. This reevaluation is based on an understanding of the nature of global opportunities for the protection and promotion of human rights, as well as their perceived impact in the post–Cold War era. To this topic I turn in the next section.

Human Rights and Sovereign Rights

The relation between sovereign rights and human rights is a fundamental issue in the world politics of the 1990s. As stated above, Third World critics often view the linkage of aid to human rights as a form of interference—albeit one that does not involve force. Structural adjustments, negotiated on the basis of state consent, involve legitimate and permissible leverage, regardless of the complexity of their implications and executions. What is needed is a consensus about when linkage is legitimate and when it is not. Thus far, the interpretational difficulties have yielded no consensus.

The basic problem centers around the meaning of intervention in world politics. To begin with, legal studies appear to be unclear as to the precise meaning of the term *intervention*. Pease and Forsythe pointed out in 1993 that "a clear, comprehensive, and consensual distinction between permissible forms of influence, and impermissible interference and intervention, eludes us."[60] Interventions of a structural sort aimed at destabilizing the political and economic structures of the target state, but operating under the guise of protecting democratic rights, gained no collective endorsement in the 1980s. However, intervention for nonstructural, rights-oriented claims genuinely directed at rescuing persons at risk have gained collective support in the last few years. The U.S. interventions in Liberia (1990) and Somalia (1992) and, to a lesser extent, that of France and Belgium in Zaire (1991), are cases in point.[61]

Although the dominant state values—independence, autonomy, impermeability—are likely to remain, according to one keen observer of international law, the character and the content of the norms of nonintervention will change as we approach the end of the century.[62] These changes will not transform the essential nature of the state; but they will transform the principle of nonintervention, which has been a central element of state sovereignty and a fundamental postulate underlying the state system. It is no longer seen as an inviolable and sacrosanct norm of international politics.

The end of the Cold War invites changes in the norm of nonintervention because intervention no longer risks leading to superpower confrontation. Intervention has growing appeal, not only as a way to prompt budding constitutional democracies around the world but also as a guarantee of their sustainability. The proponents of such a view maintain that adopting an "international guarantee clause" for constitutional democracy is now as imperative as granting moral and material support to nascent democracies. Such a clause would explicitly guarantee the use of force by the UN, the United States, and regional organizations (e.g., the OAS and the European Union) to establish or restore constitutional democracy.[63]

The legal perspectives of this topic are instructive. Some scholars maintain that, legally, the norm of nonintervention must take account of those categories of political activity that the contemporary international system treats as unacceptable.[64] Since peaceful support of political candidates, parties, and movements has evolved into a pattern of state practice, such support should no longer be regarded by international law as "prohibited conduct."[65]

Recently, there have been more overt efforts to exert transnational political influence. Whether this trend will create a new consensus on the legality and legitimacy of peaceful influence is still a subject of controversy. Lori Fisler Damrosch contends that political independence is closely intertwined with citizen participation in governance; in other words, individual rights cannot, at all times, be overriden by the sovereign rights of states. It follows that a systemic denial of fundamental political rights is not a strictly internal affair.[66] Damrosch reasons: "The nonintervention norm must not become a vehicle for exalting the abstract entity of the state over the protection of individual rights and fundamental freedoms" and "the concept of the political independence of states should be understood against the backdrop of the political rights of their inhabitants."[67]

The positions of those who defend military intervention by external powers to rectify violations of human rights are consistent with such views. Fernando R. Teson points out that "international law must be wed to notions of legitimacy associated with human rights and political consent."[68] Since the rights of governments, he surmises, are derived exclusively from the rights of individuals, intervention, if premised on such rights, can be legitimate. Teson concludes: "A justified intervention must be genuinely aimed at restoring human rights, necessary, proportionate to the evil that it is designated to suppress, and welcomed by the victims of oppression."[69]

It is argued that the traditional approach of international law (under which unmitigated support is given to the sovereign rights of states under Article II subsect. 4 of the UN Charter and under which intervention is seen as violation of the prohibition of force) can no longer properly reflect the state of international law in the post–Cold War era. The imposition of No Fly zones in Iraq to protect the Kurds and the Shi'ites (1992), the mandatory arms embargo on Liberia to prevent anarchy (1990), military intervention to secure an environment for humanitarian relief operations in Somalia, and the economic sanctions on Serbia and Montenegro to stop the massacres in Bosnia are examples of humanitarian intervention in cases where a substantial segment of the populace of a state is "threatened with death or suffering on a grand scale, either because of the actions of the government of that state, or because of the state's slide into anarchy."[70]

The case of Somalia did not constitute what Chapter VII of the UN Charter considers "a threat to international peace and security"—a threat which would be grounds for a legitimate military intervention. The UN Security Council's practice in Somalia, initiated in 1992, indicated a far greater willingness to intervene than Article VII establishes.[71] The aforementioned cases suggest the emergence of what is seen as at least a limited right of intervention for reasons of human rights.[72]

Following from such legal interpretations, some advocate the statement of a "universal democratic entitlement," including free elections and international monitoring. Democracy, they observe, is the sine qua non for the validation of governance, and a change in the norm of the international system now warrants such a move to provide international supervision of electoral rights. All this implies that the principle of noninterference has been weakened. The change is real but does not condone unilateral enforcement to compel compliance with the democratic entitlement.[73]

One argument for democratic entitlement is based on the fact that democracies are not disposed to fight each other.[74] By making democracy central to the maintenance of peace, the proponents of these views argue that democratic entitlement is evolving into a universal value and must be institutionalized so that democracy can be protected. As such, it is argued that the intrusions by the United States in the Third World (most visibly in Latin America and particularly in the name of fighting the drug war) can no longer be challenged by resort to the sovereign rights of the states.

Critics of such a view insist that the pull of the past remains strong. With the end of the Cold War, many analysts contend, the search for new ways to intervene could be based on familiar political and economic considerations but justified under the rubric of human rights. Some mention the return of Pax Americana and a new phase of neocolonial policies in this connection. Claims to national sovereignty are not likely to disappear in the near future. Echoing such a perspective, David Forsythe asserts that "the United States shows few signs of abandoning its historic unilateralism across international relations and few signs of accepting an international definition of human rights as supervised by international agencies [e.g., the Inter-American Commission and Court.]"[75] While concurring with Forsythe, I would assert that, apart from a few exceptional cases, the sovereign rights of states have been the most significant factor in interstate relations. There is little evidence that jingoistic attitudes and national politics will disappear and human rights diplomacy will never be the sole rationale for intervention. Furthermore, outside intervention always has unintended consequences: an intervention might, for example, call into question the legitimacy of the existing government. Interventions will be counterproductive if the chief economic and social ills of the country are not properly handled. When they are not, the blame is regularly placed on the foreign intervention; and future elections, even fully democratic elections, are then vulnerable to charges that the interests of foreign powers, and not those of the voters, are the primary determinants of the outcome.

State authorities still make the most important policies, but private organizations and associations can exercise a measure of influence on the ruling elites and their policies. They thus contribute to the improvement of human rights in Third World countries. Undeniably, the end of the Cold War has increased the influence of private and international institutions. These actors have become important agents for the furtherance of human rights goals, whereas in world politics, sovereign states continue to be the major players.

The Increasing Prominence of Human Rights NGOs

Broadly defined, nongovernmental organizations (NGOs) are private, non-commercial institutions (internal, regional, and international) with international influence. A human rights NGO, according to Lauri S. Wiseberg, is a private association that consigns substantial resources to the promotion and protection of human rights, that is independent of government and other political groups who intend to exercise direct political power, and that does not itself court such power.[76] The NGOs' main strategy lies in public exposure and pressure, and includes several tactics, for example, fact-finding missions and reports, urgent-action networks, human rights awards, and promotion of international action.[77]

NGOs have done much to advance human rights through diplomatic intervention. Diplomatic intervention can serve as an effective tool for influencing public policy in the wake of the changing nature of international relations. States, in this so-called new world order, are becoming more permeable, but still are among the main violators of human rights. The present international system does not protect all of the rights of individuals. As a result, NGOs, acting on behalf of human rights victims, are gaining increasing importance and legitimacy for their services, organization, education, and propaganda.[78] This has been facilitated by the rapid growth of transportation, communication technologies, democratization, and the globalization of trade. The new international conditions make greater reliance on the roles and resources of NGOs inescapable. Sustainable development requires both ecological consciousness and popular participation. The NGOs' role in promoting both of these aspects is critical.[79] Any new paradigm of world politics must acknowledge the important part played by NGOs in securing and enhancing human rights.

According to the World Bank, NGOs have become an important force in the development of Third World countries. NGOs are the outlet for large sums of government and private monies spent on international projects.[80] In 1987, NGOs transferred about $5.5 billion from industrialized to developing countries.[81] Their success lies in sensitizing governmental and international financial institutions to the social and environmental aspects of development as well as in their ability to involve grassroots organizations directly in the development process and in the alleviation of poverty.[82]

Collaboration between governments and NGOs has increased considerably, as in the cases of Togo, Gambia, Ghana, Jordan, and Malawi; cooperation has also increased between the World Bank and the NGOs, as in the cases of Bangladesh, India, Indonesia, Nepal, and the Philippines. This has expanded the role of the NGOs in reducing poverty.

NGOs raise most of their resources (approximately 60 percent) by themselves. The rest ($2.2 billion in 1987) is provided by official aid agencies.[83] The international human rights NGOs (Amnesty International, International Commission of Jurists, International League for Human Rights, and the International Committee of the Red Cross) have special "consultative status" with the United Nations.[84] However, the largest number of human rights NGOs are domestically based in a single nation—the French League for Human Rights, the American Civil Liberties Union, the Help and Action Committee being examples.

The NGOs' success in publicizing, lobbying, and disseminating information regarding the plight of victims of human rights violations has spawned the notion that the state system can, to some extent, be held in check. Human rights NGOs want to improve their effectiveness in pressuring governments on the protection of human rights, in making publicity about violations, and in providing remedies for victims. Given their limited size and resources and, most of all, their dependence on the consent, goodwill, and cooperation of governments, NGOs must be careful challengers of the vested interests of those in power in countries of the Third World. Although many NGOs do not directly seek political power, as their umbrella name and definitions of their functions implies, they inevitably voice concerns that bear on power politics in countries where they operate.

Conclusion

In summary, and by way of conclusion, in the post–Cold War era, there are a myriad of opportunities to promote lawful governance, democratization, and human rights. However, there is no single, clear direction for the promotion of democratic governance in Third World countries. Many difficulties stand in the way of transformation.

A key question concerns the role of the armed forces in turbulent transitions toward the strengthening of civil society; a carefully crafted politics of accommodation is possible. Such a politics recommends gradual political and economic liberalization initiated by civilian rule. The renewal of civil society, a prerequisite for democratization, need not be antithetical to state interests.

A plethora of collective and bilateral actions have been pursued to redress the grievances associated with human rights violations. While structural adjustments, foreign aid, and funding for democratic assistance have been tried extensively, their outcome is still problematic. There are still many questions about their relevance and propriety.

Legal perspectives that support curbing the sovereign rights of states, or even supplanting them with the dicta of multilateral institutions, have yet to produce evidence that the state of international law in the post–Cold War era has been changed drastically. Multilateral institutions such as the United

Nations now hold an increasing preeminence in the international community of nation-states. The argument that "universal democratic entitlement" supersedes the norm of nonintervention still has a tenuous bite to it. There is little evidence that international political and economic transactions will be governed by so-called democratic interventions in the post–Cold War era. The emergence of a global enthusiasm for democracy is no guarantee of its durability, much less of its potential to transform some of the time-honored principles of international law. Legal interpretations and speculations (reviewed in the chapter) are exploratory. It would be premature to draw definitive inferences from such suggestions.

It seems likely that NGOs will improve the worldwide status of human rights. They will enjoy a greater importance in the so-called new world order. Their strength and tactical powers will increase. However, NGOs will have to address questions about how long they can stay aloof from internal politics and power struggles and to what extent they can possibly get embroiled in the power politics of the nation-states within which they operate. There are legitimate concerns surrounding the legality of their involvement, but the NGOs' role in improving human rights conditions—especially if consonant with measured liberalization timetables—can prove to be decisive.

The global changes of the past few years have offered enormous opportunities for the issues of human rights and democratic governance to be addressed as subjects of international relations. But these opportunities are likely to be matched by challenges, due to structural, institutional, and situational setbacks. The strengthening of democratization and human rights may not sufficiently motivate many who fervently believe in the liberalization process and its ultimate harvest (democracy and human rights) to comply with externally prescribed policies. Liberalization may be a measure halfway between democracy and autocracy. Democratization and liberalization need to be indigenous ways of life in order to be permanent.

Notes

1. Constantine P. Danopoulos, "Military Dictatorships in Retreat: Problems and Perspectives," in C. P. Danopoulos, ed., *The Decline of Military Regimes: The Civilian Influence,* Boulder, CO: Westview Press, 1988; pp. 1–24. See pp. 19–20.

2. Bogdan Denitch, *After the Flood: World Politics and Democracy in the Wake of Communism,* Hanover, NH: Wesleyan University Press, 1992. See pp. 107–108.

3. Loveman and Davies, "Antipolitics," p. 12.

4. Danopoulos, 1988, op. cit., p. 23.

5. Weiner, "Empirical Democratic Theory."

6. Ayoob, "The Security Problematic," p. 280.

7. Tai Ming Cheung, "Soldiers and Scholars," *Far Eastern Economic Review,* Vol. 154, No. 49, 5 Dec. 1991, pp. 15–18. See p. 18.

8. For a thorough analysis of this issue, see Norton, "Future of Civil Society," p. 211.

9. Ibid., p. 215.

10. Michael Bratton, "Beyond the State," pp. 411–412.

11. Ibid., p. 412.

12. Ibid., p. 428.

13. Ibid., p. 429.

14. See Richards, "Economic Imperatives."

15. Ibid., p. 226.

16. *World Development Report 1991*, p. 114.

17. Joan M. Nelson, "Poverty, Equity, and the Politics of Adjustment," in Haggard and Kaufman, *Politics of Adjustment,* pp. 221–269. See pp. 227–228.

18. Ibid., pp. 229–231.

19. Quoted in Brian W. Welsh and Pavel Butorin, eds., *Dictionary of Development: Third World Economy, Environment, Society,* New York: Garland Publishing, 1990, Volume Two, p. 940.

20. Lewis, *Pro–Poor Aid Conditionality,* p. 4.

21. Richard Jolly, "Poverty and Adjustment in the 1990s," in John P. Lewis, ed., *Strengthening the Poor: What Have We Learned?* Washington, D.C.: Overseas Development Council, 1988, pp. 163–175. See pp. 168–174.

22. Haggard and Kaufman, *Politics of Adjustment,* p. 344. On this topic, see Ch. 7, "Economic Adjustment and the Prospects for Democracy," pp. 319–350.

23. See Nyang'oro, "Evolving Role," p. 21.

24. Nayang'oro, "Evolving Role," p. 22. Also see Carol Lancaster, "Economic Restructuring in Sub-Saharan Africa," *Current History,* Vol. 88, No. 538, May 1989, pp. 213–216, 244. See p. 244.

25. Nyang'oro, "Evolving Role," p. 24.

26. See Stephen Riley, "Africa's New Wind of Change," in Helen E. Purkitt, ed., *World Politics 93/94,* Guilford, CT: Dushkin, 1993, pp. 152–155. See p. 153.

27. Robert M. Press, "Africa's Turn," *World Monitor,* Vol. 5, No. 2, February 1992, pp. 37–43. See p. 43.

28. *World Development Report 1991,* p. 117.

29. Ibid.

30. Rothstein, "Democracy, Conflict, and Development." Rothchild and Ravenhill, "Retreat from Globalism."

31. For example, Gurr, in "America as a Model?"

32. *World Development Report 1991,* pp. 133–135.

33. See Bienen and Waterbury, "Political Economy of Privatization," p. 396.

34. Ibid.

35. Moore and Scarritt, "IMF Conditionality."

36. David P. Forsythe, "US Economic Assistance and Human Rights: Why the Emperor Has (Almost) No Clothes," in Forsythe, *Human Rights and Development,* pp. 171–195 See p. 175.

37. Michael Stohl, David Carlton, Mark Gibney and Geoffrey Martin, "US Foreign Policy, Human Rights and Multilateral Assistance," in Forsythe, *Human Rights and Development,* pp. 196–212.

38. *Christian Science Monitor,* June 17, 1993, p. 3.

39. Michael Vatikiotis, "Dollar Diplomacy," *Far Eastern Economic Review,* Vol. 153, No. 39, 26 September 1991, p. 35.

40. Arnold Kanter, "America's Commitment to Human Rights," *US Department of State Dispatch,* Vol. 3, No. 51, December 21, 1992, pp. 904–906. See p. 905.

41. *Christian Science Monitor,* March 16, 1994, p. 23.

42. *New York Times,* June 13, 1993, p. 8Y.

43. Tomasevski, *Development Aid.*

44. For example, see Lone, "Challenging Conditionality."

45. Tomasevski, op. cit., pp. 17–18.

46. Stohl et al., op. cit., pp. 208–209.

47. Joan M. Nelson, "Beyond Conditionality: Foreign Aid and the Changing Global Agenda," in Helen E. Purkitt, op. cit., 1993, pp. 177–181. See p. 178.

48. Ibid., p. 180.

49. For more on conditionality, see Miles Kahler, "External Influence, Conditionality, and the Politics of Adjustment," in Haggard and Kaufman, *Politics of Adjustment*, pp. 89–133. Conditionality occurs when policy changes and external finance are linked in a bargaining context. The concept of conditionality is associated with IMF standbys and has been formally incorporated into the amendments to the Articles of Agreement of the IMF. De facto conditionality has also become a feature of the World Bank and bilateral aid programs. Kahler (p. 31) describes the last decade's record insofar as "conditionality as influence" is concerned as mediocre (p. 133).

50. See Nelson and Eglinton, *Global Goals*, p. 31.

51. Kahler, op. cit., pp. 95–101.

52. Ibid., p. 131.

53. Ibid., p. 91.

54. Michael Pinto-Duschinsky, "Foreign Political Aid: The German Political Foundations and Their US Counterparts, *International Affairs*, Vol. 67, No. 1, January 1991, pp. 33–63. See p. 38.

55. Ibid., pp. 41–42.

56. Ibid., p. 47.

57. "President-Elect Clinton's Foreign Policy Statements," *Foreign Policy Bulletin*, Vol. 3, No. 3, November-December 1992, pp. 2–23. See p. 6.

58. Pinto-Duschinsky, op. cit., p. 63.

59. "Nicaraguan Policy Shifts Under Bush," *Congressional Quarterly Almanac*, Vol. 45, 1989, pp. 549–585. See p. 569.

60. See Pease and Forsythe, "Human Rights," p. 293.

61. Ibid., pp. 298–314.

62. Henkin, "Law and Politics," p. 207.

63. See Halperin, "Guaranteeing Democracy," p. 121.

64. See Damrosch, "Politics Across Borders," p. 6.

65. Ibid., p. 13.

66. Ibid., p. 36.

67. Ibid., p. 37.

68. Teson, *Humanitarian Intervention*, p. 244.

69. Ibid., p. 247.

70. See Greenwood, "Is There a Right of Humanitarian Intervention?" p. 34.

71. Ibid., p. 40.

72. Ibid.

73. Franck, "Emerging Right."

74. Ibid., pp. 88–89.

75. Forsythe, *Internationalization*.

76. Laurie S. Wiseberg, "Protecting Human Rights Activists and NGOs: What More Can Be Done?" *Human Rights Quarterly*, Vol. 13, No. 4, November 1991, pp. 525–544. See p. 529.

77. Ibid., pp. 532–538.

78. Lowell W. Livezey, *Nongovernmental Organizations and the Ideas of Human Rights*, Princeton, NJ: Center of International Studies, Princeton University, 1988.

79. Timothy M. Shaw, "Popular Participation in Non-Governmental Structures in Africa: Implications for Democratic Development," *Africa Today*, Vol. 37, No. 3, 3d quarter, 1990, pp. 5–22. See pp. 14–15.

80. See Denis MacShane, "The New Age of the Internationals," *New Statesman and Society*, Vol. 6, No. 250, April 30, 1993, pp. 23–26. See esp. p. 26.

81. *World Development Report, 1991*, p. 136.

82. Ibid., p. 136.

83. MacShane, op. cit., p. 26.

84. See Claude and Weston, *Human Rights in the World Community*, p. 289.

CHAPTER 4

Algeria: The End of the Beginning of Democratization

From 1965, when President Ahmed Ben Bella was replaced by Houari Boumedienne through a peaceful coup, until the late 1980s, Algeria enjoyed relative political stability with centralized and collegial governments. After independence from French colonial rule in July 1962, the Algerian economy was planned and managed by the government, which nationalized all major foreign firms. In a country where 99 percent of the population is Muslim of Arab, Berber, or mixed descent, secularism, under the leadership of the National Liberation Front (Front de liberalization nationale—FLN) prevented a close symbiosis between religion and politics. The recent Islamic political agenda spearheaded by the Islamic Salvation Front (Front islamique du salut—FIS) calls for the mutualism of religion and politics.

Algeria lacks political and ethnic cohesion, and an increasing number of Algerians today see Islam as a unifying force. This challenges the secularism of the past thirty years. As economic stagnation, massive deterioration of social conditions, and natural disasters such as the 1989 earthquake in Tipasa have continued, the Islamic resurgence has gained momentum and exerted mounting pressure on the government. More than 30 percent of Algeria's 26 million people are between the ages of fifteen and twenty-nine; 12 percent of the people are unemployed; and the annual population growth rate is 3.2 percent. The FIS, which has succeeded by providing alternatives to the grand failures of the secular governments, has had little difficulty in finding constituencies among marginalized youth. Recently, however, the growth of Islamic groups has been expedited largely by political liberalization under former President Chadli Bendjedid.

In February 1989, Algeria's new constitution permitted, for the first time since 1962, the creation of civil and political associations and a multiparty system. The history of Algeria since then has been tumultuous. Abrupt changes in social and political relations led to the breakdown of the democratic initiatives on January 11, 1992, and the cancellation of the scheduled second-round election for the National Assembly. Democratization was not successful after the brief period of 1989–1992 because civil society had not matured enough. The renewal of civil society in Algeria, the military takeover, the polarization of society, and the end of democratization are the issues this chapter explores.

Historical Overview

Independence came after nearly eight years of bloody conflict with France. The nationalist FLN led the war against the colonial power and laid down the structure of the National Liberation Army (Armée de Liberation Nationale—ALN). The ALN's guerrilla warfare and political struggles against the French won the hearts and minds of Algerians. After independence, the legitimacy of the FLN's rule was unquestioned. During this time, Algerian presidents were a part of a triangular power structure composed of the army, the state, and the FLN. In this alliance, the army's role was crucial for a president: support meant longevity; lack of support was synonymous with transiency. The heads of state, Ahmed Ben Bella (1962–1965), Houari Boumedienne (1965–1978), and Chadli Bendjedid (1979–1992) were very aware of this reality. Boumedienne and Bendjedid, both had military backgrounds—Boumedienne as head of the armed forces and Benjedid as an army officer. They were custodians of a revolution in which the armed forces played a supreme role.

Under Ben Bella and Boumedienne, the government promoted socialist development programs, including extensive state-financed modernization programs based on secular blueprints.[1] Through oil and gas exports from 1969 to 1973, Algeria achieved a 9 percent annual growth rate, which made further industrialization feasible.[2] But during the 1980s, worldwide economic stagnation, coupled with a sharp drop in oil and gas prices, aggravated the economy; and the regime's failure to distribute services caused public discontent. The demand for change compelled the government, by then headed by Chadli Bendjedid, to initiate economic and political reforms; however, Bendjedid's failure effectively to implement these reforms led to further economic troubles, culminating in an array of strikes and food riots in October 1988. Bendjedid saw the necessity for reforms designed to defuse the rising discontent among both the secular and Islamist oppositions. Behind the calls for reform, lay the public's dissatisfaction with economic hardships that had resulted from failed austerity measures in 1986. At the request of the FLN, the army restored some semblance of short-term stability.

February 1989 ushered in a new era of multiparty politics that unleashed a sudden democratization that culminated in the 1991 national legislative elections. Suddenly, Algeria went from a one-party system to multiparty political structure, with more than fifty parties. With a renewed economic liberalization and a swift political liberalization under way, Bendjedid hoped to preserve his party and its agenda amid the mounting public demands for reforms. Of course, the party that benefited the most from fast-track political liberalization programs was the FIS. Writing in early 1993, Mohammed Akacem provided a plausible explanation:

> No longer having to operate underground, [FIS] was now free to openly spread its message and recruit new members from the masses of disaffected youth who filled the mosques every Friday. Others were recruited and attracted to the movement from the ranks of the so-called "hittistes" [the unemployed and vagrants] who now have a cause and a vehicle through which to vent their anger against the establishment.[3]

Bendjedid's liberalization programs were not effective and failed to accommodate the interests of all the sectors of the society. As noted above, rapid political liberalization contributed substantially to the undermining of his party and the resurgence of Islamist groups. The failure of the economic liberalization programs of the 1980s, which culminated in October 1988 food riots, helps to explain, to some extent, the failures of the democratic experiments of the early 1990s. The liberalization programs of the 1980s mainly benefited the middle class—presumbly at the cost of the lower class—and further skewed the nation's income distribution. As Bendjedid's government launched a new, but somewhat similar, program of liberalization in the early 1990s, the poor and disenchanted segments of the society resisted fiercely (more on that later). Following the first round of elections in December 1991 (resulting in a resounding victory for FIS) and anticipation of a further defeat for the government in the second round, the army took over and Bendjedid resigned. The ensuing political instability facilitated the military's political role. These events, bringing the army back to the forefront of Algerian politics, were influenced in important ways by the nation's civil-military relationship. This relationship is the topic of the next section.

Civil-Military Relations

Born in a violent revolution against French colonial rule and riddled with political infighting and nationalistic conflicts in the post-1962 period, Algeria's politics have been intimately associated with the military's maneuverings. External security problems, such as territorial and political disputes with neighboring Morocco and Libya, as well as foreign policies sympathetic to national liberation movements in the Third World, have kept the armed forces heavily engaged in the politics of the postindependence era. Beyond its security responsibilities, the People's National Army (ANP) played a politically significant role in the top echelons of the government. The armed forces were extensively used to promote rural economic development projects—a role established by Algeria's constitution.[4] Increasingly, Algeria's secular governments, especially those of Ben Bella and Boumedienne, relied upon the army to safeguard their impotent and fragmented governments from internal threats. Over time, the military's role as the guardian of stability deepened, at times overshadowing the policies of the state and the FLN.

During the first year of independence, Ben Bella converted the external (ALN) and internal units of the army into a unified force, redesignated the People's National Army. This was an effort to consolidate the FLN's control over the army. However, an alliance between some of the FLN leaders and Boumedienne, a former defense minister, resulted in a coup on June 19, 1965. This coup removed Ben Bella and his political faction from the political scene and marked the beginning of a long period of direct military participation in Algeria's politics. Frederick Ehrenreich has documented the military's influence in Boumedienne's first government. The military dominated the Council of the Revolution, the country's supreme governing body: twenty-two of the council's twenty-six original members were military officers.[5]

After surviving a coup attempt by his chief of staff, Zbiri, Boumedienne encouraged continued military influence in national and local government; the latter being made possible through the military's direct role in national economic development projects. In 1978, Boumedienne's deteriorating health forced him out of Algeria's political scene. His successor, Bendjedid, a prominent ANP leader, gingerly moved to solidify his power by tactfully curtailing the involvement of military officers in politics. Nevertheless, the military's influence in the political arenas remained very strong.

By the mid-1980s, the declining influence of the ANP on the regime was clear. Only 16 percent of the ministers and deputy ministers in the 1984 government were military officers, compared with the 35 percent that had served in the previous administration.[6] Bendjedid intended to put an end to the military era—the state of mobilization in which military leaders, supported by a military oligarchy, had directed socialist programs. The emergence of the Algerian government out of a national liberation movement had meant, according to Morris Janowitz, that its leaders were primarily concerned with issues of political organization; thus, the military became directly and continuously involved in mass-party organization.[7]

Bendjedid's maneuverings reinforced his 1987 pragmatic economic liberalization package—policies consistent with the interests of the military oligarchy. Trouble began in 1989 when Bendjedid's swift political liberalization polarized Algerian society into two irreconcilable camps: the military and the Islamists. Traditionally a powerful institution, the military interpreted the weakening of the secular FLN and the strengthening of the Islamists as a threat. When the 1991–1992 Assembly elections favored the FIS, the military cancelled the elections and themselves completely took power. Bendjedid was forced out of politics and Mohamed Boudiaf, a veteran FLN member, became head of the High Council of State. Boudiaf's assassination on June 29, 1992, indicated that the army and some factions within the FLN found his conciliatory policies unacceptable. Soon after, Colonel Ali Kafi took charge; the effort to form a new civil-military relationship had come to an abrupt end, and secular democrats had lost the most ground. Robert Mortimer, in a 1993 evaluation of the military's comeback, quotes the Algerian historian Mohamed Harbi: "In most countries," said Harbi, "the state has its army, but in Algeria the army has its state."[8] The military's return to the forefront of Algeria's politics was a harbinger of troubles to come and a grim reminder that the civil-military relations in Algeria are far from stable.

Economic Liberalization—of Sorts

Algeria has an oil-based economy: nearly 98 percent of government revenues are derived from hydrocarbon exports. Historically, it has relied on a centrally planned and dominant public sector. From 1973 to 1984, Algeria enjoyed large gains in foreign exchange due to growth in oil revenues. Between 1962 and 1984, however, the food self-sufficiency ratio dropped from 70 to 40 percent.[9] The country's leaders managed to gain access to development assistance from Eastern and Western bloc countries and international agencies, including the Organization for Economic Cooperation and Development (OECD) and the World Bank. Domestic forces in Algeria favored an increased role for private capitalism and foreign investment. These forces—present in agriculture, services, and commerce at the time of independence in 1962—regrouped in the right wing of the FLN after independence. However, their policy prescriptions were overshadowed by the left wing of the FLN until the early 1980s.

Following Boumedienne's death in 1978, economic policy was intensely debated within the ruling circles of the FLN. The private sector's importance was emphasized early in the 1980s when a group of capitalists within the FLN criticized the Boumedienne era industrialization campaign and demanded more freedom for the private sector so it could maneuver in the economy.[10] Eventually, those who espoused a retreat from lofty industrialization and socialized agriculture prevailed. The promotion of moderate liberalization measures began. The first five-year plan (1980–1984) was intended to shift economic priorities away from basic industry and balance the needs of industry, agriculture, and consumers. The second five-year plan (1985–1989), while continuing the priorities of the first, emphasized the private sector and the necessity for optimal efficiency.[11]

Some scholars maintain that economic liberalization was embarked on during the first five-year plan, under the direction of Abdelhamid Brahimi, a Western-educated economist.[12] Others assert that—although during that period the government expressed interest in the liberalization of agriculture, social infrastructure (housing, education, and public health), and light industry—the overall economic record of Algeria indicates that the actual liberalization programs were implemented by the private sector during 1985–1989. Supporting the latter view, John Ruedy notes that Bendjedid and his advisers had not planned to relinquish a major part of state economic control to the private sector during the first plan. Rather, their principal aim was to decentralize the system in order to make the institutions of state capitalism "more reactive to economic forces and more responsive to the needs of the society."[13]

Ruedy also argues that the policy simultaneously served political goals. The large state corporations, such as SONATRACH, ESDNC, and SNS, had developed into centers of power and become increasingly defiant of the central government, and the reformers of 1980–1984 wanted to break them into smaller companies.[14] An alternative view on the political implications is offered by some historians. In this view, Algeria's efforts at economic liberalization are not taken seriously due to the fact that in oil-producing states like Algeria, the regime counts so much on oil and gas prices rising in the future that it may decide to stall any major implementation of liberalization policies.[15] According to this view, although the regime goes through the motions of liberalization, it counts on price increases to defuse tensions in society.

Having argued that the move toward reform and privatization measures was deliberately sluggish, Dirk Vanderwalle divides the liberalization programs into four distinct periods: 1980–1982, characterized by a few, isolated liberalization measures; 1982–1985, when the integrated directives were stressed; 1986–1988, characterized by an intensification of the earlier measures and ended by the riots; and the last period, 1988 to the time when Vanderwalle was writing—1992—when the remaining political opposition to infitah, the open-door policy, was rejected and the government went ahead with additional reforms.[16]

The austerity measures associated with the earlier period failed drastically to change the country's economy. Cuts in national income resulting from the austerity measures imposed colossal hardship on the poorer sections of the population, while the well-to-do segments remained protected. In the latter part of the 1980s, notes Vanderwalle, several restrictions were lifted: the banking sector was reformed and renewed, monetary policy was shaped by an independent central bank, and most public companies became legally autonomous.[17] Throughout 1991, the government continued attempts to deregulate the economy by devaluing the Algerian dinar (at one point by 22 percent).[18]

By the time the second five-year plan was put into effect, the sharp plunge in oil revenues (in 1986) and the subsequent fall of the dollar against European currencies on which Algeria's imports were heavily dependent created a dismal economic situation for the Bendjedid government. Facing a severe crisis, in 1987 Algeria, upon the advice of the IMF, started moving toward a market economy. The Ministry of Planning was abolished; the state monopoly on credit, banking, and financial institutions was terminated; private investment (both domestic and foreign) in all these sectors was permitted.[19]

Although the IMF's ties with Tunisia and Morocco were traditionally stronger than those it had with Algeria, insofar as structural adjustment programs were concerned, Algeria's domestic policy changes in agricultural, commerce, and service sectors were consistent with the IMF's guidelines. For instance, the austerity measures of 1983 and 1986–1987 were initiated by the domestic planners. Although compatible with IMF policy requirements, they were not a direct result of them. Additionally, the U.S. Agency for International Development was not operative in Algeria;[20] thus, external influences were not directly linked to these early developments.

Economic Liberalization and the Internal Crisis

The economic crisis of the 1980s caused the Bendjedid government to initiate some economic reforms. More atttention was given to private investment. Tim Niblock writes that the 1982 code des investissements sought to promote private investment in light manufacturing, craft industry, and hotel infrastructure by providing a range of guarantees and incentives such as tax advantages and credit facilities. The creation of the domaines agricoles socialisters was accomplished by a limited privatization of agrarian land.[21] Economic liberalization measures coincided with the beginning of the second five-year plan. In February 1985, Bendjedid lobbied a special congress of the FLN to adopt a new national charter promoting the private sector and a balance between socialism and Islam as a state ideology—an obvious departure from the centralized planning of his predecessor, Boumedienne. In the January 1986 referendum, with an incredibly high voter turnout (95.92 percent of those eligible), 98.37 percent of the votes were cast in favor of adopting a new charter. Bendjedid's liberalization gained further approval on February 26, 1987, when a record 87.9 percent of the electorate voted for the FLN candidates in a general election for the National Assembly. The composition of the newly elected assembly made the liberalization program viable.[22]

The move toward market mechanisms and strategies, according to Niblock, gave the Banque Centrale d'Algerie more freedom from bureaucratic control, gave state-owned companies greater freedom in determining their sales and investment policies, and gave smaller agricultural cooperatives (exploitations agricoles cooperatives—EACs) more usufruct rights. These included the right to utilize and enjoy the profits and advantages of the land without owning it, so long as damage was not done to the property. These measures were accompanied by austerity measures in July 1988. They resulted in zero growth in GDP and a 20 percent unemployment rate.[23] The domestic unrest of October 1988 and the government's weakened position forced the Bendjedid government to negotiate a standby credit with the IMF. The latter's support for Algeria in 1989 totalled about $1 billion and gave the IMF a new degree of influence over economic policy changes in Algeria.[24]

Reorienting the economy toward market-based precepts led to rising unemployment and declining industrial output. Consistent with the rules of the international financial institutions, austerity measures were imposed to reduce the volume of imports and to ameliorate the trade and budget deficits by markedly reducing the social welfare programs. These measures hit the poorest and unemployed segments of the population the hardest, but still failed. The long-term national debt rose from $16.5 billion in 1985 to $25.5 billion in 1992.[25] Deepening poverty, combined with government corruption and inefficiency, substantially eroded the legitimacy and popular mandate of the FLN. For the young, unemployed and impoverished, "what counted was not the one million martyrs of a generation ago, but the abject poverty brought by a generation of FLN rule."[26] Economic liberalization had been moderate, its pace deliberately slow, and its execution poor. It is regularly maintained that, by not moving fast and far enough in implementing broad macroeconomic reforms, governments risk succumbing to politicoeconomic difficulties; or, at best, they simply "change the principle of allocating goods and services within the economy"[27] without improving anything.

The economic liberalization of 1986–1987 included cuts in government subsidies and the state bureaucracy as well as decentralization of production. The poor results of the reforms in the latter part of 1980s spelled disaster for the regime. Beginning in 1987, the Bendjedid government had introduced measures designed to increase privatization in agriculture and other economic sectors. Joint ventures in the production and exports of oil and gas were launched. The government's 1987 slogan, "Autonomy for enterprises," announced a new economic initiative. New legislation was enacted in December 1987 allowing the state-controlled enterprises to adopt their own annual plans, determine their products' prices, and freely invest their income. These newly autonomous companies were called entreprises publiques economiques (EPEs). By mid-1989, 75 percent of state-controlled enterprises were EPEs.[28]

The loss of government revenues in 1986, largely due to a drop in oil prices from $40 a barrel in 1979 to under $10 in 1986, substantially curtailed the investment opportunities envisaged by the 1985–1989 plan. Algeria's foreign income declined from $13 billion in 1985 to $8 billion in 1986. Early in 1988, a series of economic reforms was introduced in which more than seventy state-controlled companies became EPEs, including banks, insurance companies, and industrial, commercial, and service companies.[29] In October 1988, economic distress and social unrest caused crises of unmanageable proportions for the regime, and the Bendjedid government had to use force to restore order. Economic liberalization resumed shortly afterwards, but this time it was blended with constitutional reforms. Some have suggested that the principal aim of the 1990–1994 development plan, had it been implemented, would have been fully to liberalize the economy; but as the revenues from oil and foreign remittances dwindled and foreign debt mounted toward the end of the 1980s, the government's task was interrupted.

Sensing a growing tension in the country because of economic decline, the architects of the economic reforms sought refuge behind a sudden liberalization and sweeping democratization. The latter complicated the attempts to accommodate the interests of the secular and religious sectors of the society. Democratization was premature and lent credence to the proposition that only gradual, piecemeal political liberalization could, in the long run, have incorporated the interests of different groups, from the FIS and the Islamic Alliance, to the Movement for Democracy (MDA), the FLN, the army, and other secular groups in the society.

Aside from the difficulties associated with political liberalization, the execution of economic liberalization plans and their implications for the economically deprived segments of the populace were disturbing. Economic liberalization entailed social costs that many groups or parties in Algeria were not willing to pay. Thus, attempts to promote market reforms predictably reinforced the fundamentalist wing of the FIS under the Imam Alin Belhadj, who opposed increasing the financial burdens on the poor.[30]

Constitutional Revisions: Some Implications

The constitutional alterations approved in February 1989 renewed Algeria's civil society by establishing in Article 40 the terms of an associational life for Algerians. The constitutional reforms and revisions undertaken to reshape the state-society relationship denoted, in the words of John P. Entelis, "a veritable democratic revolution."[31] Reelected as Algeria's president for a third term in 1988, Bendjedid acknowledged the political and economic limits of state socialism and opted for a dramatic break with the country's official economic philosophy and political ideology. Change was needed to resurrect the civil society and press for democratization. Bendjedid's determination to seize opportunities for political reform was praiseworthy—given Algeria's structural and institutional constraints—they were not practicable, as the consequences of his abrupt democratization programs soon showed. John P. Entelis described the pace of these changes: "In only nine months, from October 1988 to July 1989, the Algerian political system was fundamentally transformed from a single-party authoritarian state to a multiparty, pluralistic nation of laws."[32] Representing a major break with the past, the revised constitution established the right to form civil and political associations. The constitution's wording was unambiguously straightforward, recognizing the citizens' right to found "associations of a political character." This provision opened the way for the FIS to enter the political fray.

The FIS established a reputation as an organized and credible agent of social service by helping the poorest of the shantytowns in Algeria's urban areas, as well as the victims of the 1989 earthquake. In urban areas, it gained access to a large pool of disaffected young people who were looking for an alternative to the discredited secular policies of the FLN and its bloated state bureaucracy. The first free elections since independence were held in June 1990. The FIS won 54 percent of the popular vote in the municipal and provincial elections; the FLN only 28 percent. In December 1990, the Bendjedid government promised legislative elections for the next year. In March 1991, Prime Minister Moulud Hamrouche gerrymandered district boundaries to bolster the FLN's standings in future southern elections. The Islamist groups challenged him and dubbed his tactics a "malapportionment practice." Violence erupted, forcing the army to become directly involved. The summer of 1991, writes Robert Mortimer, saw a crisis that "thrust the army to the apex of the triangle [FLN-State-Army] once again as the new system of relating state and society became overburdened."[33]

In the first legislative elections, held on December 26, 1991, the ruling FLN party won only 15 seats of the 430-seat National Popular Assembly (APN). The FIS secured 188 seats. This result meant that the FIS was only 28 seats short of a parliamentary majority, and could be expected easily to attain this position in the second round of the elections. Democratization was dealt a fatal blow on January 11, 1992, when the army, wary of the possibility of a rapprochement between the FLN and the FIS, leading to power-sharing, annulled the first-round election results and cancelled the scheduled second-round of elections. The army and other parties feared that FIS control of the National Assembly would lead to the installation of an Islamic fundamentalist state and the Arabization of Algeria.

This threat, frantically exaggerated and blown out of proportion, put an end to the first instance of a truly democratically elected Islamic government via an electoral process. Islamist groups, as the dominant opposition voices in Algeria, have in recent years offered legitimate challenges to the performance of the authoritarian state. In fact, Islamist and human rights groups share both practical and political interests against government repression. Jill Crystal, who argues that the impulse toward authoritarianism lies not in something primordial in Arab culture but instead in a more complex sociostructural, economic, ideological, and institutional dynamic of growth and modernization, makes a convincing case:

> Both [Islamist and human rights groups] oppose an element at the core of authoritarianism: arbitrariness. . . . At the heart of both movements is a denunciation of arbitrary government and a promise to replace it with the rule of law (God's or men's). Human rights groups aim to change not just the players but also the rules and . . . the rules about the rule making. So, too, the Islamists.[34]

The nullification of the second round, which would have led to a major victory for the FIS in the National Assembly, escalated the conflict and the polarization of Algeria's political landscape. Bendjedid, who resigned, was forced from the political scene. Mohamed Boudiaf, a veteran FLN member and founder who spent twenty-eight years in exile, became head of a five-member High Council of State on January 14, 1992. This provoked a new era of violence and terror. On February 9, 1992, the FIS was officially banned. On March 4, 1992, the FIS was dismantled and its leaders, Abbas Madani and Imam Alin Belhadj, were jailed and banned from political life. However, this failed to prevent further trouble. On June 29, 1992, Boudiaf was assassinated, allegedly in accordance with a plan engineered by the army and some circles within the upper echelons of the FLN. This signalled the rising divisions within and conflicts between the old factions of the FLN, and was an omen of the turbulence to come in Algerian politics.[35]

The 1989 experiment with democracy, started by Bendjedid, ended quickly. Ali Kafi, Boudiaf's successor, vowed to promote a platform combining military and theocratic interests. The appointment of Abdesselam Belaid as the new prime minister initially shattered the optimism of those who believed that economic liberalization would resume in the near future: Abdesselam had a reputation for being a staunch critic of Bendjedid's market-oriented economic reforms. But, contrary to his reputation, Abdesselam pursued market-oriented policies with a vengeance. The Presidential Council on August 21, 1993, ousted him and appointed in his place Foreign Minister Redha Malek, after Belaid's austerity policies failed to win the support of the regime and did nothing to alleviate Algeria's $26 billion foreign debt. Economic uncertainty, along with the political impasse surrounding the return of multiparty electoral activity, has accentuated, in the words of Jonathan G. Farley, "the general lack of international economic confidence in Algeria's medium term future and the country at present finds it exceedingly difficult to borrow money in the world's financial markets."[36]

Despite this lack of confidence, a group of eight international banks, led by Credit Lyonnais, approved on February 26, 1992, a $1.5 billion foreign loan to ease Algeria's debt repayments. This loan reportedly had been in the making since October 1991. The refinancing of Algeria's debt paved the way for disbursement of a $510 million loan from the European Community (now the European Union).[37] Offers of credits from the World Bank (US$1 billion), France (US$877 million) and Italy (US$300 million), as well as joint venture proposals by Italian firms for Algeria's public and private sectors were all aimed at soothing the country's economic distress.[38]

In January 1994, Algeria reportedly removed restrictions on the importation of several consumer products. A new, unspecified tariff on imports was applied, and import buyers were required to pay with money from their foreign exchange bank accounts.[39] Further, Algeria consented to carry out strict economic reforms as part of an agreement with the IMF. In early 1994, Algeria had a 22 percent inflation rate and at least 22 percent of workers were reported to be unemployed. Approximately 10 percent of Algeria's gas and oil industry proceeds were supposed to be earmarked to help pay interest on its external debt, which at that time totaled $27 billion.[40] Despite economic reforms, tension between secular and Islamic groups continues to narrow the "middle ground." The battle for supremacy persists relentlessly and—as Mortimer wrote in 1993—secular democrats agonize over the narrow space left.[41]

Human Rights Setbacks

Several trends have persisted since Boumedienne's death, some encouraging and others disheartening. The liberalization measures of the 1980s under the Bendjedid government increased the civil rights of Algerians. The pressing need to obtain public acceptance of renewed austerity measures in 1986–1987 forced the Bendjedid regime to make concessions in the civil liberties area. The government officially recognized the Algerian League for the Defense of Human Rights and an Algerian branch of Amnesty International and conceded that both these associations would be independent of the FLN—a meager but marked departure from previous practice, in which the party had a formal monopoly of public life.[42] Recognition of the nongovernmental organizations' presence and legitimacy was very encouraging to human rights advocates. The repression after failed democratization entailed gross violations and the social order of the emerging civil society crumbled.

Some socioeconomic areas have made considerable strides since independence. Life expectancy in Algeria increased from 47.0 in 1960 to 65.1 in 1990. The adult literacy rate rose from 25 percent in 1970 to 57 percent in 1991. The combined enrollment in primary and secondary schools rose from 46 percent in 1970 to 79 percent during the 1987–1990 period. Real GDP per capita (purchasing power parities, ppp$) increased from $1,676 in 1960 to $3,011 in 1990. The financial commitment to education as percentage of GNP was significantly enhanced, advancing from 5.6 in 1960 to 9.1 during 1988–1990.[43] The riots of 1988, however, reflected the failure of the government's economic policies in certain areas. The dramatic increases in underemployment and in the annual rate of inflation from 6.6 percent (during the period from 1980 to 1990) to 50 percent (in 1991)[44] indicate that Algeria's economic troubles played a key role in the upsurge of the Islamist opposition and the rejection of the FLN's secular politicians. Other elements of the conflict—now to be considered—are minority politics and issues.

Minority Rights

The Berber-speaking Kabyle minority, who constitute almost one-fifth of Algeria's population, have frequently complained of oppression and discrimination.[45] Threatened a decade ago by Islamist demands for Arabization under Chadli Bendjedid and recently by the growing appeal of the FIS, the Berbers maintain that they have the most to lose if an Islamic state is formed in Algeria.

Such fears heightened in January 1990, when the Arabization of the media and schools was legally sanctioned. The new law rendered it illegal for the main news organs of the new parties to publish in any language other than Arabic. However, the Rally for Culture and Democracy (RCD) and the Front of Socialist Forces (FFS) chose to disregard the law and published their newspapers in Berber.[46] The Kabyle's insistence on expressing themselves in their native language has strengthened in recent years. Islamic opposition groups have portrayed Kabyle as a Western-influenced group whose people have relinquished Islam. As an Islamic minority, Berbers see their cultural survival endangered by the FIS.[47] It is not clear, however, if their demands will be sufficiently heeded under the present military regime.

Failed Democratization and Its Dire Consequences

Following the cancellation of the 1992 election, the Algerian government abrogated all political freedoms granted during the liberalization of 1988–1991 and held thousands of Islamists in detention camps, clearly violating habeas corpus rights and the right to due process.[48] There have been massive human rights abuses, including torture of prisoners. The military-backed government has justified its actions in the name of preventing a repressive theocracy from assuming political power and has freely used emergency powers to detain civilians. Human Rights Watch reports that "detainees were not informed of the reasons for their detention, the length of the detention order, or the criteria for determining when they would be released."[49] In late October 1992, there were approximately sixteen thousand detainees in camps. By March 1, 1993, according to Amnesty International, government use of torture and other abuses had increased drastically. More than nine thousand prisoners suspected of being Islamic activists had been detained in desert camps without charges being laid.[50]

Since 1991, the boundaries of free expression have been severely limited.[51] Algeria's independent press, which until 1991 was the freest in North Africa, has lost considerable ground. The only source of information is a single press agency, the state-owned Algerian Press Service (APS), which has demonstrated more loyalty to the ruling body than to truth.[52] Censorship persists, and journalists' only way of printing the news hinges on the availibility of the three rotary printers owned by FLN publishers.[53] The Association of Algerian Journalists (AJA) has condemned the clampdown as "veritable judicial harassment."[54] Repeated requests by Middle East Watch to visit places of detention have been denied by the government. Access was granted to the International Committee of the Red Cross (ICRC), but the ICRC discontinued its visits when the government failed to meet the ICRC's standard stipulation that such visits be allowed on a regular basis.[55]

U.S. aid to Algeria was limited to an annual grant of $150,000 for military training, but even this small amount contradicted the rhetoric linking foreign aid to democratization. U.S. reticence concerning the coup and its aftermath has proved that, to the U.S. government, pro-Western authoritarian regimes are preferable to elected—but not necessarily pro-Western—regimes. This tacit support of the new regime may account for, among other things, why no resumption of political liberalization seems to be in the offing.

What Lies Ahead?

The political upheavals in 1991–1992, precipitated by a sudden political liberalization and a premature democratization, placed Algerian politics at a crossroads. During democratic transitions, often unstable and volatile, leaders' strategic choices and tactical measures can debilitate or exacerbate the extent of the volatility. The truncated and poor implementation of economic liberalization in Algeria, together with the abrupt political liberalization and democratization of the 1980s, propelled social decline, political decay, and economic torpidity. These factors finally led to violent politics and a takeover of power by the army. The army's intrusion into civilian politics was prompted by the gross miscalculations of a ruling civilian elite that overlooked the nature and history of the Algerian political structure, of which the army historically was a major part. Ali El-Kenz, an Algerian economic sociologist, aptly describes the political history:

> After the country's independence, by act of force and coup d'etat, the political structure crystallized upon the *command function* to the detriment of *leadership function* and within the former, upon the function of public order to the function of politics, properly speaking. Its fire power developed but in inverse proportion to its power to persuade, and when, with the 1980s, came the dark years of depression and nondevelopment, it was the former that was called upon to respond to the demands of a civilian society that no longer had any means of expression except the street, violent strikes, or riots. October 1988 was the final round of this tragic confrontation by a state whose organizational logic had amputated the political dimension and reduced its social mediation of its apparatus of order and repression, while the society, its political dimension also totally amputated, was also reduced to expressing itself only by violence.[56]

What can one reasonably anticipate for Algeria's future, given the constraints and obstacles faced by democratization? Because it is an energy-based economy, Algeria's economic conditions will be vulnerable to the vagaries of oil prices on the international markets. Its domestic conditions point to the types of structural problems characteristic of many Third World countries: government mismanagement, corruption, social cleavages, demographic strains, political instability, and susceptibility to external problems. The expansion of Algeria's civil society needs to proceed in tandem with measured economic liberalization. The social costs of the changes for different segments of the society need to be tolerable. For the long-term effects of economic liberalization to sustain a move toward democratization, a measured political liberalization must be enacted as well. Economic liberalization, in the long run, enhances national unity only if it is accompanied by a measured political liberalization program.

Lynette Rummel argues that the economic costs of privatization and economic liberalization in Algeria have been high. Nevertheless, she and others are mistaken in attributing all of Algeria's economic difficulties to privatization. The global decline in the price of oil, a severe housing shortage, and the 1987 drought are other causes of Algeria's serious economic difficulties. Ultimately, economic reforms are critical for an effective democratic transition and privatization must accordingly be encouraged.[57]

While economic liberalization lasted more than a decade and was gradually implemented by state technocrats, political liberalization was precipitated under political duress, instead of through a measured and incremental fashion. Bradford Dillman maintains that the weak link in Algerian experiments with democratization is civil society. Algeria's civil society, composed of workers' unions, feminist groups, professional unions, and alternative political parties, did not have a long evolution. Rather, the institutional reforms of 1989 took place in a society lacking organized groups outside of the extended family and patron-client structures. The lack of organized and collective bargaining in Algerian society was patent.[58]   In retrospect, it can be said that a swift, wide-ranging restructuring of the economy accompanied by a gradual process of political liberalization aimed at expanding Algeria's civil society, would have been the correct formula. The suppression of civil society since 1962, along with the legacy of French colonialism and a severe economic crisis, complicated the Algerian democratic experiment. The swift political liberalization process in 1990–1991 dashed even further the hopes of building the infrastructure for a successful democracy.

The Paralyzed Government

All the indicators in the aftermath of the 1992 military takeover suggest that the present government is in a state of paralysis. On January 14, 1993, Ali Kafi, then acting head of state, promised to hold a referendum to decide the future direction of the nation; but the five-man High State Council, acting as a collective-style presidency, extended a state of emergency to counter the Islamic dissidents and Kafi's promise was delayed until 1994.

On January 31, 1994, a retired general, Liamine Zeroual, was named to Algeria's new top post, "president of state." Zeroual's assumption of power from the interim High State Council, as Algeria'a sixth president, brought the country under full overt control of the military. Zeroual made it clear that he was committed to serious dialogue and compromise between the opposition groups, especially the army and the Islamists. It remains unclear if these negotiations will pull Algeria back from the spiral of violence and economic collapse in the near future.[59] A crucial sticking point in these negotiations is, of course, the issue of amnesty for the military.[60]

The outlawed FIS, which became a guerrilla movement after the coup under Sheik Abdel Kadir Shabouti and Al Said Makhloufi, will also find it imperative to compromise in certain areas.[61] Kate Zebiri maintains that, in the Algerian context, the function of the FIS and other Islamic political parties has been one of sociopolitical protest. They are, however, widely criticized for lacking a coherent political program, "but apparently no one is prepared to give them the opportunity to discredit themselves by actually exercising power gained through the ballot box."[62]

Anwar Haddam, the FIS parliamentary leader in exile, has set three conditions for entering into a dialogue with the government of President Zeroual: recognition of the FIS as a political party; the release of political prisoners; and commitment to a democratic process for Algeria.[63] Furthermore, as militant armed Islamic groups have gained popular appeal since the 1992 coup, the army has become wary of potential splits in its own ranks: while the top brass have remained vehemently antifundamentalist, some junior officers and conscripts are said to have leaned toward the Islamists.[64] Some even contend that "all lieutenants and sergeants are pro-FIS."[65] The army has been weakened by the defection of an estimated 20,000 from its ranks to the Islamist side.

With further increase in the number of defectors, the army could risk disintegration by losing control of the country.[66] In late 1994, a state of paralysis prevailed. The government was so divided that it was unclear how it would be able to impose conditions on the opposition. The country was barely functioning and was rapidly unravelling in an atmosphere of escalating violence and fear.[67] This could potentially open prospects for compromise between the FIS and the army. Still, many argued that the prospects for a national dialogue and an end to the violence were bleak.[68] The two-year period following the coup left four thousand dead, a state of full-fledged civil war, and a country paralyzed.[69]

Conclusion

Algeria's brief experiment with democratization came to an abrupt halt when the army cancelled the second round of parliamentary elections on January 11, 1992. Fearing that an FIS majority in the National Assembly would lead to the emergence of an Islamic state, the army stepped in to prevent such a change—a takeover tacitly supported by some secular groups who similarly feared Islamization and Arabization.

Earlier—in 1989—sudden political liberalization and democratization had been initiated by socioeconomic turmoil and the October 1988 food riots.

Democratization lasted only briefly. Its hasty end is accounted for by structural constraints and three decades of rule by authentic national authoritarian regimes. The damage resulting from the unsuccessful democratization will most likely outweigh any of the short-term gains achieved during the 1989–1991 political opening.

Among the former Maghreb countries, Algeria has the longest legacy of French colonial occupation (1830–1962), of postindependence regime turnovers, and of preeminent and protracted military involvement in national politics. But why did a fairly enduring process of liberalization fail in Algeria? In the absence of necessary economic reforms, social contract, and political compromises, the sudden hurling of Algeria into democratization led the nation to the brink of civil war. The swift political liberalization and democratization further polarized Algeria, creating irreconcilable political camps, or, in the words of Robert Mortimer, two nondemocratic alternatives: the military and theocratic rule.[70] The lack of prior consensus on acceptance of election results, and leadership miscalculations regarding the election, led to the cancellation of the electoral process.

Economic failure, too, was a significant factor. The liberalization measures of the early 1980s were not followed by the measures necessary to build a civil society. Political liberalization was delayed until the late 1980s, and when it came it was in response to an economic tinderbox and the strife of October 1988. The young civil society was thus not prepared effectively to absorb the shocks of democratization. The elections, instead of uniting society, polarized it.

The Algerian situation is typical of Third World countries with social and structural handicaps. The democratization process—supposed to spur economic prosperity and the protection of human rights—failed and all efforts to renew the process have stalled. Democratization, as introduced, was not the solution for the political, economic, and social ills of the society. Instead, it did fatal political damage as the army reclaimed its dominant role. Measured, gradual political liberalization earlier in the 1980s, when support for the Bendjedid government was evident, could have prepared Algerian society for a sustainable transition. Now, the setbacks caused by that abrupt process of political liberalization have enormously complicated the expansion of civil society. A double-track approach to liberalization (political and economic) with different emphasis over a longer period would have been a better solution.

The crisis in Algeria appears to have vindicated the fears of many of the leaders of the Islamic countries about the speedy promotion of democratic reforms. Moreover, as Chris Hedges wrote in 1994, it has "tied the West even closer to governments that may be stumbling further away from democracy, even as the West calls for more freedom as the basis for global stability."[71] Democracy deserves a fair chance in Algeria. The military's illegitimate takeover is unlikely to withstand popular and social pressures for long. For now, one can only hope that the politics of national reconciliation will fairly soon be reinvented by Algeria's leaders.

Notes

1. See Mortimer, "Islam and Multiparty Politics," pp. 576–577.
2. See Evans, "Algeria: Thirty Years On," p. 4.
3. See Akacem, "Algeria: Search," p. 52.
4. Frederick Ehrenreich, "National Security," in Harold D. Nelson, ed. , *Algeria: A Country Study*, Washington, D.C.: U.S. Government, 1985, pp. 295–347. See pp. 296–309.
5. Ibid., p. 314.
6. Ibid., p. 318.
7. See Janowitz, "Some Observations," pp. 436–437.
8. See Mortimer, "Algeria: The Clash," p. 37.
9. Parvez Hasan, "Structural Adjustment in Selected Arab Countries: Need, Challenge, and Approaches," in Said El-Naggar, ed. , *Adjustment Policies and Development Strategies in the Arab World*, Washington, D.C.: International Monetary Fund, 1987, pp. 49–72. See pp. 52–56.
10. See Pfeifer, "Economic Liberalization," pp. 107–109.
11. Ruedy, *Modern Algeria*, p. 231.
12. See Roberts, "The Algerian State," p. 448; John P. Entelis, "Introduction: State and Society in Transition," in Entelis and Naylor, *State and Society*, p. 18; also Pfeifer, "Economic Liberalization," p. 110.
13. Ruedy, *Modern Algeria*, p. 234.
14. Ibid., p. 235.
15. Pool, "Links Between Economic and Political," p. 48.
16. Dirk Vanderwalle, "Breaking with Socialism: Economic Liberalization and Privatization in Algeria," in Iliya Harik and Denis J. Sullivan, eds., *Privatization and Liberalization in the Middle East*, Bloomington: Indiana University Press, 1992, pp. 189–209. See p. 193.
17. Ibid., p. 192.
18. *Facts on File*, Vol. 51, No. 2661, November 21, 1991, p. 883.
19. Ibid., p. 247.
20. "Algeria," *Background Notes*, November 1988, U. S. Department of State, Bureau of Public Affairs, pp. 1–8. See p. 8.
21. Tim Niblock, "International and Domestic Factors in the Economic Liberalization Process in Arab Countries," in Tim Niblock and Emma Murphy, eds., *Economic and Political Liberalization in the Middle East*, London: British Academic Press, 1993, pp. 55–87. See p. 72.
22. *Middle East and North Africa 1991*, 37th ed., London: Europa Publications, 1990, p. 269.
23. Niblock, op. cit., pp. 73–75.
24. Ibid., p. 76.
25. See *World Debt Tables*, supplement, Washington, D.C.: World Bank, 1991, p. 38. For related data, see Bradford Dillman, "Transition to Democracy in Algeria," in Entelis and Naylor, *State and Society*, pp. 31–51; esp. p. 41.
26. See Entelis and Arone, "Algeria in Turmoil," pp. 25–26.
27. Vanderwalle, op. cit., p. 192.
28. *Middle East and North Africa 1991*, 37th ed., London: Europa, 1990, p. 304.
29. Ibid., p. 305.
30. See Daniel Brumberg, "Islam, Elections, and Reform in Algeria," *Journal of*

Democracy, Vol. 2, No. 1, winter 1991, pp. 58–71; esp. p. 70.

31. John P. Entelis, "State and Society in Transition," in Entelis and Naylor, *State and Society,* pp. 1–30. See p. 19.

32. Ibid., p. 19.

33. Mortimer, op. cit., p. 592.

34. Crystal, "Authoritarianism and Its Adversaries," p. 285. For a relevant discussion, see Kevin Dwyer, *Arab Voices: The Human Rights Debate in the Middle East,* Berkeley: University of California Press, 1991.

35. See Roberts, "The Algerian State and Democracy," *Government and Opposition,* Vol. 27, No. 4, Autumn 1992, p. 454.

36. Jonathan G. Farley, "Algeria: Democracy On Hold," *Contemporary Review,* Vol. 262, No. 1526, March 1993, pp. 130–135. See p. 135.

37. *Facts on File,* Vol. 52, No. 2678, March 19, 1992, p. 198.

38. Jean-Pierre Audoux, "Algeria: Dramatic Change," *Energy Policy,* Vol. 20, No. 11, November 1992, pp. 1060–1062. See p. 1061.

39. *Facts on File,* Vol. 54, No. 2776, February 10, 1994, p. 88.

40. Ibid.

41. Mortimer, "Algeria: The Clash," p. 41.

42. Hugh Roberts, "In Troubled Waters," *Africa Report,* Vol. 32, No. 5, September–October, 1987, pp. 52–56. See p. 54.

43. UN Development Programme, *Human Development Report 1993,* New York: Oxford University Press, 1993, pp. 142 and 164.

44. Ibid., p. 188.

45. George Thomas Kurian, ed., *Encyclopedia of the Third World,* Third Edition, New York: Facts on File, 1987, p. 51.

46. Kusyel Tissas, "Berber By Any Other Name," *Index on Censorship,* Vol. 21, No. 5, May 1992, p. 21.

47. Ibid.

48. *Human Rights Watch Report 1993,* p. 290.

49. Ibid.

50. *Facts on File,* Vol. 53, No. 2732, April 8, 1993, p. 253.

51. *Human Rights Watch Report 1993,* p. 291.

52. Anne Dissez, "Still under the Influence," *Index on Censorship,* Vol., 21, No. 5, May 1992, pp. 22–23. See p. 23.

53. Ibid.

54. Lek Hor Tan, "Judicial Harassment," *Index on Censorship,* Vol. 21, No. 5, May 1992, p. 23.

55. Ibid., p. 293.

56. Ali El-Kens, *Algerian Reflections,* pp. xi–xii.

57. Lynette Rummel, "Privatization and Democratization in Algeria," in Entelis and Naylor, *State and Society,* pp. 53–71. See pp. 57–59.

58. Bradford Dillman, op. cit., pp. 49–50.

59. *Christian Science Monitor,* February 4, 1994, p. 6; see also *Middle East,* No. 232, March 1994, pp. 16–17.

60. Ibid.

61. For an informative commentary-essay on the major factions within the FIS, see Mamoun Fandy, "West Must Back Reform Efforts in Algeria," *Christian Science Monitor,* April 26, 1994, p. 19. Fandy writes that FIS is comprised of three major factions. The nationalist faction, generally considered "moderate," is led by Abdelkader Hachani and includes intellectuals, nationalists, and former socialists disappointed in the FLN's approach to solving Algeria's problems. The traditionalist group follows Ali Belhadj, a charismatic preacher who is similar in style to the Egyptian cleric Omar Abdul Rahman. Between these is the mainstream group. Led by Abbasi Madani,

this faction is closer to the policies of the mainstream Egyptian Muslim Brothers than to either of the other groups.

62. See Zebiri, "Islamic Revival," p. 221.

63. *Arab News,* May 8, 1994, p. 4.

64. Lara Marlowe, "Algeria: Faith's Fearsome Sword," *Time,* Vol. 143, No. 6, February 7, 1994, pp. 48–49. See p. 49.

65. "Algeria: Army Thrust into the Front Line," *Middle East,* No. 232, March 1994, pp. 16–17. See p. 17.

66. *Christian Science Monitor,* April 26, 1994, p. 19.

67. See "Algeria: Paralysed by Fear," *Middle East,* No. 233, April 1994, pp. 10–11.

68. *Christian Science Monitor,* January 5, 1994, pp. 1 and 18.

69. *New York Times,* April 4, 1994, p. A7.

70. Mortimer, "Algeria: The Clash," p. 37.

71. *New York Times,* February 6, 1994, p. E5.

CHAPTER 5

Pakistan: Political Crisis and the Democracy Conundrum

Since the partition of British India in 1947 and the development of Pakistan as a federated parliamentary democracy, this Muslim state in the northern part of the subcontinent has undergone a turbulent process of nation-building, consensus-building, and institutionalization of internal politics. The struggle for democracy has been handicapped by interethnic strife, social strains, elite fragmentation, and praetorian rule, and it has been influenced by external powers at both regional and global levels. In the postindependence era, military men have three times administered martial-law governments in Pakistan to gain legitimacy en route to democratization.

The failure of democracy to take root in Pakistan has been attributed to, among other things, the leaders who have followed Jinnah since 1948. Instead of promoting the tradition of civilian supremacy bequeathed by Britain, civilian rulers have relied on the military for their own survival.[1] That is independent Pakistan's tradition: military rulers have been arbiters of the nation's destiny. The Punjabi-dominated military, which represents landed and industrial interests, regards intrusion into Pakistani politics as a right; more than that: as an obligation that safeguards the territorial integrity of the country in the face of lingering ethnic, linguistic, and religious fissures.[2] Such praetorian interventions in the name of order and stability have largely been predicated on an alleged commitment to improving the economic development of the nation.

However, regardless of the military's role, other factors have, in fact, largely shaped the nation's politics: problems of subnational identity, organizational ineptitude, socioeconomic disparity, and crises of governance. Current theoretical treatments of the process of Pakistan's democratizing experiences are preoccupied with economic growth and development. This preoccupation presents a serious problem in analyzing contemporary Pakistani politics.

Many intricacies are associated with Pakistan's experience of democratization. Numerous internal and external factors have hampered the process in recent years, making it desirable to present a historical overview of

91

Pakistan's volatile politics. This forms the content of the next section of the chapter, to be followed by an assessment of civil-military relations. The chapter then moves on to explain the democratic chaos of Benazir Bhutto's first administration (1988–1990), in which the injection of dramatic democratic measures exacerbated ethnic strife while having but limited impact on Pakistan's elitist power structure.

Later sections deal with the upheavals of Nawaz Sharif's administration (1990–1993) and the return of Benazir Bhutto to Pakistan's politics in 1993. Finally, human rights conditions and the process of liberalization are investigated to ascertain why Pakistan's experiments with democratization have been tenuous and transitory.

Historical Overview

Born of the idea of a separate Muslim state on August 14, 1947, Pakistan, under Muhammad Ali Jinnah, leader of the Muslim League, opted for partition from the rest of the Indian subcontinent. After British withdrawal in 1947, Muslim-majority districts of western British India, along with parts of Bengal, formed the nation-state of Pakistan. The Muslim nation was bifurcated, separated by Indian territory. It was a turbulent partition.

West Pakistan comprised four provinces: Baluchistan, North-West Frontier (NWFP), Punjab, and Sind, which hosts the capital, Lahore. East Pakistan consisted of only one province: Bengal. Since the partition, Pakistan and India have been involved in hostilities over religious, border, and political disputes. Communal and strategic disputes led to the wars of 1948 and 1965 over Kashmir; then rigid perceptions, misperceptions, and distorted information caused a third war, in 1971, culminating in the national disintegration of Pakistan and the creation of Bangladesh (formerly East Pakistan).[3]

Pakistan's Islamic heritage began with transactions with Muslim traders who arrived in the eighth century. During the sixteenth and seventeenth centuries, the Moguls integrated a vast part of South Asia "in an empire marked both by its administrative effectiveness and cultural refinement."[4] Lawrence Ziring's *Middle East Political Dictionary* notes that the Muslims tend to view themselves as the supreme conquerors and rulers of India. This was especially true during the Mogul period, but in the nineteenth century the Moguls were displaced by the British. Nevertheless, such beliefs nurtured the two-nation theory that, with other political considerations, furnished the logic for the creation of a Muslim state within the subcontinent.[5]

The postindependence era in Pakistan was marked by ethnic tensions, political instabilities, and economic hardship. Four dominant ethnic groups (Punjabis, Sindhis, Baluchis, and Pushtuns) formed the main ethnic composition of the country. Each of these major ethnic groups is divided into a variety of subgroupings and there are also ethnolinguistic, occupational, and caste divisions. As a mosaic of ethnic groups held together only by a common religion (Islam), Pakistani ethnic strife and tribal tensions have made it virtually impossible for the central government to enjoy long periods of stability. Pushtuns, or Pathans, the dominant ethnic group in NWFP, and Punjabis, the nation's majority group, are the groups most heavily represented in the armed forces and bureaucracy.

Unlike the technocratic elites with obvious connections with the old British bureaucrats, the military elites, as the guardians of independence, have always found their ways in the political chambers of the establishment. The wars with India (1948, 1965, and 1971) carved out for the armed forces a relatively constant space in Pakistan's political affairs. In addition, the failure of the civilian governments to generate a broad support base and a practical vision for the country's future generated several military takeovers. The extensive influence of the military in Pakistan's politics accounted for the persistence of the secular state. The administrations of Ali Khan (1948–1951), Mohammad (1951–1955), Mirza (1955–1958), Ayub (1958–1969), Bhutto (1971–1977), Zia (1977–1988), Benazir Bhutto (1988–1990, and 1993), and Sharif (1990–1993) have all remained secular, while including Islamic measures to varying degrees.

Pakistan's return to democracy followed the suspicious death of Zia on August 17, 1988. In a fair and orderly election, Benazir Bhutto was elected prime minister and formed a government on December 1, 1988. Regional ethnic strife and political differences about constitutional interpretations of presidential authority marked Bhutto's brief tenure in office. The dismissal of the Bhutto government in 1990 by President Ishaq Khan, for nepotism, corruption, and inefficiency, and the dissolution of the National Assembly led to a new election, culminating in the victory for Muhammad Nawaz Sharif. The Sharif administration lasted into 1993, when differences between Sharif and the president (still Ishaq Khan) led to a government paralyzed by constitutional gridlock. At the army's insistence, both the president and prime minister resigned. In new elections, on October 19, 1993, Benazir Bhutto regained a majority of votes and was again named prime minister.

The turbulence associated with the transition to democratic civilian governments in Pakistan has repeatedly cast its shadow on the nation and the politics of liberalization has yet to find a way to adjust itself to Pakistan's desire for democracy. The democratization process, coupled with efforts to bring the private sector to the forefront of economic activity in Pakistan, made Benazir's task difficult. In a nation with a history of staggering political crises, Benazir's attempts during 1988–1990 to reinvigorate the democratic process ran into fundamental difficulties.

Civil-Military Relations

Since 1958, the military's involvement in Pakistani politics has been constant: the military has either ruled directly, as under General Ayub Khan (1958–

1968), General Yahya Khan (1969–1971), and General Zia (1977–1988), or indirectly to maintain its power in the politics of the country. The transfer of power to civilian political leaders (as in 1963, 1971, and 1988) appears to be only a tactical retreat by the army from politics. The old tradition of the military's role continues.

Some analysts argue that democracy emerged by default when the military elites withdrew temporarily after the sudden death of Zia in 1988. The army's exit from power occurred when the democratic movement was nascent and unable to dominate the political environment.[6] The greatest subsequent danger to democracy stemmed from political decay and the ensuing crisis of governability that surfaced following the advent of the democratic process.[7]

The military's deepest penetration into civilian society and the state institutions took place under the martial law of President Zia (1977–1988), when, for more than a decade, a system of military rule shaped Pakistani politics. Such dominance in all sectors of society and polity led to what Hasan-Askari Rizvi describes as the "civilization of military rule."[8] Even when the army allowed democratic order to function under Benazir (1988–1990), it did so mainly because the election, acting as a safety valve following Zia's eleven years of authoritarian rule, vented pent-up frustration.

Examining power relations in post-Zia Pakistan, Ashok Kapur writes that the Pakistani military-bureaucratic oligarchy has in the past supported representative democracy, but not to the point of sharing power with political parties or organizing "transfer of power" to civilian leadership. "The function of the democracy advocacy in Pakistan by the oligarchy," says Kapur, "is to make the Army's central position in political affairs palatable and legitimate."[9] Historically, except for Jinnah's brief rule (1947–1948), the civilian elites of Pakistan in the postindependence period lacked the vision and power to effect a national consensus on the political foundations of the state and the emergence of the "participant society." Politics in Pakistan during 1947–1958, in the view of some scholars, was marked by nonconsensus and a series of unsuccessful efforts at institution building, including the drafting of three constitutions.[10] Summarizing the earlier causes of the erosion of civilian rule in Pakistan, Rizvi points out:

> Serious disagreements on several constitutional and political issues (federalism and autonomy for the provinces, the Islamic state, the national language and the electoral system) delayed the formulation of the Constitution. By the time the first permanent Constitution was framed in 1956, a strong pattern of violation of parliamentary and democratic norms had been established. The Constitution could not restrain the political drift and degeneration which made it possible for the military to dislodge fragile institutions.[11]

The military's nucleus was formed in Pakistan even before the state and society. As in Algeria, the armed forces in Pakistan were the guardians of state sovereignty. As in Algeria, where the armed forces were one part of a triple alliance (FLN-state-army), in Pakistan, too, the military was part of a ruling troika (president–prime minister–army). But in Pakistan the military either blatantly overrode the state and party politics through direct rule or indirectly influenced the policymaking of the civilian regimes. This can be amply demonstrated in the civilian regimes' compromises and appeasement policies toward the military in Pakistan. Salamat Ali, a prominent Pakistani journalist, maintains that the sacking on July 19, 1993 of Prime Minister Sharif by President Ishaq Khan with the tacit approval of the army indicated again that the real power in Pakistan lies with the president and the army.[12] The army's discreet intervention to broker the Sharif–Ishaq Khan resignation pact, and to guarantee future elections under a neutral administration, again showed that the army's role in Pakistani politics is active. The army still holds the power to defuse political crises.[13] However, the military showed its commitment to free and fair elections and its willingness to reconcile itself somewhat—though not entirely—to civilian rule when, in the October 19, 1993 election, Benazir Bhutto was again elected prime minister.

Pakistan's geostrategic location and security environment have made it crucial for the military to remain engaged in the country's domestic and foreign policy. But in addition to the external factors, the internal cohesion of the armed forces has been maintained by their essentially Punjabi and Pathun ethnic makeup. [14]

Traditionally, capitalist farmers, private importers, and the military have played an important role in forming Pakistan's dominant ruling coalition. Standing to benefit the most from structural adjustment and economic liberalization, these partners have played, and will continue to play, a significant part in the country's adjustment to both the social and bureaucratic costs of privatization.[15]

Democratic Beginnings: Independent Pakistan

With Jinnah at the helm as governor general, Pakistan's first experiment with democracy involved the colossal task of creating a secular modern polity. To attempt this in a country created by the British Raj on the basis of a religio-nationalist identity crisis was no mean feat and Jinnah died on September 11, 1948, without having confronted this, his major obstacle. On assuming power, all his successors—Liaquat Ali Khan (1948–1951), Ghulam Mohammad (1951–1955), and Iskander Mirza (1955–1958)—struggled unsuccessfully with postindependence socioeconomic and ethnic tensions and with the political elites' personal and provincial loyalties.[16]

The failure of the democratic experiments from 1947 to 1958 can be attributed to several factors, ranging from factional strife and the inability of the Muslim League to be an all-encompassing national party to the bitter contest between the president and prime minister over the leadership of the central government.[17] Short terms of office created unstable policies. Several administrations have ruled since 1958 with longer terms—the notable exception being Yahya Khan's brief reign (1969–1970), which culminated in a free and competitive election. The 1970 election brought Zulfikar Ali Bhutto and the Pakistan People's Party (PPP) to power in 1971 as Pakistan's first effective civilian government since the early 1950s.[18]

The military regime of Ayub Khan (1958–1969), despite its rhetoric of "basic democracy," was a syncretic regime in which both types of elites—the modernizing, urban-based nationalists and the tradition-bound, rural aristocracy—ruled as a coalition for eleven years. Such coalition governments had appeal and endured for many years, ending with Benazir Bhutto's rule in December 1988.[19] Zulfikar Ali Bhutto (1971–1977), who until Benazir Bhutto was the only prime minister to be democratically elected, rose to power on populist appeals and promises. In his second term, however, he opted for a close association with the military and bureaucratic elites. Toward the end of his two terms, Zulfikar Ali Bhutto's nationalistic program to uplift the masses ground to a halt. Many private industrial firms had been adversely affected by his policies. In 1977, Bhutto was removed by General Mohammed Zia Ul-Haq and in 1979 was hanged on charges of murder.

Zia, who assumed power in a military coup in 1977, ruled until 1988, in what came to be one of the longest presidencies in the country's history. Between 1977 and 1985, political parties were banned. In the early and mid-1980s, Zia pursued religiocultural legitimacy by giving prominence to Islamic jurisprudence. He saw Islam as a mobilizing force that could expediently be utilized to bypass the nation's tensions. In hindsight, it is evident that the emphasis on the Islamic state proved to be poor public policy: Zia failed to realize that the major problem for national integration lay not in the theme of Islam-in-danger but rather in forces of parochialism and subnational identities.[20]

After Zia's death in a plane crash in 1988—a crash surrounded by many suspicions as to its cause—Mohtarma Benazir Bhutto came to power. She was the first woman to lead the government of a Muslim nation. In her twenty-month tenure (1988–1990), Benazir insisted on a new brand of democracy for the Pakistanis—one that was carefully crafted not to violate the integrity of the Islamic legacy or the de facto role and influence of the army in the politics of Pakistan, and one that was predicated on secular premises and advancement of the individual's basic rights. Fractious and boisterous Pakistani politics appeared to be an inappropriate context for such a brand of democracy.

The Benazir Regime: A Surge Toward Democracy

In the national election held in November 1988, the Pakistan People's Party (PPP) won 92 of the 215 seats in the National Assembly. Benazir formed a government over the opposition of the Islamic Democratic Alliance led by

Nawaz Sharif, chief minister of Punjab. Having come to power more as a result of the people's desire for a change than as a result of a transparent ideological vision or a landslide voting mandate, Benazir knew that she had to be conciliatory toward the army and its bureaucracy. Her shaky majority in the assembly and inexorable dependence on the army as a stabilizing influence on the national scene, most observers agree, deflected considerable energies from national and regional exigencies. Thus, matters of social justice and the repeal of fundamentalist laws degrading to women, bureaucratic corruption, and economic difficulties had to be downplayed.[21] The inability of Benazir to act on these fronts was attributed, according to Ziring, "to back-door politics wherein the Pakistan People's Party (PPP) [had to] satisfy different constituencies lest it lose its slim majority, but the failure to confront these matters [was] also due to structural limitations and financial constraints."[22]

The army's confidence in the civilian government of Benazir Bhutto seemed to remain high, at least throughout the first year of her premiership. However, differences between Benazir and the army intensified over ethnic tensions in Sind. The conflicts between the Sindhi nationalists and the Mohajirs (Urdu-speaking Indian immigrants from Karachi and other urban areas of Sind) took a heavy toll in May 1990. The army's involvement was deemed inevitable. But where Benazir favored a more restricted role for the army in Sind—lest the army's actions discriminate against the Muhajirs in the process of restoring order—the army saw an opportunity to reassert its influence beyond the restoration of order. Some army commanders closely associated with the Zia strategy of direct military rule demanded an unrestrained role for the military in Sind: carte blanche in dealing with communal violence. This was, according to some observers, a turning point in the crisis of state power that eventually led to the dismissal of the Benazir Bhutto government.[23]

Further differences grew over Bhutto's Afghan and Kashmir policies, in which she pressed for limited involvement in Afghanistan and a political settlement for Kashmir. Her policy with regard to Afghanistan and India alienated the army. She preferred a negotiated settlement in Afghanistan. The army and the Inter-Services Intelligence (ISI) were not in a mood to settle for anything less than a defeat of the Afghani regime by the mujahidin. Similarly, Benazir's desire to tone down Pakistan's support for the insurgency in Kashmir met with fierce opposition in the army, which was interested in bolstering its capacity vis-à-vis India. In both cases, the army viewed Benazir's preferences as unpatriotic.[24] Such discords indicated that Benazir was bent on reasserting civilian authority by overriding the army. Had she succeeded, her policies could have carried far-reaching implications for the premiership and the future of Pakistan.[25]

In May 1989, the dismissal of Lieutenant General Hamid Gul, chief of the ISI, over disagreements about Pakistan's role in supporting Afghan guerrilla forces, the mujahidin, in the post-Soviet withdrawal, was seen not only as an attempt by Bhutto to signal a change in Pakistan's foreign policy toward

Afghanistan (in the direction of a negotiated settlement), but also to assert further domestic consolidation of the prime minister's powers and civil authority over the military.[26] A no-confidence motion was defeated on November 1, 1989 (107 of the 236 members of the assembly voted no-confidence, 12 short of a majority). The vote was pushed on the floor by Nawaz Sharif, who represented the Islamic Jamhoori Ittehad (or IJI). Bhutto sustained her tenuous majority in the assembly and also took pride in gaining credibility in the Assembly for democratic procedure under a civilian government—an event unprecedented in Pakistan's history since independence.

In general, the political atmosphere under Benazir allowed freedom for the press and individuals, tolerance for divergent political ideologies and opinions, and independence for the judiciary. Having spent twenty-four months in detention without a trial between the imposition of martial law in July 1977 and September 1981, having been placed under house arrest on several occasions under consecutive detention orders, and having been expelled as well as banned from the Punjab on one occasion,[27] Benazir had developed deep distaste for oppression and a real commitment to the reconstitution of civil society.

The patron-client relationships of the syncretic political structure, which for three decades had characterized Pakistan's personalized politics, effectively ended. Pakistan appeared to be on the verge of a transition to a new era of institutionalized politics. Unlike her father's policies of nationalization and public sector expansion, Benazir attempted to place the private sector at the forefront of economic activity. She gave her approval to a deal with the IMF already negotiated by the Zia regime, and accepted its pressures to restructure Pakistan's economy in accordance with IMF guidelines.[28]

Bhutto's political victories, however, were offset by her reliance on the army. The ethnic tensions in the Punjab, Sind, and Baluchistan and ensuing demands for the devolution of sovereignty to the several "nations" of Pakistan made it necessary for Bhutto to work in close harmony with the military establishment.[29] Benazir's political status in the midst of pressing socioeconomic problems was precarious. Lack of consensus within the government and between the army and the Bhutto administration on key issues of expanding civil society drastically undermined the democratic process she had so painstakingly implanted.

Beseiged by structural, institutional, and societal challenges, the Benazir government was increasingly unable to solve the country's problems. While admiring Benazir's ability to survive in such turbulent times, and arguing that she needed more time to build up the democratic framework to cope with these challenges, John Bray mentions several constraints on the Bhutto regime:

> Tax evasion on a massive scale and the expansion of the drugs trade have produced an enormous alternative economy. In Sind the government has proved unable to provide basic security so that increasingly private citizens

are buying their own weapons or seeking protection from vigilante groups. Meanwhile, the failure of national politics is encouraging ethnic chauvinist movements and will foster radical Islamist politics, albeit among a minority. All this weakens the country's social cohesiveness.[30]

Further clouding Benazir's political prospects was a power struggle with the president, Ishaq Khan, over the eighth amendment to the constitution, passed in 1985 under Zia's rule. Under this amendment, the president retains full powers to appoint a caretaker government for holding elections, to nominate any member of the National Assembly to be the nation's prime minister, to appoint judges and military commanders, to disqualify elected members of the National Assembly, and to dissolve the National Assembly. This amendment incapacitates the office of prime minister, giving an inordinate share of the power to the president. On August 6, 1990, the president, with the consent of the armed forces, dismissed Benazir Bhutto from her office as the nation's prime minister. Thus ended Pakistan's fledgling democratic order. The specter of the army again loomed over the country's political destiny. With the dramatic rise in socioeconomic deterioration, political polarization, and ethnic turmoil, the optimism and enthusiasm with which a new wave of democracy swept the country when Bhutto was elected came to a standstill. The consensus among the region's observers appears to be that the Gulf crisis of August 2, 1990, caused by the Iraqi invasion of Kuwait, facilitated President Ishaq Khan's removal of Benazir. Washington's attention shifted to the Gulf and Pakistan's relation with the Gulf states demanded sharp attention.

Nawaz Sharif: Back to Traditional Politics

In the ensuing October 24, 1990 election—described by some as fairly open and by others as rigged and manipulated by the army—IJI defeated the PPP. On November 6, 1990, Mian Nawaz Sharif was sworn in as prime minister. The Nawaz victory, made possible by an alliance including the conservative Muslim League and Jammath-i-Islami parties, precipitated the military's regaining of its legitimacy and a freer reign in the national politics.[31] In addition, Sharif's government represented for the first time in Pakistan's history a ruling party that enjoyed more than a two-thirds majority in the National Assembly and also ruled at the center (Islamabad) as well as in all four provinces.[32] Unable to reconcile his differences with the president and to fulfill his promises to the Islamic groups within the IJI, Sharif's uncertain journey began. In 1992, the IJI's convenient alliance began to distintegrate: some groups broke ranks with the alliance. As a result, Sharif's government lost the two-thirds assembly majority, pivotal for any constitutional amendment.[33]

Sharif's government had promised privatization and economic liberalization, mostly in industry, banking, and insurance, and soon privatized some of the government institutions by providing incentives to foreign investment. The primary focus of the government was privatization of industry and increased exports. Numerous measures expedited the pace of economic growth through privatization. Industrial policy reform included the opening of several industries to private enterprise, the offering of liberal tax and tariff incentives for new industries, the promotion of liberalization of the foreign exchange regime, the opening of export trade to foreign firms, and the return of almost all industrial units and financial institutions to the private sector. New banks were also opened in the private sector.[34]

But new strains developed between Islamabad and Washington. There was a cutoff of aid to Pakistan due to the latter's developing nuclear weapons. The once-close ties between allies had weakened. Understandably, Pakistan had lost the strategic importance it enjoyed in the geopolitical context of the Cold War. The Gulf crisis seriously affected remittances from and exports to Iraq and Kuwait. This meant that military aid and geopolitical configurations would no longer figure prominently in Pakistan's aid programs and security imperatives.[35]

Meanwhile, the adversarial relationship with India, particularly over Kashmir and about disarmament issues, resumed, with no major accord in sight. On December 6, 1992, 200,000 Hindu militants attacked the sixteenth-century Babri Mosque in Ayodhya, a city in north India. The mosque, on a site that had long been disputed as to who should control it, was destroyed. The Hindus hope to build a temple to Ram in its place. The violence touched off by this incident jeopardized the position of the Indian prime minister, Narasimha Rao. As reports of the demolition of the mosque spread, Muslim mobs attacked and burned Hindu temples in neighboring Bangladesh and Pakistan. More than thirty Hindu temples in Pakistan alone were attacked and in some cases demolished.

Sharif denounced the Ayodhya assault in no uncertain terms. Beyond public condemnation, however, his reaction to the assault was mild and reserved. Sharif, who the following year (April 18, 1993) was ousted by President Ishaq Khan, only to be reinstated by the country's supreme court (May 26, 1993), found himself in the midst of a leadership and constitutional crisis. As this power struggle unfolded, Sharif became too preoccupied to react to the Ayodhya incident vigorously. The national crisis demonstrated that the dynamics of Pakistani internal politics overshadowed the developments related to the Ayodhya affair. Nevertheless, one should not overlook Sharif's pragmatic, prudent approach: underplaying the Ayodhya tragedy meant he was not provoking nationalistic sentiments. The desecration of the Babri Mosque is likely to add new, intractable complications to Indo-Pakistani relations. The destruction did, however, alert Sharif to new possibilities in foreign relations: in working with a centrist, secular Indian government on issues such as Kashmir, coexistence is a desirable alternative, worthy of reasonable political compromise.

Overall, after Sharif took office, ethnic-related violence in Sind Province heightened, freedom of the press was restricted, and arbitrary arrest and detention of opposition groups increased. Although Sharif initially supported measures to Islamize Pakistani society, his foreign policy toward Afghan mujahedin and the decision to support the UN peace initiative for Afghanistan displayed a disposition to hold back more radical forces.[36]

The widely held view regarding Sharif's pragmatic approach toward a settlement in Afghanistan is that, since Afghanistan is Pakistan's land corridor to the Central Asian republics, peace and stability in Afghanistan is crucial. It became a matter of practical policy. Given the significance of Central Asia to Pakistan for gas, energy, and market availability, and given the fact that the Afghani crisis led to the influx of more than three million Afghani refugees to Pakistan, such a policy is understandable. It is fair to argue that, insofar as a transition to market economy was concerned, governmental measures adopted under Sharif (1990–1993) were fairly effective. Nevertheless, the reconstitution of civil society (political liberalization) was relegated to a lower priority. Essentially, it lacked the driving force needed for a sustainable move toward democracy. On July 19, 1993, Sharif's differences with the president and continued legal and political crises over presidential powers brought the military back into Pakistan's politics. The military convinced both Sharif and Ishaq Khan to resign in the interest of political stability. Moeen Qureshi was named prime minister of a caretaker government. On October 6, new elections resulted in victory for Bhutto.

Benazir's Second Chance: A New Era

Benazir Bhutto's Pakistan People's Party (PPP) won by a slim margin in the national elections in October 1993. Benazir was appointed prime minister again on October 19, when the National Assembly voted for her, 121 to 72. Bhutto built a coalition government with the support of minor parties in the assembly, including all of the country's religious parties. She appeared confident of forming a similar coalition in the parliament of Punjab.[37] Having lost the 1990 election because of her failure to cope with the country's crushing economic decay, ethnic violence, and her shaky majority coalition, Benazir appeared determined to avoid past mistakes.

Those who had argued that Benazir would devote her second term to the reinvention of Pakistan's government and economy were proved wrong. On February 25, 1994, the Bhutto-installed president, Farooq Leghari, suspended the provincial assembly of the North-West Frontier Province, sacking the chief minister and his cabinet. This move, which was primarily directed against the political opposition and its leader, former prime minister Nawaz Sharif, has put an end to the anticipation that she would unite the country. Recent events have revealed that it is politics as usual in Pakistan. The recent power struggle could very well drag the army into the business of governing, further complicating the future of democracy in the country. Sharif's recent assertion that Pakistan possesses a nuclear bomb was clearly aimed at embarrassing Bhutto and providing an opening for the army to intervene in the politics of Pakistan.

Unlike in her first term, when she toned down Pakistan's support for the insurgency in Kashmir and refused to give the army carte blanche in dealing with the communal violence in Sind, this time Benazir opted for a markedly different approach, linking the Kashmir issue with Pakistan's nuclear programs. Shortly after the election, Bhutto vowed that Pakistan would continue its nuclear weapons program, despite pressures from the United States. Without resolution of the Kashmir issue, Bhutto said, there could not be peace in the region.[38] Later, Bhutto reiterated those views, assuring the army that the government was fully sensitive to the country's defense needs and requirements.[39] But, still stressing that Pakistan would not accept unilateral pressure on its nuclear program or on its Kashmir policy, she entered into a dialogue with the United States.[40] This dialogue marked the beginning of a new, quiet diplomacy between the two countries.[41]

During the first few months of her second term, Bhutto realized that it was difficult to keep the army out of the fray and that the army was virtually running Sind. The army's continued mistreatment of the Muhajir Quami Movement (MQM), which it suspects of having connections with Indian intelligence, has fuelled speculation about their active role in the country's politics. The prospects of an open revolt, with fighting between the military and the MQM, frightens Bhutto's administration.[42]

Bhutto's new tenure comes at a time when Pakistan faces serious economic problems. Achievement of the government's 1993–1994 GDP growth target, 7.5 percent, and bringing inflation, the inefficient banking system, and interest rates under reasonable control remained largely dependent upon a global recovery.[43] Bhutto's 1994/95 budget aimed at reducing the deficit and liberalizing the economy in order to attract greater foreign investment. The budget forecast a deficit of 4 percent of GDP, down from a projected 5.8 percent in 1993/94 and 7.9 percent in 1992/93. Import duties were reduced and import-license fees were called off in an effort to eliminate smuggling. The budget confined defense spending despite present tensions with India. A rise in austerity meant a rise in taxes as well. The budget doubled the price of gas, and a 15-percent sales tax on 169 domestically produced items and 108 imported items caused an outcry. Business and industry went on strike in protest of the tax. Bhutto temporarily backed down, withdrawing some of the powers of tax officers and declaring a moratorium on the tax until the end of August 1994.[44] Late in 1994 it was still too early to judge what her victory meant for Pakistan's socioeconomic and educational reforms. Edward Gargan reported that many Pakistanis doubted whether Benazir could equal the accomplishments of Moeen Qureshi, a former World Bank vice-president who acted as a transitional prime minister after Sharif's abdication. Qureshi, a political unknown and outsider, ignored politics as usual, laid the ground for economic liberalization and reform, oversaw the transition to a new government with considerable neutrality, and expanded his mandate by initiating wide-ranging reforms:

> He devalued the country's overvalued rupee, moved to free the Central Bank from political influence, introduced the first tax on large rural landowners (Ms. Bhutto's allies), ended capricious government spending and went after loan defaulters, including Ms. Bhutto and her husband. He also increased prices on subsidized commodities and utilities, measures that would be difficult for any elected government to enact.[45]

The extensive reforms introduced by Qureshi were regarded as necessary by many development economists. They put Pakistan back on a sustainable economic course. Pakistan's federal budget deficits, which have amounted to 7.5 percent of GDP annually in the past two fiscal years, and service to the public debt, which has amounted to Rs121.4 billion per year, cried out for tough economic decisions.[46] The Qureshi caretaker government launched a number of tax reforms, thus creating considerable financial resources for the government. In addition to supplying a significant increase in revenue for the government, these reforms were Pakistan's initial step in qualifying for $1.2 billion in loans from the International Monetary Fund.[47]

A public opinion poll conducted the week prior to the national elections indicated that 85 percent of those polled were eager to see Qureshi, although he had not been elected, remain in office.[48] This demonstrates the way complexities involved in democratization, including constitutional, social, and political crises, could inhibit the process of economic liberalization and recovery. As a little-scrutinized political outsider, obliged to few, Qureshi initiated measures aimed at eroding Pakistan's endemic political corruption and economic mismanagement. They were effective and gained the respect of many Pakistanis.[49]

Some of Qureshi's political steps, such as making public the list of bank loan defaulters and the decision to disqualify them from contesting the elections, drew wide applause from the public. But there was a widespread perception among the Pakistani public that Qureshi was an "imported prime minister," attempting to implement an agenda favored by the World Bank and IMF.[50] However, Qureshi's main targets—reduction of the budget deficit, improvement of the balance of payments, and mobilization of additional resources—set the tone for economic recovery. His firm measures, such as efforts to facilitate recovery of bank loans, tax dues, and utility charges, and suspension of a transport scheme and channeling of credit from the public to the private sector, tangibly improved the country's economic conditions.[51]

Benazir's return to office may mean that some of these policies will be tampered with. Benazir's government has reasserted its control of the State Bank of Pakistan (SBP), which was given autonomy by Qureshi.[52] The next section examines the economic liberalization measures undertaken by both Bhutto and Sharif and illustrates the inadequacies and strengths of each of these governments.

Economic Liberalization in Perspective

By the mid-1980s, the public sector's inefficiency in industry, agriculture, energy, banking and finance, and telecommunications convinced the Zia government to give serious consideration to privatization of public sector industries. Government attention turned to reform and privatization of the major state-owned enterprises (SOEs)—manufacturing, chemicals and ceramics, engineering, and others. Privatization actually began under the Seventh Five-Year Plan (1989–1993), centering initially on the energy sector. Larger incentives were introduced for private sector activities in the exploration and development of oil and gas. The deregulation and privatization of other sectors, such as telecommunications and power, followed.[53] A clear electoral victory for the IJI (encompassing the interests of the army, the president, and members of the IJI coalition) meant that the economic liberalization programs would continue.

Following the Gulf crisis, repatriation of Pakistani workers from Kuwait and Iraq resulted in a loss of $100 million in workers' remittances. On October 1, 1991, U.S. foreign assistance to Pakistan was suspended. However, Pakistan, by fulfilling the conditions of the IMF and the World Bank, received $1.168 billion from these sources.[54] Sharif's government used its consolidated power to carry out a series of reforms based on deregulation and privatization.

In 1992, investments rose by 17.6 percent and exports by 12.6 percent. The budget deficit was brought down from 8.8 percent of GDP in 1990/91 to 6.9 percent—well short, however, of the IMF target of 5.8 percent. Benazir's government budget is designed to get the deficit down from 6 percent in 1994 to 4 percent in 1995. This renders possible the government forecast that growth will recover to 7 percent in 1994, although some analysts find that figure optimistic.[55] Following privatization plans, 57 of 115 industrial units were sold by September 1992.[56] Notwithstanding its liberal industrial policy, Pakistan's approach to reducing the deficit, Ahmad Khan wrote in 1993, was predicated on cuts in social sector allocations and in the annual development plans. If the decline in social sectors and the population growth rate of 3.1 percent was not expeditiously harnessed, he argued, economic development could sink in socioeconomic chaos.[57] The World Bank offered $200 million for undertaking an energy project in Pakistan on the pattern of the Hub power project in Balochistan; it also announced a $125 million public sector adjustment loan.[58]

Pakistan's economic troubles lend credence to speculations such as Khan's. Pakistan's largest recent budget deficits, following large-scale crop losses from flood damage in 1992 and a drop in economic growth rate from an expected 6 percent to slightly over 3 percent, have intensified the economic problems of the country.[59]

Some writers have argued that there appears to be no strong correlation between the economic performance of a particular regime and its political destiny in Pakistan. Impressive economic growth rates have proved inconsequential as far as government survival is concerned. Leo E. Rose underscores this point:

> There may be a general principle in Pakistani politics: a government can suffer marginally from a poor economic record but it receives few tangible benefits from a flourishing economy. But then this may be fair, as the Pakistan economy still is heavily dependent upon forces beyond the government's control—the weather, the affluence of the Islamic OPEC countries, and foreign aid.[60]

Development (and economic growth, if the terms can be equated) does not always necessarily generate democratization and the connection between democracy and economic growth remains flimsy and uncertain in the case of Pakistan. A crisis of governability, not of economic performance, appeared to account for the inability of the Sharif government to restore democracy. After the supreme court's decision to overturn Sharif's dismissal by Ishaq Khan (on May 26, 1993), the administrative crisis became a constitutional crisis. Pakistan remained, to borrow a term from Salamat Ali, a "kingdom without power."[61] Sharif became aware that he must accord as much priority to broadening sociopolitical opportunities as to promoting growth, if democracy was to stand a better chance of taking root. The promotion of a civil society, an essential part of any democratization process, rests largely on a sustained liberalization program. In the face of the crisis of governability, Sharif's attempts to advance economic liberalization did not, in the end, further the cause of democratization.

Human Rights Setbacks

Pakistan, which has yet to ratify any United Nations covenants on universal human rights, has been under constant attack by the international community for its dismal human rights record. During Zia's presidency, human rights conditions, especially individual human rights, deteriorated. The independence of the judiciary system was denied; presidential powers to dissolve the National Assembly were bolstered. Free and fair elections at both provincial and national levels were banned, as were the parties' efforts to campaign and to participate in local and national elections. The legal status of women, insofar as effective protection of rights was concerned, suffered serious setbacks. Minority cultures and religions were further eclipsed as Zia pushed Pakistan one step closer to becoming a theocratic state.

Under Zia, with Islamization, minorities' rights were further restricted. Islamic courts were given wide powers to interpret Muslim "personal laws." In 1979, a bill known as the Hudood Ordinances was enacted that made the penal system harsher. These ordinances criminalized adultery and fornication and prescribed cruel and inhuman punishments and even discrimination on the basis of gender. For the most part, non-Muslims were not exempted from the application of this new law. On April 26, 1984, ordinance 20 was enforced, providing severe penalties for a minority Muslim group called the Ahmediya, whose Islamic status is denied under Pakistani law. The Ahmediya cannot practice or proselytize their faith. Many international sources voiced concern about minorities' rights in Pakistan after the government declared the Ahmediyas "heretics." Although the Sharia Act stipulates that minorities may practice their religion and that sharia (Islamic law) will not constrain non-Muslims' activities, in practice, non-Muslims endure economic and political discrimination with no legal remedy.[62] Shi'ite and Ahmadi Muslims are also at a disadvantage. They are not immune from discrimination in this predominantly Sunni nation.[63]

In 1985, non-Muslims were also excluded from contesting general elections to the National Assembly. Further, the ninth amendment was added to the constitution, aimed at interpreting all laws in order to bring them in conformity with the injunctions of Islam as laid down in the Qur'an and Sunnah.[64]

In sum, civil society suffered reverses under Zia. Student and labor unions were banned. The media was severely restricted and professional and associational life was denied to individuals. Civil rights (life, liberty, and integrity of person) were constantly disregarded in the interest of government stability. The partyless elections of 1985 was a prime example of restraints on democratization.

The first Benazir government was not very successful in reversing such trends, although many aspects of civil society were emphasized under Benazir. A printing press and publication ordinance allowed newspapers to appeal to the civil courts in cases of confiscation by the government.[65] The political atmosphere was described as "open" and "competitive." Associational life was renewed and party politics rejuvenated. However, corruption in and mismanagement of government, economic frustrations, and lack of a strong support by the army continued to hurt Benazir's administration. The democratic chaos propelled by Benazir's crippled government facilitated Sharif's ascendancy to power.

While successful in economic liberalization and privatization, Sharif's policies failed to strengthen civil society. During his premiership, Pakistan's human rights standing registered many reverses. Many members of the PPP and other opposition groups were arrested; successive false charges were, it was alleged, used to imprison political opponents. Torture of criminal and political suspects in police custody was frequent. Flogging and public executions of convicted of rape and drugs offenders continued under severe Islamic laws.[66]

Civil society encountered many setbacks. The right to peacefully associate and assemble was ended, with curfews being periodically imposed. Many meetings were banned. Detentions without charge, up to one year under article 10 of the constitution, were common. Religious observance and the teaching of state ideology was commonly made compulsory in schools. Censorship of mail and telephone tapping was rampant.

The members of the Mohajir Quami Movement (MQM) complained that they had suffered much discrimination. Today, such complaints are still widespread in many spheres, especially in jobs, education, and political life.[67] Discrimination against Baluchis, Pathans, members of the Ahmedi religious sect, and Christians continued. Fewer than 10 percent of workers belonged to trade unions, and unions had limited rights. Strike restrictions were endemic. Personal rights to interracial marriage and marriage between people of different religions, to equality of the sexes during marriage and divorce, to the practice of any religion, and to noninterference by the state in private affairs were denied under the requirements of Sharia law.[68] Women's rights suffered serious setbacks, and in some sense the Islamic legacy of Zia was resurrected. Asia Watch has documented that in 1991 between 50 and 80 percent of all female detainees in Pakistan were imprisoned under the Hudood ordinances. Over two thousand women were imprisoned under these laws. Such a rise in the number of female prisoners enhanced the opportunity for police misconduct toward women, as was shown in numerous cases of custodial violence and gender-discrimination.[69] With an eye toward improving the status of women, Benazir opened the first police station with an all-female staff in early 1994. The women are to receive salaries equal to their male counterparts.[70]

Other indicators can be used to measure the status of socioeconomic rights and physical quality of life: the percentage of GNP spent by the state on health was 0.2 percent; on the military, 6.7 percent; on education, 2.2 percent. Socioeconomic rights clearly did not figure prominently in Sharif's administration.[71]

Overall, the trend toward the improvement of socioeconomic conditions in Pakistan's postindependence history has been mixed. Life expectancy (at birth) increased from 43.1 years in 1960 to 57.7 years in 1990. Infant mortality (per 1,000 live births) decreased from 163 in 1960 to 101 in 1991. The percentage of population with access to safe water doubled from 25 in the 1975–1980 period to 50 in the 1988–1990 period. The adult literacy rate rose from 21 percent in 1970 to 35 percent in 1990.[72] Education spending as percentage of GNP soared from 1.1 percent in 1960 to 3.4 percent in the

1988–1990 period.[73] But military expenditure as percentage of GNP increased from 5.5 percent in 1960 to 6.6 percent in 1990.[74] The average annual rate of inflation jumped from 6.7 percent (1980–1990) to 10.7 percent (1991).[75]

Conclusion

Pakistan, a country handicapped by clientelist politics, subnational identities, ethnic division, crises of legitimacy and constitution, a political history of abortive democratic attempts, and an authoritarian legacy of praetorian rule, in 1990 saw democracy fade for the third time in its postindependence history. To date, the balance between reconstituting a civil society and enhancing economic liberalization has not been established by Pakistan's ruling elites. Civil society has lagged far behind economic liberalization and Pakistan's fledgling democratic order needs to be strengthened by its leaders' commitment to renewing civil society. Without such a commitment, economic liberalization programs will not create the conditions necessary for long-term stable democracy.

Zia's attempts to foster economic growth at the expense of civil society woefully delayed Pakistan's movement toward democratization. Benazir Bhutto's endeavors (1988–1990) to resurrect civil society without decisive economic reforms, and in a political environment inimical to national consensus, were bound to fail. Nawaz Sharif promoted economic liberalization, but gave low priority to renewal and expansion of civil society. Tacit approval by the army and the president provided the necessary support for Sharif's administration. In many respects, Sharif continued and even fostered Zia's legacy of economic growth. Commitment to the promotion of civil society was unbalanced at best. Fast-paced economic growth was not accompanied or followed by a measured renewal of civil society. Those in power were reluctant to concede to the evolutionary process of liberalization. Elections proved unable to restore democracy. There was a crisis of governability, political decay, ballot fraud, and the military's political role.

Pakistan under Sharif represented a fairly successful case of economic liberalization but a poor case of broadening civil society, as evidenced by the military's continued influence in regional and national politics, the ruling elite's manipulative resort to Islamization of the laws, and Punjabi dominance over other ethnic groups in the bureaucracy and the army.

In Bhutto's second term, a balanced economic and political liberalization program, along with prudent accommodation toward the military, can sustain her government's longevity. Benazir must be careful in pushing the country toward more-liberal policies designed to aid the consumer as the events of mid-1994 pointed to the persistent threats of strike by Pakistan retailers. Pressing ahead with austerity programs to reduce the budget deficits must be tolerable for the poor. Failure to fulfill economic expectations could in the long run destabilize Bhutto's fragile government. In Pakistan, democratization has not translated into the expansion of civil society and an end to human rights violations. Islamic bonds have frequently been inadequate in subduing ethnic and sectarian anguish.

A wide array of structural and social obstacles has limited the capacity of virtually every Pakistani government in implementing a full-scale democratization process. Elections—in the absence of a well-entrenched civil society and necessary economic reforms—have plunged Pakistan into endless trouble—political horse trading, paralyzing cycles of polarization and confrontation, reversals of economic policy, and constitutional crisis. Benazir's continuing conflict with Sharif over the issue of party-hopping by legislators and the suspension of the provincial assembly of the North-West Frontier Province (NWFP) and the sacking of its chief minister and his cabinet by the Benazir-installed president of Pakistan, Farooq Leghari, are but a few examples of the uproars that have plagued Pakistan since 1988.[76]

Benazir Bhutto's success might depend on her seeking to reconcile the army's interests with those of the civil society and the expansion of the latter well beyond formal, periodical elections. How the military would react to such a process, were it to be initiated and were Bhutto to stay in office, is a question worth pondering. History teaches us to guard against favorable (but by no means unrealistic) expectations.

Notes

1. Rathnam Indurthy, "The Fragility of Democracy in Pakistan: The Military as the Root Cause," *Indian Journal of Political Science*, Vol. 52, No. 3, July–September 1991, pp. 295–326. See pp. 301–302.

2. Ibid., pp. 321–322.

3. Richard Sisson and Leo E. Rose, *War and Secessions: Pakistan, India and the Creation of Bangladesh*, Berkeley, Calif.: University of California Press, 1990.

4. *Background Notes: Pakistan*, June 1992, pp. 1–8. See p. 2.

5. Lawrence Ziring, *The Middle East Political Dictionary*, Santa Barbara, CA: ABC-CLIO Information Services, 1984, p. 83.

6. For an illuminating analysis on this subject, see Nasr, "Democracy and Crisis of Governability," p. 523.

7. Ibid., p. 537.

8. Rizvi, "Military and Politics," p. 31.

9. Kapur, *Pakistan in Crisis*, p. 205.

10. For example, Veena Kukreja, *Civil-Military Relations in South Asia: Pakistan, Bangladesh and India*, New Delhi: Sage Publications, Inc., 1991. See p. 41.

11. Rizvi, "Military and Politics," pp. 32–33.

12. For more details on this, see Salamat Ali, "Presidential Putsch," *Far Eastern Economic Review*, Vol. 156, No. 17, April 29, 1993, pp. 10–11.

13. See Ali, "Soldier's Solution."

14. Ibid., p. 34.

15. See John Waterbury, "The Political Management of Economic Adjustment and Reform," in Alan Roe, Jayanta Roy, and Jayshree Sengupta, eds., *Economic Adjustment in Algeria, Egypt, Jordan, Morocco, Pakistan, Tunisia, and Turkey,* Washington, D.C.: World Bank, 1989, pp. 55–65.

16. Surjit Mansingh, "Historical Setting," in Richard F. Nyrop, ed., *Pakistan: A Country Study,* Washington, D.C.: Foreign Area Studies, 1984, pp. 1–63. See pp. 36–40.

17. See Rose, "Pakistan: Experiments," pp. 110–114.

18. Ibid., p. 119.

19. See Bertsch, Clark, and Wood, *Comparing Political Systems,* pp. 588–590.

20. Ziring, "Public Policy Dilemmas," pp. 795–812.

21. Ziring, "Pakistan in 1989," p. 127.

22. Ibid.

23. See, for example, Alavi, "Nationhood and Communal Violence," p. 178.

24. Anwar H. Syed, "The Pakistan People's Party and the Punjab: National Assembly Elections, 1988 and 1990," *Asian Survey,* Vol. 31, No. 7, July 1991, pp. 581–595. See p. 592.

25. Shazia Rafi, "Benazir Bhutto: Her Rise, Fall—and Rise?" *Ms. Magazine,* Vol. 1, No. 3, November–December, 1990, pp. 16–20. See p. 19.

26. Marvin G. Weinbaum, "War and Peace in Afghanistan: The Pakistani Role," *Middle East Journal,* Vol. 45, No. 1, winter 1991, pp. 71–85. See p. 81.

27. For more details see an Amnesty International report on *Pakistan: Human Rights Violations and the Decline of the Rule of Law,* London: Amnesty Inernational, 1981, pp. 46–47.

28. See Richter, "Pakistan Under Benazir Bhutto," p. 449.

29. See Ziring, "Pakistan in 1989," p. 131.

30. John Bray, "Pakistan: The Democratic Balance-Sheet," *World Today,* Vol. 46, No. 6, June 1990, pp. 111–114. See esp. 114.

31. Weinbaum, op. cit., pp. 83–83.

32. Rais A. Khan, "Pakistan in 1991: Light and Shadows," *Asian Survey,* Vol. 32, No. 2, February 1992, pp. 197–206. See esp. 197.

33. For further details, see Rais Ahmed Khan, "Pakistan in 1992: Waiting for Change," *Asian Survey,* Vol. 33, No. 2, February 1993, pp. 129–140; esp. 130.

34. Rais A. Khan, 1992, op. cit., pp. 201–202.

35. For an excellent analysis, see Lawrence Ziring, "Pakistan in 1990: The Fall of Benazir Bhutto," *Asian Survey,* Vol. 31, No. 2, February 1991, pp. 113–124; esp. 123.

36. See Asia Watch and the Women's Rights Projects, *Double Jeopardy: Police Abuse of Women in Pakistan,* New York: Human Rights Watch, 1992, p. 23.

37. *Christian Science Monitor,* October 20, 1993, p. 2.

38. *New York Times,* November 21, 1993, p. Y4.

39. *Dawn,* Karachi, May 9, 1994, p. 1.

40. *Dawn,* Karachi, April 8, 1994, p. 16.

41. *Dawn,* Karachi, April 10, 1994, p. 1.

42. Ahmed Rashid, "Roll of Dishonour," *Far Eastern Economic Review,* Vol. 157, No. 19, May 12, 1994, p. 20.

43. "Great Expectation," *Far Eastern Economic Review,* Vol. 157, No. 3, January 20, 1994; pp. 48–52. See p. 52.

44. Ahmed Rashid, "Getting Tough," *Far Eastern Economic Review,* Vol. 157, No. 25, June 23, 1994, p. 61.

45. *New York Times,* October 24, 1993, p. E3.

46. Salamat Ali, "An Uphill Task," *Far Eastern Economic Review,* Vol. 156, No. 42, Oct. 21, 1993, pp. 16 and 18. See p. 16.

47. *Facts on File,* Vol. 53, No. 2761, October 28, 1993, p. 815.

48. *New York Times,* October 24, 1993, p. E3.

49. Ibid.

50. Amin, "Pakistan in 1993," p. 195.

51. Ibid., p. 197.

52. Ahmed Rashid, "Bhutto Backtracks," *Far Eastern Economic Review*, Vol. 157, No. 2, January 13, 1994, p. 79.

53. Ibrahim Elwan, "Privatization, Deregulation, and Macroeconomic Policies: The Case of Pakistan," in *Structural Adjustment and Macroeconomic Policy Issues*, Washington, D.C.: IMF, 1992, pp. 84–106. See pp. 92–94.

54. Khan, 1992, op. cit., p. 200.

55. *Economist,* June 18, 1994, p. 45.

56. Khan, 1993, op. cit., p. 133.

57. Ibid., pp. 133–134.

58. *Dawn,* April 17, 1994, p. 1.

59. *Christian Science Monitor,* July 20, 1993, p. 6.

60. Rose, "Pakistan: Experiments," p. 129.

61. See Salamat Ali, "Kingdom Without Power," *Far Eastern Economic Review*, Vol. 156, No. 23, June 10, 1993, pp. 10–11.

62. The Pakistani supreme court uses trademark law to justify laws prohibiting Ahmediyas the use of Islamic phrases and merchandise marks, thus encouraging religious intolerance against Ahmediyas. See *Christian Science Monitor,* Jan. 5, 1994, p. 23.

63. R. Bruce McColm, ed., *Freedom in the World: The Annual Survey of Political Rights and Civil Liberties 1992–1993,* New York: Freedom House, 1993, p. 400.

64. Asma Jahangir, "Protection of Religious Minorities and Women: The Impact of Islamic Law in Pakistan," in Claude E. Welch, Jr., and Virginia A. Leary, eds., *Asian Perspective on Human Rights,* Boulder, Colo.: Westview Press, 1990, pp. 206–217. See pp. 210–214.

65. Manfred Nowak and Theresa Swinehart, eds., *Human Rights in Developing Countries: 1989 Yearbook,* Kehl: N. P. Engel, 1989, p. 272.

66. See *Amnesty International Report: 1992,* New York: Amnesty International USA, 1992, pp. 206–209.

67. *Dawn,* April 21, 1994, p. 13.

68. See Humana, *World Human Rights Guide,* pp. 241–244.

69. For further details, see *Double Jeopardy: Police Abuse of Women in Pakistan,* op. cit., p. 3.

70. *Facts on File,* Vol. 54, No. 2780, March 10, 1994, p. 172.

71. Ibid., p. 241.

72. United Nations, *Human Development Report 1993,* Oxford: Oxford University Press, 1993, p. 143.

73. Ibid., p. 165.

74. Ibid., p. 177.

75. Ibid., p. 189.

76. Ahmed Rashid, "Divide and Rule," *Far Eastern Economic Review,* Vol. 157, No. 10, March 10, 1994, p. 23.

CHAPTER 6

Peru:
The *Autogolpe*
in Perspective

Four significant, interrelated factors have shaped Peru's political dynamics in recent years: the failure of its democratic governments; economic decay and burgeoning corruption; a continuing leftist insurgency; and the war on drugs. The executive takeover by President Alberto Fujimori in 1992—the *autogolpe*—largely supported by both the military and civilians, has spawned a large dose of skepticism about democratization in Peru. The deterioration of economic conditions and poor management of the market economy have called into question the relevance of democratic measures for a country whose economic uncertainties and inequitable distribution of wealth render any stable progress extremely precarious if not impossible. In addition to the dismal economic situation, the rise of revolutionary organizations such as the Sendero Luminoso (the Shining Path) since the early 1980s has thrust Peru's internal politics into chaos. And finally, the drug war has caused widespread searches and seizures by the Peruvian military and police, culminating more often than not in blatant human rights violations.

The complexity of Peruvian politics presents a clear example of a country experimenting with political democratization in the midst of an economic shambles. Called a country of *todas las sangres,* of all bloods, Peru has a variety of immigrants and a racial mix that few countries of Latin American duplicate.[1] The racial makeup of whites, Indians, mestizos, and others, has led to intense polarization of the Peruvian society, with serious consequences for both economic and political aspects of governance. Peruvian politics and the causes of the 1992 executive coup reflect the history of civil-military ties in Peru. The policies and circumstances surrounding the coup's aftermath must be understood within the context of economic liberalization programs that Fujimori has unleashed. Peru's economic and political dilemmas account for the country's agonizing experiments with democracy. This chapter scrutinizes Peru's latest crisis of democratization and its consequences for human rights.

Historical Overview

The colonial period, following the Spanish conquest with all of its legalistic, centralist, and authoritarian ramifications, spawned a polarized society with inequitable socioeconomic structures as well as political leaders diametrically opposed to the evolution of civil society and, by extension, democracy. Peruvian history reveals that, from the time of independence (1821) until 1968, the criollos, a group of whites descended from the Spanish conquerors, ruled the native Indian masses. During the nineteenth century, civilian constitutional governments heavily influenced by the aristocracy ruled the country. Changes and turnovers, however, have marked the politics of twentieth-century Peru. During the early part of twentieth century (until 1930), nearly all presidents were civilian. Since 1930, only three presidents out of fifteen have taken office by election, and most have been military men.[2]

In 1930, a civilian, Luis Sánches Cerro, won election by a considerable margin, only, after slightly more than a year in office, to be assassinated by an Aprista—a member of the American Popular Revolutionary Alliance (APRA). Established by Haya de la Torre, APRA was outlawed, and remained so until 1945. After this, however, its strength became obvious and it began to control the congress.[3] In the 1950s and 1960s, the military assumed control of the presidency, out of fear of the popular appeal of APRA.

The Latest Military Rule

In 1963, the armed forces came down on the side of Fernando Belaúnde Terry. He was elected president, but by 1968, inefficiency, a poor economic record, corruption, and the soaring popularity of APRA led the army to remove Belaúnde in 1968 and assume complete control. Stressing a socialist platform, the military initiated sweeping agrarian reforms and worker participation in the ownership of industry. These changes were promoted in a revolutionary spirit and manner; but by the mid-1970s, the military reformers had grown extremely unpopular. The economic system was dysfunctional. The army then restored Belaúnde in a democratic transition to civilian rule in 1980.

The reforms initiated by the military had led to hyperinflation and economic collapse. Inequalities, associated with subcultural cleavages, were manifest in both the social and political structures of the country—inequalities exacerbated by geographical forces. Peru's statist policies enriched the elites and kept real reform at arm's length. As Cynthia McClintock writes, until 1980 there were but the trappings of democracy. Peru's so-called elected regimes, in fact, were often less congenial to social reforms than were authoritarian regimes. Writing in 1988, McClintock noted that the Peruvian military continued to be the most politically progressive in Latin America and the most sympathetic toward social reform. This was due in part to the fact that the majority of military officers are from the highlands, an area hit hard by the economic collapse of the early 1980s, resulting in a certain degree of sympathy for sociopolitical discontent. Nevertheless, even the authoritarian governments have suffered from a lack of political institutions and sustained legitimacy.[4]

The frequency with which Peru's military leaders have been involved in politics can be explained by the fact that they were constantly involved in wars of independence. The country's colonial aristocracy, on the other hand, were estranged from these wars, leaving the armed forces as the sole arbiter of Peruvian politics.[5] For more than fifty years after independence (1821), rule by caudillos prevented the natural evolution of civilian politics in Peru. During the period 1821–1980, fifty-two of Peru's seventy-eight presidents were military men. The civilian presidents and civil institutions lacked a sound power base and often ruled at the discretion of the military.[6] The most recent period of military rule (1968–1980) involved a junta-dominated government led by General Juan Velasco Alvarado, whose revolutionary promise to transform the oligarchic society into a democracy was not fulfilled. Velasco's extensive agrarian reform and nationalization programs failed to address the country's rapidly deteriorating socioeconomic problems and, in 1975, General Francisco Morales Bermúdez Cerrutti replaced Velasco as the chief of the junta. But the nation's problems were far too complex to be solved by a change in the presidency.

Transition to Democratic Rule

Unable to cope with the inherited economic difficulties and demands for the formation of a civil society, Bermúdez presided over a transition to civilian government. This was provided for by a new constitution drawn up in 1979: Peru appeared to have halted the conventional pattern of military intervention in politics. The elections of 1980 marked the assumption of power by the center-right Popular Action (AP) and the apparent departure of the military from the political scene. President Fernando Belaúnde Terry was restored to office.

However, the Belaúnde government's free-market approach failed to address the core economic issues of the country. His support declined; economic problems, drug trafficking, insurgency, and hyperinflation undermined his government and 1985 brought Alan García Pérez (1985–1990) of the center-left American Popular Revolutionary Alliance (APRA) to office. The García administration resorted to unorthodox adjustments and drastically changed the economic policies of the Belaúnde government. By 1990, the country had lost its access to foreign credit and the use of government funds to subsidize consumption and investment brought the government to the brink of bankruptcy. Poverty in Lima increased astronomically and consumption became even more unequal.[7]

García, who came to power in "Peru's first exchange of power from one democratically elected leader to another in 40 years,"[8] initially launched a

massive attack on the Marxist left, comprised of two terrorist organizations—
Sendero Luminoso and the Tupac Amaru Revolutionary Movement–Movement of the Revolutionary Left (the MRTA–MIR). He also attempted to reform
the centralized and bloated Peruvian bureaucracy and the old governmental
structures. Despite early success (1985–1987), García's austerity-based
economic programs led (as had those of his predecessor) to worsening
economic conditions. Toward the end of its tenure, the García government
encountered several difficulties: continued poor economic conditions,
skyrocketing inflation, unstable currency markets, diminishing support among
the armed forces, and a widespread guerrilla war. The latter compelled García
to grant the armed forces excessive latitude in dealing with the insurgency.
Their officially sanctioned violence not only failed to crush the Sendero
Luminoso but also led to the continuation of widespread human rights abuses
of civilians.

Sendero Luminoso—the Shining Path

Founded by Abimael Guzmán, Sendero Luminoso derived its membership
from the Ayacucho Regional Committee of the Communist Party, especially
Bandera Roja. The Bandera Roja, Peru's first Maoist party, was founded after
the Sino-Soviet split in 1964.[9] The rise of rightist paramilitary death squads
with links to the government, to the ruling APRA party, and to the armed forces
and the police has intensified the bloodshed.[10] During an interview with El
Diario, a Lima daily newspaper and the official organ of the Shining Path,
Gonzalo (the "nom de guerre" of Guzmán) was asked if his campaign had
trapped the peasantry between two fires: military raids and the guerrillas'
psychological warfare and terror tactics. He responded by noting that "it is
precisely the peasantry that makes up the vast majority of the People's
Guerrilla Army. What must be understood is that the Peruvian State, with its
armed forces and repressive apparatus, wants to drown the revolution in
blood."[11] Regular clashes between the army and Sendero Luminoso, with
peasants and civilians caught in the middle, continued throughout the 1980s.
Elected governments felt threatened by the destabilizing and destructive tactics
of not only Sendero Luminoso but also other guerrilla groups and the military.

The Fujimori Era

In the 1990 elections, the rightist Vargas Llosa lost to Alberto Keinya Fujimori,
a political unknown who captured the protest vote of the center and the left.[12]
Fujimori, who inherited a dismal economy, an unrestrained military, and the
continuing Sendero agitation, seemed foredoomed to encounter difficult
choices ahead. In contrast with his predecessor, Fujimori lacked a broad base
of support in civilian society. The sources of his support were not clear, hence

there were fears that the military's influence in government was widespread. After less than two years in office—on April 5, 1992—Fujimori rejected the democratic principles of the 1979 constitution. He suspended the constitution itself, dissolved the elected congress, purged the judiciary, and, with the military's explicit approval, seized complete control of the political apparatus. The fears were vindicated. Fujimori cited his reasons for the takeover: drug overlords, leftist terrorists, hyperinflation, a weakened judiciary, and an impotent congress. The fate of democracy in Peru is still an open question.

The nation, strongly influenced by three hundred years of Spanish colonial rule, oligarchical traditions, and governmental paternalism and authoritarianism, has a diverse ethnic makeup: 46 percent Indian, 38 percent mestizo, and 15 percent white, plus 1 percent of others.[13] It has nagging regional disparities and identification, terrorist insurgencies, little experience with the tradition of electoral politics, and counterinsurgency death squads linked with the establishment. Hopes for a democratic transition to civilian rule in the 1980s did not last long. The early years of the 1990s have not been different. To understand what led to Fujimori's takeover—the *autogolpe*—after twelve years of electoral politics (1980–1992), it is essential to ascertain why civilian-military ties have lasted so long.

Civil-Military Relations

Between 1821 and 1992 Peru had thirteen constitutions, the last of which was enacted in 1979 (the one nullified by Fujimori in 1992); yet military regimes frequently ruled the country by decree, isolating themselves from civilian society and rejecting the constitutional authority when they deemed it necessary. The military government that took control in October 1968 initiated several agrarian reforms and established itself as an institution, lasting for twelve years. As documented by James D. Rudolph, in the post-1968 government, supreme authority was formally vested in the junta. This consisted of the commanders of the three military services and the president, who was himself appointed by the military commanders. That the president had to enjoy considerable political support from the top-ranked caudillos was a given, as shown in August 1975 by the junta's removal of President Velasco. In his place the junta appointed the prime minister, Morales Bermúdez.[14]

In 1969, the military government created the National Justice Council. The powers of this body, especially those related to the selection of the judges and investigation of their conduct, were intended greatly to reduce judicial independence.[15] In the mid-1970s, rampant corruption, a worsening economic situation, and free-falling currency markets lessened popular support for military intervention in politics. The growth of civilian pressure groups (particularly organized labor) proved to be a decisive social force against the military regime. The 1979 constitution, under which a civilian government began to rule on July 28, 1980, made the judiciary markedly independent, excluded legal justification for a coup, and limited the political role of the military.[16]

Subsequently, and largely as a result of the economic and agrarian reforms of the 1968–1980 period, newly mobilized socioeconomic groups pushed oligarchical elites to the margins. A new elite—that has been described as entrepreneurial, nationalist, and developmentalist—emerged. This new class in 1985 threw its support behind the reconciliation government of García and achieved a national consensus.[17] By the 1980s, the expansion of the educated middle classes greatly increased democratic openings. These new social classes favored transition from authoritarian rule and the expansion of civil society.

The initial manifestations of a move toward civil society had become evident under the Velasco government. These included the emergence of trade unions (e.g., the Confederation General de Trabajadores del Peru—the CGTP), agrarian cooperatives (e.g., the National Agrarian Confederation—the CNA), small landowner peasants, labor elites, popular organizations such as the Marxist Peruvian Peasant Confederation (CCP), and a teachers' union. Support for democracy during the 1980–1988 period continued unabated, with many social groups favoring a democratic political regime over socialist revolution or a military coup.[18] Nonetheless, the exclusionary approach of the neoliberal teams under the Belaúnde administration reinforced the regime's disdain for civil society and the state.[19] The key components of the neoliberal experiments were enacted by executive decrees: "of the 675 laws publicly promulgated between 1980 and 1984, 463 were issued by the executive branch."[20] Using market discipline, the government's economic teams tried to uproot businesses grounded in the unorthodox and centralized policies of the previous administration. These businesses had little say in the formulation of economic policy during most of the Belaúnde administration. In short, the neoliberal economic package (e.g., stabilization programs) was not accompanied by an expansion of civil society. It called for an authoritarian mode of operation.

García's imposition of a heterodox economic alternative contained many aspects of the exclusionary approach of his predecessor's government. However, his reduction of military expenditures by almost half (as a percentage of GDP), despite the fact that Peru's military expenditures remained comparatively high for the region,[21] was an indicator of the high priority accorded to building civil society—albeit within an unorthodox economic context. By 1988, however, it was evident that the poor state of the economy, with negative growth and high inflation rates, had already doomed the succession of democratic regimes in place since 1980—a telling illustration of democratic failure in the context of an ailing economy.

A massive trade deficit in 1987 nearly exhausted Peru's reserves of foreign currency. Between 1987 and 1989, Peru's GDP dropped 28 percent, and real wages plunged 60 percent. In July 1990, at the end of García's term, the government's expenditures were three times larger than its revenues, and inflation had risen to an annual rate of more than 3,500 percent. The foreign debt approached $24 billion. Peru had defaulted on $2 billion in loans from the IMF and other international lending institutions.[22]

The 1990 election culminated in Alberto Fujimori's victory and the general perception that the success of any economic stabilization program depended in part on the explicit support of the military and in part on swift economic progress itself. Unwilling to attack the drug economy, on whose revenue rested his economic reforms, Fujimori sided with the armed forces in their distaste for a militarized drug war and in their persistent efforts to eradicate Sendero Luminoso. The aftermath of his executive coup consolidated support for Fujimori among the armed forces, opening a new chapter in the tumultuous history of the civil-military relationship—a role for the military that refuses to disappear from the Peruvian political landscape.

Democracy Reconsidered: The Road to *Autogolpe*

On April 5, 1992, President Fujimori's takeover closed the elected congress, suspended the constitution, and purged the judiciary—a phenomenon unparalleld in the nation's brief democratic history. Vladimiro Montesinos, a former army officer and close adviser to Fujimori, effectively mobilized the support of the military. Fujimori announced his self-styled government of emergency and national reconstruction and justified his self-coup-from-above (*autogolpe*) in the name of combating judicial corruption, legislative inefficiency, bureaucratic incompetence, narcotics trafficking, increased terrorism, and social chaos. With substantial military and popular support, Fujimori embarked on a different path.

Escalation of Violence

What led to such a change of mind in a man who had been properly elected only twenty months earlier? This is an interesting question. In part, the answer lies in the fact that, since 1980 when the first presidential elections were held, Peruvian living standards had plummeted and guerrilla-related violence had escalated. The Peruvian GNP dwindled significantly, falling below that of the mid-1960s. Foreign debt (estimated at $20 billion) and capital flight (associated with García's earlier nationalization program) precipitated the collapse of the economy during the first two years of Fujimori's rule.[23]

The tremendous surge in guerrilla raids and drug-related violence led to extreme laxity in judicial responses to violence; moreover, it was becoming obvious that the Sendero Luminoso and the Tupac Amaru Revolutionary Movement (MRTA) were heavily involved in the drug economy. José E.

Gonzales has pointed out the significance of the drug industry in a poor society experiencing harsh economic conditions. Writing in 1992, he stated:

> There are no reliable figures on how widespread coca cultivation is—figures range from 150,000 to 300,000 illegal hectares of coca production, with a general consensus of around 200,000. However, Peru has become the world's largest producer of coca for cocaine—about 65 percent of the total. This production generates about $1.2 billion in foreign exchange per year—about half of legal exports. Estimates on employment generated directly and indirectly by coca production fall in the 300,000-to-400,000 range, or over 5 percent of the work force in a country with 50 to 60 percent underemployment in recent years. Thus massive antidrug operations carried out by coordinated U.S. and Peruvian efforts in the UHV [Upper Huallaga Valley], where most of Peru's coca for export is now grown, adversely affected political and economic situations at both local and national levels.[24]

Both guerrilla movements derive income from the drug industry—though not directly through drug trafficking—as well as from kidnapping for ransom and extortion. Faced with continual attacks by specialized antidrug police forces and the traffickers' bands of hired guns (the *sicarios*), residents of the coca growing regions turned to the Sendero Luminoso for protection. The Senderistas' actions to safeguard the farmers and peasants, coupled with the peasants' appreciation, left Sendero Luminoso virtually unchallenged as the de facto government of the Huallaga Valley. It is estimated that Sendero taxation on the region's $600 to $800 million economy brings them $30 to $40 million per year.[25]

Executive-Legislative Tensions

Fujimori, who was already enjoying autocratic powers due largely to his constitutional unilateral authority over economic policy, found himself in the midst of an executive-legislative power struggle, centered on the decree laws. Some of these laws were repealed. But the legislature and the executive disagreed on more than implementation of counterinsurgency measures: there was trouble over the budget, and charges of illicit financial gain against Fujimori's family. On balance, however, as McClintock points out, the political context in 1991 was far from obstructionist: over a period of twenty months, only one minister was censured; and 78 percent of Fujimori's decrees were passed. In general, legislators wanted to negotiate with Fujimori.[26]

In addition, there was the prospect of García's return to the presidency in 1995 following his acquittal of embezzlement charges. The future was uncertain for both the military and Fujimori. Although structural adjustment programs and market-based reforms—dubbed Fujishocks—had been successful in curtailing inflation rates and deficit levels and in raising foreign exchange reserves, Fujimori nonetheless had failed to curb the overall economic recession.

Backsliding to Autocracy

Compounding the dismal economic outlook was the failure of Fujimori's "emergency social program"—measures designed to keep in check the adverse effects of structural adjustment policies on the poorest segments of the Peruvian society. By 1992, government estimates showed that 70 percent of the population lived in poverty. These continuing economic strains led to burgeoning support for Fujimori in the months prior to and even after the autogolpe.[27] The road to the autogolpe faced no major setbacks. The international response in the wake of Peru's backsliding to autocratic rule was ambivalent.

The ambivalence, according to McClintock, can be accounted for in several ways. First, more than 75 percent of the people reportedly approved Fujimori's actions against the legislature and the judiciary. Second, the failure of Peru's democratic institutions to perform effectively and the simultaneous failure of sanctions to restore democracy in Haiti were important factors in generating international apathy toward the developments in Peru. Third, any threat to suspend aid or loans by the International Monetary Fund and the World Bank could have increased problems for the Fujimori government in its fight against the Shining Path and other guerrilla forces. Fourth, the special friendship between Fujimori, who is of Japanese descent, and the Japanese government contributed to international tolerance of the coup.[28]

After *Autogolpe*

In the postcoup era, Fujimori has enjoyed qualified backing from the business community and the armed forces and massive public support. As stated above, the international reaction to the coup, however swift, was not harsh. There were some costs: between $200 and $300 million of foreign economic assistance was suspended; the process of reinsertion into the international financial community was delayed (evidenced by the postponement of some $500 million in credits promised by international financial institutions); U.S. military aid was temporarily suspended; and the 30 U.S. military advisers in the country were withdrawn. Nonetheless, the counterdrug program and humanitarian aid continued.[29] At a meeting of the Organization of American States (OAS)—the meeting of foreign ministers known as the Bahamas Meeting or the Nassau Talks—Fujimori promised to return to elections in the foreseeable future. This gave him some time to restore his credibility with international financial institutions. In June 1992, the United States confirmed a $400 million World Bank loan for Peru's financial sector. In the immediate aftermath of the April coup, the United States had opposed an Inter-American Development Bank loan of $221 million. Supporting the larger loan, the United States cited Fujimori's announcement of elections in the near future as being progress toward restoration of democracy.[30]

Fujimori's New Majority-Change 90 (Cambio 90) bloc, which won a slim majority (44 of the 80 seats) in the election of a constituent assembly on November 22, 1992, gave him a convenient cushion of stability till the next assembly elections in July 1995, when he will face former United Nations secretary-general Javier Perez de Cuellar as a presidential challenger. The election, however, was boycotted by the APRA, the AP, the Freedom Movement, and other major leftist parties. The new Democratic Constituent Congress had no power to reverse presidential orders and was confined essentially to rewriting the constitution. The election was a well-orchestrated move to legalize Fujimori's autogolpe, and not a real effort soon to restore democratic rule. As decreed by Fujimori, the congress is unicameral, the eighty representatives being elected to terms terminating in July 1995. After these 1992 elections, the U.S. State Department restored economic assistance to Peru. The OAS's position vis-à-vis the reinstatement of democracy also softened, conferring further legitimacy on the Fujimori administration. But on October 31, 1993, balloting for a new constitution did not indicate strong public endorsement. Only about 53 percent of the voters supported the charter drafted by Fujimori appointees. This narrow approval of a new consitution, which paves the way for Fujimori's reelection bid in 1995, demonstrated that the opposition to the regime cannot be overlooked.

The Opposition

A coup attempt against Fujimori, led by a retired general, Jaime Salinas, was foiled in Lima on November 13, 1992, but it demonstrated that Fujimori did not have complete support in the military. His early, unwavering support from two-thirds of Peru's population made it possible for Fujimori to effect the kind of changes he deemed necessary in the constitution.

Opposition groups claim that Fujimori's army-backed "institutional coup" of April 1992, along with the new constitution that would guarantee his tenure of office until the year 2005, will perpetuate Fujimore's authoritarian rule for many years.[31] Particularly alarming to the opposition are the constitution's centralizing tendencies and the impact that these would have on the 46 percent of Peru's population who are indigeneous Indians. Fujimori claims that centralization programs will cut waste and improve government efficiency and will pave the way for the urgent economic liberalization. Regionalization of authority and decisionmaking undertaken during the García period will be dismantled under the new constitution.[32] The new constitution allows for the confiscation of some Indian lands. Supporters of these new measures contend that allowing native land to be mortgaged would stimulate economic development in the Amazon and alleviate the region's poverty. Many believe, however, that a weakening of regional government will infringe on indigenous rights, political participation and land tenure. A consensus among observers is that Fujimori's constitution perpetuates indigenous communities' problems and delays ethnic reconciliation.[33]

Some observers also contend that neither the majority of the so-called Democratic Constituent Congress (CCD) nor President Fujimori is the least bit interested that this constitution is the fruit of consensus and even less interested that it expresses a long-term political pact. The authoritarian character of the constitution is expressed in growing presidential and military prerogatives and in consequent diminishment of legislative power. The new constitution does not signify a move from an authoritarian state of affairs to a strengthened civil society. It is, rather, a perpetuation of Peru's traditional troubles; that is to say, there will be a prolongation of the war—the war in which, with Sendero Luminoso now defeated, Peruvians will continue to fight one another to pay homage to the market and to survive.[34]

Other observers argue that the economic aspects of the new constitution are perhaps its most ideological part. This view sees the neoliberal orientation of the Fujimori government expressly written into the constitution. The text does not, in fact, emphasize enough the pluralistic character of the economy and property; instead it maintains that the principal form of property is private. The constitution consecrates market economics. On the other hand, it ends the state's participation in the economy as well as the state's role as a promoter of development. Private selfishness thus displaces social interest as the norm that the state promotes and defines as a part of the search for democratic consensus.[35]

The introduction by Fujimori of the death penalty for convicted terrorists appears to stand a good chance of being approved by the legislature. Sendero leader Abimael Guzmán Reynoso was captured on September 12, 1992, and other key guerrilla leaders have since been seized. This has contributed significantly to the decline of political violence. The complexities associated with the politics of drugs continue and Fujimori's approach seems no different than that of the army: reluctance to militarize the drug war. Peruvian military officials, according to one source, are less than enthusiastic about the drug war, which they perceive as driving peasants into the arms of the guerrillas. The Senderistas won their base of peasant support in the Upper Huallaga Valley by serving as a shield against antidrug operations sponsored by the United States and by demanding higher coca prices from Colombian traffickers on behalf of small producers.[36]

Moreover, the success of economic stabilization programs has depended on a thriving drug economy.[37] It seems unlikely that Fujimori's approach in this regard will be different. All indications suggest that Fujimori's policies will primarily center on narcoterrorism as opposed to a militarized drug war. As long as coca continues to be Peru's most important export, a viable source of employment, and, increasingly, a source of foreign exchange badly needed for servicing the country's foreign debt, many sectors of the Peruvian polity will oppose militarization of the drug war.

Stabilization Programs

The neoliberal policies of the Belaúnde regime, including privatization, trade liberalization, public investment, and macroeconomics, failed to alleviate Peru's economic problems. They were not properly initiated or implemented. The price shocks stemming from the world economy, the curtailment of external credit, and adverse weather conditions in the early 1980s considerably weakened the economic performance of the government.[38] Implementation was further stifled by "weaknesses inherent in the Peruvian bureaucracy, the configuration and balance of power between the main state financial and planning institutions, the unstable nature of the coalition backing the program . . . [and] the fragmented politics."[39]

The macroeconomic austerity measures and orthodox policies of the Belaúnde government deepened social divisions, leading to a disproportionate burden on the poor classes—fertile ground for the emergence of poverty-related insurgent factions such as Sendero Luminoso in the early 1980s.[40] The García administration (1985–1990) represented a reversal of the orthodox policies of its predecessor. García's main policies, including debt service limits, inflation and demand management, and relations with private capital, were premised on a strong interventionist blueprint. Such policies came to a halt as a bewildering draining of reserves, hyperinflation, recession, and interagency conflicts undermined the administrative capacity of the government. By the late 1980s, the failure of the heterodox experiment was obvious. In effect, both the neoliberal Belaúnde regime and the interventionist García administration adopted highly autocratic styles of policymaking, bypassing the state institutions that typically monitor economic policy.

The Fujishock: An Abrupt Prescription

Fujimori's early campaign vows not to create abrupt orthodox shocks were reversed. He shifted from "gradual stabilization" to so-called Fujishock. In August of 1990, Fujimori announced a series of dramatic measures, including

> a 3,000 percent increase in gasoline prices (to raise government revenues), sharp upward adjustments in food and public-sector prices, elimination of the multiple exchange-rate system and thus an effective devaluation, and a generally unsupportive approach to any wage compensation for the resulting 397 percent monthly inflation.[41]

These shocks have been made possible by a harsh stabilization program consistent with traditional IMF stabilization guidelines. The IMF restored Peru to its list of nations to which it will lend by approving a $1.4 billion, three-year loan package. The money, which would be available until March 1996, would be used to support Peru's medium-term economic program. The IMF said the package was approved due in large part to the fact that the Peruvian government made various efforts to remedy the economy and clear debts owed to the IMF and other foreign creditors.[42] The stabilization programs that Peru adopted pushed inflation down to 2 percent a month, and the economy grew 7 percent in 1993, with 4 to 5 percent growth expected in 1994. The state sector was privatized. In February 1994, Spain's Telefónica picked up 35 percent of the state telephone company for $2 billion. The inflow of foreign money into Peru has been steady since 1992, yet infrastructure and political institutions (especially judiciary and legislative) have not been properly rebuilt.[43] If future moves in the direction of reform are not based on an effective, direct targeting of assistance to the poor—especially the most vulnerable—Fujimori's hope for reelection in 1995 will be dashed.

In Peru most of the poor live in rural areas. Although less than half (44 percent) of all Peruvians live in rural areas, 70 percent of the poorest 30 percent and 83 percent of the poorest 10 percent of the population are rural. The effect of structural adjustments on Peru's poor is pronounced in the rural areas, but those poor who do live in urban areas are even more negatively affected by structural adjustment programs than are the rural poor.[44]

Privatization: A Return to Orthodoxy

Fujimori's insistence on privatization has helped reshape Peru's markets. It has been widely reported that Peru plans to auction off virtually all its state-owned companies over the next two years (an estimated 70 by July 1995)—including oil, electric, telephone, and mining companies and the railroad that takes tourists to the Inca ruins at Machu Picchu. On February 28, 1994, the Peruvian government received $2 billion from a consortium of Telefónica de España, the Spanish telephone company, for 35 percent of the state telephone company.[45] And, in June 1994, the Houston law firm of Andrews and Kurth announced that it was involved in the $3 billion privatization of Petroperu, Peru's government-owned oil monopoly.[46] In order to facilitate the sale of state companies to private investors, the Fujimori government restored public utility rates to profitable levels and slashed costs and payrolls. The cutbacks have reduced state company losses to about $300 million in 1992 from $3 billion in 1990.[47] In February 1993, the government let a $360,000 contract to Booz, Allen, and Hamilton to develop a strategy to privatize Petroperu and study the petroleum law the government is drafting. Petroperu estimates Peruvian oil production will surge to 127,000 barrels per day in 1993 and 133,200 barrels per day in 1994 from 115,900 barrels per day in 1992.[48]

Further, the United States has agreed to participate in a financial-support plan for Peru after Peruvian ministers assured the United States that Peru would improve its human rights record. The United States joined Japan in funding a $2 billion loan program to help Peru refinance its debt to international financial

organizations, thereby making it possible for Peru to reestablish its creditwor-
thiness.[49] On March 18, 1993, the IMF restored Peru's eligibility to receive
IMF loans and approved a $1.4 billion, three-year loan package in support of
the country's medium-term economic reform program. The IMF's justification
was grounded in the fact that Peru's inflation rate had been drastically reduced
to 57 percent in 1992 from 7,600 percent in 1990; its international reserves had
been increased; and its public-sector deficit had been cut from 6.5 percent of
its GDP in 1990 to 2.5 percent in 1992.[50] On the same day, the World Bank
approved a $1.03 billion loan to Peru after the latter had cleared its $900 million
of arrears with the multilateral bank. Fujimori later announced that the two-
year residency requirement preceding application for citizenship would be
waived for foreign investors who made a $25,000 nonrefundable cash con-
tribution.[51] These economic liberalization measures show Fujimori's strong
inclination to advance orthodox solutions. Whether such abrupt liberalization
has been accompanied by a simultaneous buildup of civil society (and consequent improvement in human rights conditions) is an issue to which I now turn.

Human Rights Setbacks

In the last decade or so, the promotion of civil society and democratic rule in
Peru has been complicated by the draconian activities of the Shining Path
guerrillas and by the free hand with which the military, security forces, and
paramilitary groups have carried out violent antiterrorist and counterinsurgency campaigns. The atrocities committed by those guerrilla-hunters in recent
years have received little or no judicial attention. In numerous cases, the courts
have failed to withstand pressure to grant immunity to the armed forces and
other state-related agents.[52]

The recent state-sponsored coverup of the La Cantuta killings—described
below—shows that the Fujimori regime is bent on protecting its armed forces.
In this incident, on July 18, 1992, nine students and one professor from La
Cantuta University were abducted and brutally executed by the army during
an antiguerrilla raid. A military court sentenced Major Martín Rivas and Major
Carlos Pichilingue to twenty years' imprisonment.[53] The military tribunals,
which were closed to public scrutiny, left considerable doubts about whether
the sentences against the perpetrators of these heinous crimes will ever be put
into effect.[54] What is more, President Fujimori recently signed controversial
legislation passed by the Congress on February 8, 1994, stipulating that a secret
supreme court vote would settle jurisdiction in nonnarcotics cases. This, many
contend, would allow the army to conceal incriminating evidence, thus
precluding a thorough investigation of the abuses of human rights by the
military. The ensuing cabinet crisis and resignation of Premier Alfonso Bus-
tamente in protest over the government's enactment of the controversial law
did not change many of the systematic protections granted to the armed

forces.[55] Some have interpreted Fujimori's moves (such as signing such controversial legislation and turning over a high-profile human rights case to a military court) as a way of ensuring his reelection in 1995.

The Counterinsurgency Alibi

The carte blanche given to the military to conduct their counterinsurgency campaign has profoundly undermined Peru's constitutional structure, creating, in the words of Cornell and Roberts, "a state within a state where the military exercises de facto authority insulated from civilian institutions or political control."[56] What sets Peru apart from the majority of Latin American countries is the fact that the counterinsurgency measures that have resulted in the granting of inordinate power to the military, even greater than previously, have been adopted under democratic governments. The frail democratic order in place since 1980 has been blamed for many of the impotencies associated with the civilian courts and civil bureaucracies. The judicial system has been a major impediment to the development of civil society, protection of human rights, and democratization.

Despite repeated pledges by President Fujimori to promote respect for human rights in the coup's aftermath, little improvement has been reported; and suppression of peaceful protest, raids and massive detentions, disappearances, torture, and extrajudicial executions have increased considerably. Fujimori's increasing dependency on advisers with close ties to the military and security forces (e.g., Vladimiro Montesinos) has aggravated the human rights debacle. Many years of counterinsurgency strategy have already placed the military forces in an unchallengeable position. The military combats terrorism at the cost of blatant human rights violations. A substantial majority of "disappearances" and extrajudicial executions have been carried out by the security forces. Operation Aries—conducted by the army as a so-called final offensive against the guerrillas—on a riverbank at Aucayacu is another recent (1994) sad chapter in the seemingly unending story of the army abuses—rape, torture, and extrajudicial execution—in Peru.[57]

Human Rights Watch reports that the Peruvian government continues to stress the role of civil defense patrols (rondas campesinas) in areas where Sendero Luminoso is active. Whereas some are formed by villagers themselves, others are mandated and controlled by the army. These patrols are frequently accused of serious human rights violations.[58] In the Apurimac Valley, the Human Rights Watch report continues, civil defense patrols have effectively defeated the guerrillas at the expense of permitting a booming trade in cocaine. Farther north, the army has helped an expanded Ashaninka army, controlled by local leaders, to defeat guerrillas. But Ashaninka units have also been implicated in raids against peasant families in attempts to regain traditional hunting lands.[59] The Shining Path's reaction to civil defense patrols has been violent. Forty-seven people, including thirty-three women and children, were killed in the Ayacucho village of Huayao apparently as punishment for the formation of a civil defense patrol.[60] Such reactions by Sendero are commonplace.

The difficulties inherent in monitoring the civil patrols have resulted in the lack of any effective constraint on patrol actions. This exacerbates the human rights conditions of the civilians:

> Unfortunately, just as in other countries where civil defense patrols have been part of a counterinsurgency strategy, in Peru the formation of such patrols tends to create paramilitary forces that function principally to punish other civilians—on the theory that this "drains the sea" in which subversives swim like fish—and in the process, local forms of democracy are ruptured, the most violent members of a community benefit, and even when abuses are committed by patrols independently of the military, it is not in the military's interests to punish those abuses, because that would mean dismantling a patrol. In Peru there is hardly a need for another force to prey upon the rural civilian population.[61]

The spiral of guerrilla-versus-government violence led to the promulgation on May 4, 1992, of "emergency rules" that had disastrous effects on the rural civilian population. Americas Watch has concluded that, given the isolation of many areas under state emergency and the lack of oversight of the civil defense patrollers, many curbs on patrol activities are unenforceable.[62] Decree Law 25744, so-called antiterrorist legislation, has left Peruvians virtually unprotected from the abuse of power by the armed forces and security agents. The right to habeas corpus no longer seems to exist for those accused of terrorism.[63] Domestic and international human rights monitors have come to be the new targets of threats posed by these decrees as well. Labor unions remain the target of political violence. Unionists, according to one source, continue to be murdered or "disappeared" at a rate of more than one per month.[64] In short, the elements associated with civil society are being inexorably weakened.

Corruption and Economic Decay

The state of socioeconomic and cultural rights is reflected by several indicators and trends. The Human Development Index, a composite of longevity, knowledge, and income, provides some measure of socioeconomic human rights. Life expectancy increased from 47.7 in 1960 to 63.0 in 1990; infant mortality (per 1,000 live births) fell from 142 in 1960 to 80 in 1991; the daily calorie supply (as percentage of requirements) decreased from 98 in 1965 to 87 in 1988–1990; the adult literacy rate increased from 71 percent in 1970 to 85 percent in 1990; real GDP per capita increased from $2,130 in 1960 to $2,622 in 1990.[65]

Trends in economic performance also reveal interesting results. The annual percentage growth rate of GNP per capita decreased from 0.8 during 1965–1980 to minus 2.0 during 1980–1990; the average annual rate of inflation rose from 233.7 during 1980–1990 to 386.0 in 1991; the overall budget surplus/deficit (as percentage of GNP) increased from minus 0.9 in 1972 to minus 5.0 in 1990.[66] While it is difficult to distinguish between the performance of the civilian-democratic and the military regimes insofar as the trends in human development are concerned, and while it is erroneous to attribute the economic performance of a particular period entirely to its regime, the trends in economic performance illustrate that the performance of the military regimes (1968–1980), especially of Velasco's regime (1968–1975), has been generally superior to that of civilian-democratic regimes (1980–1990).

Fujimori's emphasis on the improvement of the living conditions of the people is grounded in the widespread perception in Peru that freedoms associated with democratic systems will carry little or no weight in the face of massive corruption and economic collapse. When Fujimori successfully managed to bring the rate of inflation down from over 7,000 percent in 1990 to 57 percent in 1992, Peruvians were convinced that such a success was related to his aggressive authoritarian style and his neoliberal, autocratic approach.

Civil Rights: Off the Beaten Path

Fujimori's lack of an institutional base in spite of surprisingly high popular support in the coup's aftermath is a grim reminder not just of the complexities of politics in Peru but also of the reduced importance of civil-political rights in the minds of the Peruvian people. Peruvians have lost the sympathy and patience necessary for democratic tolerance. Such a public mood particularly reflects the extent to which Peruvian society has been overwhelmed by the rampant corruption of an elite and gruesome terror and violence.

Today, Peru, according to Freedom House, is "partly free" with little prospect for improvements in sight. A 1993 tally by the Lima-based nongovernmental Human Rights Commission (COMISEDH) found that forty-seven of the first seventy-two decrees issued by the new government in the aftermath of the coup fired members of previously autonomous institutions; all institutional protection against arbitrary state actions has been removed.[67] Americas Watch reports indicate that violent human rights abuses by state agents have continued at roughly the same level of intensity as in previous years. In 1992, the Coordinadora Nacional de Derechos Humanos registered 178 unresolved "disappearances"—a figure that in 1991 was reportedly 301. Peru's Public Ministry, however, registered a total of 242 disappearances in 1992.[68] Undeniably, civil rights conditions have suffered many setbacks. Although it is premature at this juncture to judge the economic performance of the Fujimori administration, continuing popular support for him points to yet another case of the popularity of an autocratic style at a time when "perceived" and "potential" economic gains loom tangible on the horizon.

Conclusion

The complexity of the Peruvian politics can be traced to several factors. First, the polarization of Peruvian society renders any swift-acting economic policy virtually useless. The claim that redistribution of wealth is better accomplished within "heterodox" economic programs fails to correspond to the reality that in the polarized context of Peru such redistribution would pose the greatest challenge for any government adopting such policies.[69] The military's sweeping agrarian and industrial reforms from 1968 to 1980 led to growth of an educated middle class, paving the way for political and economic liberalization in the early 1980s. But the exclusionary approach of the Belaúnde and, to a lesser extent, García economic teams denigrated the role of civil society—and, in the process, obstructed the gradual process of democratization.

Second, the success of any economic liberalization program depends largely on an immediate effort in which assistance provided directly to the poor and the most vulnerable takes precedence over other priorities. Finding ways to cope effectively with Peru's socioeconomic ills could prove to be the best counterinsurgency strategy that the Fujimori government could conduct. The civil patrol and other methods to combat narcoterrorism cannot succeed solely through a militarized drug war, which has so often resulted in a greater violation of human rights. Given the increasing degree of poverty and politicization in the country, the ultimate outcome of Peru's current guerrilla war will hinge more upon the response and legitimacy of the Peruvian state than upon any other factor.[70]

Third, the formation of civil society must be pursued concomitantly with liberalization. The continuing tenacious civil-military rule in Peru can be gradually eroded as civil society expands its space. Preoccupation with elections to the exclusion of civil society has made the successful working of democratic order in Peru unlikely.

Fourth, liberalization has in recent years been complicated by the disruptive activities of the Sendero Luminoso; it also seems to have no correlation with what type of government—democratic or authoritarian—is in control. The oligarchical traditions, the continuing deference of civil authorities to the military, the polarized political culture, and the marked inequalities associated with racial and cultural cleavages pose profound obstacles to the effective functioning of democracy in Peru. In Peru, the space in which democratic rule and economic liberalization can be simultaneously pursued is very narrow. The functioning of liberalization programs is complicated by the process of democratization.

The key to democratic development is the extent to which civil society has previously been formed and elevated. If the Fujimori economic team adopts an exclusionary method of operation, as did their predecessors, old problems will surface. Problems of inequality, in both the economic and social senses, need to be effectively addressed if Fujimori is to stay long in office. Fujimori's narrow approach to liberalization, characterized by pursuing orthodox economic policies without regard for the gradual expansion of civil society and associational life, appears to be headed for an uncertain future. The conclusions drawn here reinforce the claim that it is not enough to have formal channels for democratic procedures and participation. These channels are necessary, but not sufficient, conditions for true democracy.[71] The case of Peru illustrates yet another example of a system in which a crumbling economy, along with the absence of a sense of citizenship and civil community, severely undermine the popular support for democracy.

Notes

1. Gustav Gorriti, "The Unshining Path," *New Republic,* Vol. 208, No. 6, February 8, 1993, pp. 19–23. See p. 20.

2. Wesson, *Democracy in Latin America,* p. 32.

3. Ibid, p. 33.

4. See McClintock, "Peru: Precarious Regimes," pp. 337–364.

5. Ibid., p. 338.

6. James D. Rudolph, "Government and Politics," in Richard F. Nyrop, *Peru: A Country Study,* Washington, D.C.: U.S. Government Printing Office, 1981, pp. 167–208. See p. 182.

7. Paul Glewwe and Gillette Hall, "Unorthodox Adjustment and Poverty in Peru," *Finance and Development,* Vol. 29, No. 4, December 1992, pp. 10–13.

8. U.S. State Department, background notes, December 1987, pp. 1–10. See p. 5.

9. Sergio J. Chávez, "Sendero and the Political, Economic, and Social Situation in Peru," a paper presented at the Center for Latin American and Caribbean Studies, Michigan State University, October, 9, 1991, pp.1–14. See p. 2.

10. Petras and Molley, *US Hegemony Under Siege,* pp. 13–14.

11. *Interview with Chairman Gonzalo,* Berkeley, CA: The Committee to Support the Revolution in Peru, 1991, p. 50.

12. Carol Graham, "Government and Politics," in Rex A. Hudson, ed., *Peru: A Country Study,* Washington, D.C.: U.S. Government Printing Office, 1993, pp. 225–257. See pp. 245–248.

13. George Thomas Kurian, *Encyclopedia of the Third World,* 3d ed., New York: Facts on File, 1987, p. 1589.

14. James D. Rudolph, op. cit., p. 169.

15. Ibid., p. 171.

16. Ibid., pp. 174–189.

17. McClintock, "Peru: Precarious Regimes," pp. 356–357.

18. Ibid., p. 359.

19. Catherine M. Conaghan, James M. Malloy, and Luis A. Abugathas, "Business and the 'Boys': The Politics of Neoliberalism in the Central Andes," *Latin American Research Review,* Vol. 25, No. 2, 1990, pp. 3–30. See p. 19.

20. Ibid., p. 21.

21. McClintock, "Peru: Precarious Regimes," p. 370.

22. See Werlich, "Fujimori," pp. 61–62.

23. Radu, "Can Fujimori Save Peru?" p. 16.

24. See José E. Gonzales, "Guerrillas and Coca," p. 120.

25. Sergio J. Chávez, op. cit., p. 7.

26. See McClintock, "Peru's Fujimori," p. 115.

27. Eduardo Ferrero Costa, "Peru's Presidential Coup," *Journal of Democracy,* Vol. 4, No. 1, January 1993, pp. 28–40. See p. 33.

28. Ibid., pp. 115–116.

29. See Palmer, "Peru, The Drug Business," p. 79.

30. *Human Rights Watch: World Report 1993,* p. 1410.

31. *Christian Science Monitor,* July 27, 1993, p. 6.

32. *Christian Science Monitor,* October 29, 1993, p. 18.

33. Ibid.

34. See Adrianzén, "Un Paso Atrás."

35. See "Régimen Económico," p. 22.

36. See Andreas and Sharpe, "Cocaine Politics," p. 78.

37. Ibid., p. 75.

38. See Pastor, and Wise, "Peruvian Economic Policy," p. 91.

39. Ibid., pp. 91–93.

40. Ibid., pp. 94–95.

41. Ibid., p. 111.

42. *Wall Street Journal,* March 19, 1993, p. 7.

43. *Economist,* May 7, 1994, p. 8.

44. See Glewwe and de Tray, "The Poor in Latin America," p. 36.

45. *New York Times,* March 1, 1994, p. D2.

46. *Houston Cronicle,* June 17, 1994, p. 4.

47. *New York Times,* April 19, 1993, pp. D1–D3.

48. "Peru Turnaround Tied To Privatization," *Oil and Gas Journal,* Vol. 91, No. 16, April 1993, pp. 30–31. See p. 30.

49. *Facts on File,* Vol. 53, No. 2728, March 11, 1993, p. 173.

50. *Facts on File,* Vol. 53, No. 2734, April 22, 1993, p. 299.

51. Ibid.

52. For details on specific cases, see Americas Watch, *Peru Under Fire: Human Rights Since the Return to Democracy,* New Haven, CT: Yale University Press, 1992, pp. 29–34.

53. *Facts on File,* Vol. 54, No. 2780, March 10, 1994, p. 173.

54. *Christian Science Monitor,* March 15, 1994. p. 19.

55. *Facts on File,* Vol. 54, No. 2780, March 10, 1994, p. 173.

56. Angela Cornell and Kenneth Roberts, "Democracy, Counterinsurgency, and Human Rights: The Case of Peru," *Human Rights Quarterly,* Vol. 12, No. 4, November 1990, pp. 529–553. See p. 530.

57. *Christian Science Monitor,* May 17, 1994, p. 7.

58. *Human Rights Watch: World Report 1993,* pp. 135–136.

59. Ibid., p. 136.

60. Ibid., p. 137.

61. Americas Watch, *Peru Under Fire,* op. cit., p. 113.

62. Ibid.

63. *Human Rights Watch: World Report 1993,* pp. 137–140.

64. McColm, *Freedom in the World,* p. 411.

65. *Human Development Report 1993,* Oxford: Oxford University Press, 1993, p. 142.

66. Ibid., p. 188.

67. See Americas Watch, *Human Rights in Peru,* p. 1.

68. Ibid., p. 9.

69. Eva A. Paus, "Adjustment and Development in Latin America: The Failure of Peruvian Heterodoxy, 1985–90," *World Development,* Vol. 19, No. 5, May 1991, pp. 411–434. See p. 427.

70. See McClintock, "Peru's Sendero Luminoso Rebellion," p. 96.

71. For an interesting view on the subject, see Ascher, "Democracy, Equity, and the Myth," p. 222.

CHAPTER 7

El Salvador:
New Experiments
with Democracy

The twelve-year civil war in El Salvador finally terminated in 1992, with 75,000 dead or "disappeared," many human rights abuses unpunished, ungovernable economic and social inequalities, and a war-ravaged economy. During the war, El Salvador received $6 billion in U.S. military and economic aid. The ensuing peace process and national reconciliation were facilitated in part by the process of liberalization that was initiated (however irregularly) in the early and mid-1980s amid the ongoing civil strife.

In 1984, electoral democracy had given the highly polarized political life of El Salvador false hopes of national and political reconciliation, agrarian reform, and economic development. The fledgling democracy encountered many difficulties and sociopolitical distortions when the country became more deeply embroiled in what was to be a prolonged civil war. Opposition leftist groups stayed on the sidelines and vehemently denied the legitimacy of the elections and so negated the credibility of their outcome. Hence, the restricted, authoritarian electoral politics represented only a narrow segment of Salvadorans.

This was a country where economic and military elites had ruled together for many years; where, since the 1930s, every president but one had been an army officer. In such a setting, José Napoleón Duarte's victory in the 1984 presidential election was, regardless of the U.S. role and some irregularities, a heartening turn of events. Several important developments in the late 1980s led to a reassessment of the leftist groups' position vis-à-vis electoral politics, including the return to power of the right (the ARENA party), in allegedly fair elections in March 1988 (for the assembly) and March 1989 (for the presidency). There was also mounting regional pressure for peace in the drastically changing context of international politics following the end of the Cold War. The latter diminished the viability of the strategy of low-intensity warfare in the region and convinced leftist groups such as the Democratic Convergence and the Farabundo Martí National Liberation Front (FMLN) to fundamentally reexamine their positions. The FMLN had boycotted elections; the Democratic

Convergence, which was formed as a political party to contest elections, grudgingly participated.

The return to El Salvador of Democratic Revolutionary Front (Frente Democrático Revolucionario—FDR) leaders Guillermo Ungo and Rubén Zamora and the ensuing participation of the FDR in the 1989 elections were also important changes. Despite some political distortions and irregularities, the 1989 elections encouraged a pluralist climate. And they were, in part, preceded by an expansion of civil society. In 1991, the Salvadoran Legislative Assembly was expanded to afford smaller political parties a greater opportunity to win access to the legislative process.

However, despite elections and several political reforms, the standard of living of the majority of Salvadorans has continued to decline since the 1980s, in part due to the lack of means to reach political accommodation between different social groups, and in part because of the absence of viable economic reforms. There are many fundamental questions as El Salvador enters a new era and seeks negotiated solutions to its armed conflicts. Will the shifting realities of world politics and the democratic process in El Salvador bring Salvadorans a better life? Will the military abandon its past methods of intervening in civilian politics? What are the terms under which the military will allow civilian control? Will El Salvador evolve into a civilian democracy? Will political pluralism culminate in economic pluralism and profound reforms in the agrarian structure of the country? And what are the realistic chances of democratization in a polarized country such as El Salvador, where for centuries there have been serious difficulties in bringing together the diverse interests of campesinos, workers, the military, the right-wing oligarchy, guerrillas, and government officials? These questions are key for El Salvador. The evolution of civil-military relations in El Salvador is crucial if there is to be a transition to democracy. Socioeconomic and civil-political rights are the most important evidence of the state of democratic electoral politics. This chapter addresses some of these questions.

Historical Overview

A backwater of the Spanish Empire, El Salvador declared its independence from Spain in 1821. When other Central American provinces joined Mexico in early 1822 to form the Central American Federation, El Salvador resisted. From 1822 until 1838, this federation, also known as the United Province of Central America, was comprised of five Central American states (El Salvador, Guatemala, Honduras, Nicaragua, Costa Rica). In 1838, El Salvador became an independent republic and the turbulent era of the Central American Federation ended.

Except for the period from 1900 to 1930, the history of postindependence

El Salvador has been marked by lingering upheavals and instabilities. By monopolizing the economy and controlling export crops, the landed oligarchy dominated the new state: the entire power structure came to reflect the interests of wealthy landowners. This landed oligarchy realized that their interests would best be served if they forged an alliance with the military. Together, the economic and military elites ruled the country for a long time: "From General Maximiliano Hernández Martínez's 1932 coup, following his brutal suppression of rural resistance, until 1980, every president, with the exception of one provisional executive who served four months, was an army officer. Periodic presidential elections were seldom free or fair."[1] The roots of this system by which elites got rich can be traced to the Spanish colonial structures that bequeathed to modern El Salvador a legacy of socioeconomic inequality and political authoritarianism—conditions clearly antagonistic to the building of a democratic state.[2] Centuries of external dependence and control by elites account for the extreme maldistribution of resources in El Salvador.[3]

In the midnineteenth century, new competition with cheaper European chemical dyes had limited El Salvador's main export: indigo dye. El Salvador's elites turned to coffee production and used their influence to gain access to coffee land. Communal landholdings occupied by mestizos and Indians were legislated out of existence. Several rebellions in the late nineteenth century expressed the deep anger of the peasants at this illegal seizure of their lands and their subsequent forced labor on the coffee plantations. Would-be coffee growers, note Booth and Walker, led El Salvador into the twentieth century "with one of the most unequal patterns of land distribution in all of Latin America. A coffee elite, henceforth known as the 'fourteen families,' controlled a lion's share of the country's resources."[4]

The rebellions failed, but peasant unrest continued well into the twentieth century. In the uprisings of January 1932, Augustín Farabundo Martí, a charismatic Marxist intellectual who was the chief organizer of these peasant revolts, was captured and later brutally killed. This was when, to safeguard their interests from peasant rebellions, the landowning elites, instead of relying on civilian dictators, shifted their alliance to the military. During 1930–1980, a series of military regimes, essentially defending the interests of the oligarchy, ruled El Salvador. In the mid-1960s, the opposition Christian Democratic Party (Parido Demócrata Cristiano—PDC) was born. The PDC's leader, José Napoleón Duarte, supported incremental reforms in line with the United States–created Alliance for Progress and the Central American Common Market.[5] Duarte won the 1972 election, but the army-oligarchy alliance negated the election's results; Colonel Arturo Armando Molina took over the presidency and Duarte was sent into exile.

When, in the 1970s, the country experienced a series of severe economic, political, and social setbacks, the military leadership reasserted itself. Subsequent protests and an attempted coup were suppressed. In the late 1970s, guerrilla warfare erupted in both the countryside and urban areas. The guerrilla groups were diverse—a coalition of intellectuals, students, leftists, peasants, some elements of the liberationist Catholic Church, and factions linked to groups outside the country. The new revolutionary Sandinista government in Nicaragua, in power since the fall of the Somoza regime in 1979, supplied arms to guerrilla groups in El Salvador. The Salvadoran armed forces launched a vicious nationwide offensive—a brutal overreaction to the opposition.

The army's indiscriminate bloodletting took a dreadful toll in the rural areas as the possibility of military victory by the guerrillas loomed. It is estimated that the economic burden of the civil war during the 1979–1988 period reached approximately $2 billion and severely inhibited any effective restructuring of the economy. Economic distress boosted the importance of coffee exports as a major source of foreign exchange and the sole viable, short-term alternative to continued economic aid from the United States.[6] With Washington's support and involvement, the army withstood the pressures of civil war and guerrilla warfare. In 1980, the military-civilian junta permitted the formation of a provisional government comprised of civilian leaders. The intention was to isolate the guerrillas. Several so-called unorthodox policies, such as the nationalization of banking and exports and land reform, were adopted. The elections of March 28, 1982, led to the formation of a constituent assembly with sixty members. On December 20, 1983, the assembly drafted a new constitution. Many of the newly enunciated reforms, however, fell short of fulfilling the guerrillas' demands as put forth by the FMLN.[7]

In March of 1984, Duarte, one of the founders of the PDC, won the first presidential election by defeating Roberto D'Aubuisson of the Nationalist Republican Alliance (ARENA). In the next election (March 1989), ARENA's Alfredo Cristiani won the presidential election, taking office in an unprecedented peaceful transition. The expansion of the assembly from 60 to 84 seats in 1990 considerably broadened the representational base. Although ARENA lost its assembly majority in the March 1991 elections, it won 44 percent of the vote (39 deputies) and 177 municipalities.[8] In the early 1990s, under UN auspices, the Cristiani government and guerrillas engaged in a regular dialogue to incorporate FMLN members into Salvadoran political and social sectors. Agreement between the parties was reached under the auspices of UN Secretary-General Pérez de Cuellar on December 31, 1991. The agreement (the accords of Chapultepec) was signed in Mexico City on January 16, 1992, and took effect on February 1, 1992. At last, the civil war ended. A cease fire was finalized on December 15, 1992. The FMLN military structure was largely demobilized and demobilization of Salvadoran military forces proceeded immediately.[9] The UN mediation efforts, backed by Colombia, Mexico, Spain, and Venezuela, further paved the way for a political resolution to the longstanding conflicts of the country. In September 1993, a UN-brokered agreement established a three-phase blueprint to grant land to former guerrillas, their peasant supporters, and former soldiers.

Civil-Military Relations

Historically, the interactions between the armed forces, the state, and civil society have been marked by either military dominance or tutelary patterns of governing. More recently, the internal guerrilla wars created substantial pressures for adoption of the tutelary model as military authorities carved out for themselves a de facto political space in some areas.[10] A quick look at the evolution of the military's alliance with right-wing forces is instructive.

Alliances on the Right

Traditionally, the military supported the coffee oligarchy by suppressing peasant rebellions in the coffee growing areas of western El Salvador. In return, the landowners protected the military's interests and financed its growth and professionalization, nurturing what came to be the most powerful institution in El Salvador for most of the twentieth century (1931–1984).[11] Maximiliano Hernández Martínez (1932–1944), the first Salvadoran president, enjoyed the longest tenure in office of any of El Salvador's many presidents. Relations between Hernández and the oligarchy suffered a setback when the president adopted economic policies costly to the landowners. Hernández found he was unable to ignore the organized peasant rebellions. The succeeding regimes of Menéndez, Castaneda, Osorio, and Lemus grappled with widespread dissatisfaction associated with the implementation of so-called guided reforms, all the while distancing themselves from the oligarchy. These moves led the military to adopt the mission of preserving the country's national law and sovereignty.

The Military's Institutional Autonomy

Traditionally, the ties between the military, the church, and the oligarchy were fairly strong and the basis of elite power in El Salvador. Oscar Arnulfo Romero removed the church from this nexus in the late 1970s. By the late 1960s, the Roman Catholic Church had taken a new stance in favor of the oppressed peasants and liberation theology had become a mobilizing force against exploitative policies. Increasingly, progressive clergy were committed to the politics of change and the church became a revolutionary influence among the masses, facilitating movement toward liberation and choice.[12] Through vehicles of popular participation known as base communities, local movements of agrarian and political reform grew in rural areas, providing one of the bases of peasant mobilization for land reform in the mid-1970s.[13]

At a nationwide level, the armed forces appeared to be more independent, probably because their power increased relative to both the oligarchy and the church. The change in the role of the military from the oligarchy's private army to that of guardian of the constitution gave it a more independent influence.[14] After 1959, the nationalist revolutionary movement in Cuba, led by Fidel

Castro Ruz, inspired similar movements in El Salvador. In response, Salvadoran army officers refocused on national security, mostly on counterinsurgency strategies and doctrines, which implied further expansion of military tasks in politically based operations. President Lemus resorted to repressive measures and the outcome was further political instability. Lemus was deposed in a coup on October 26, 1960 and a shift to a military-civilian junta became inevitable. Rivera's election to the presidency in April 1962 did little to advance economic reforms.

In the 1967 election, the presidency was won by Colonel Fidel Sánchez Hernández, representing the National Conciliation Party (Partido de Conciliación Nacional—PCN), the conservative "official" party of the Salvadoran military that had dominated politics since 1949. In 1969, war with Honduras (sometimes referred to as the Soccer War) politicized the issue of unequal land distribution. The election and the ensuing coup of 1972 led to more turmoil. The government of President Molina soon confronted a growing upheaval caused by the People's Revolutionary Army (Ejército Revolucionario del Pueblo—ERP) and the Farabundo Martí Popular Liberation Forces (Fuerzas Populares de Liberación Farabundo Martí—FPL). During the 1970s, guerrilla war began to engulf the country:

> The military began to focus more on internal security than on political manipulation. Consequently, elements of the military adopted the doctrine of national security, emphasizing anticommunism, state autonomy, and limits on the exercise of civil liberties through heavy reliance on the state of siege and other security decree powers. Civil-military relations changed accordingly. In an attempt to reassert its control and protect its own institutional integrity from leftist subversion and rightist attempt to take power, the military tried to increase the distance between itself and civil society. The oligarchy encouraged the government's efforts to reinstate policies that characterized the traditional authoritarian model.[15]

By the mid-1970s, popular support for leftist groups had expanded throughout El Salvador. General Carlos Humberto Romero's reaction to the spread of guerrilla activities led to further human rights abuses by the armed forces and to the use of death squads. The extent of the internal crisis and human rights violations convinced Washington that the Romero dictatorship should end. The overthrow of the Somoza regime in Nicaragua in July 1979 by a broad-based social movement awakened Washington to a new reality: a similar revolution might be unfolding in El Salvador.

Post-1979 Civil-Military Juntas

On October 15, 1979, Military Youth, a group of junior and reformist army officers, deposed President Romero. The U.S. responded positively to the coup, if for no other reason than that the change symbolically decimated the agent of terror. Yet the new government remained under military control and the leftist groups remained isolated from political power.[16] The governing junta consisted of Colonel Adolfo Majano (refomist military), Colonel Jaime Gutiérrez (rightist military), Román Mayorga (civilian liberal), and Guillermo Ungo (civilian social democrat). The junta government subsequently failed to contain violence and it became clear that the armed forces and the death squads allied with it were uncontrollable. There were also divisions within the junta government. The regime collapsed in January 1980.[17]

A second junta, a civil-military regime, took office on January 19, 1980. Washington helped to broker an agreement between a conservative group of Christian Democrats and the rightist military in the junta so as to rationalize its foreign aid policy toward El Salvador and secure congressional assent for sustained funding. Such a policy, Petras and Molley point out, made it possible for the Carter administration to label the regime in El Salvador as reformist and moderate. President Carter argued that the Salvadoran regime was torn between the "extremes of left and right" and—despite overwhelming evidence to the contrary—that "the state was separate from and unable to control the death squads."[18]

In 1980, a third junta offered Duarte a position in the transitional government. Meanwhile, the active U.S. role in El Salvador in the form of economic aid in the wake of guerrilla attacks continued unabated. With U.S. influence and assistance, a Duarte administration (1984–1989) took office and adopted several reformist measures. Having relied heavily on U.S. material and political support, the military found itself under pressure to adjust to Washington's new orientation. The threat of a cutoff in U.S. economic and military aid compelled the military to forge an uneasy alliance with Duarte's Christian Democratic government.

Blachman and Sharpe argue that the transition to pseudoelectoral politics was part of the military's and oligarchy's response to the severe constraints created by the civil war. In effect, the military allowed the transition to occur under controlled circumstances because it wanted to curb emerging social movements and to avoid greater grassroots pressure that could jeopardize its existence as an institution.[19] Given the situation, some change in the military's traditional role in politics was inevitable. However, civil-military relations continued to be marked by covert conflicts over government policies and the methods by which warfare against the FMLN guerrillas was conducted.[20]

Some have questioned the nature of such changes in the civil-military relations. They argue that the post-1979 period can be characterized as one of transition from authoritarian rule. Yet prior to 1992, when peace accords were signed, this period in no way constituted a transition toward democracy. Indeed, several pacts signed between civilian leaders and the military actually served to consolidate the dominant position of the armed forces, as well as its institutional autonomy. During this period, the Salvadoran army greatly expanded and became more sophisticated organizationally, for which the United States was largely responsible. The military's ongoing control of the state set back efforts to democratize civil-military relations. The armed forces lacked democratic professionalism: the military's *tanda* system played a significant role in promotions and appointments, irrespective of the individual's merit, shielding officers from accountability and prosecution.[21]

Changes in the Post–Cold War World

Changes in the post–Cold War era had a dramatic impact on civil-military relations. Superpower bloc politics and rivalry in Latin America ended. Both the Salvadoran armed forces and the guerrilla groups realized that they had lost easy access to cheap weapons and diplomatic support from the superpowers. They no longer even had regional patrons. The new era also underscored the decline of security-based concerns and the emerging prominence of issues of economics, trade, environment, democratization, and human rights. The Cristiani government, dating from 1989, found itself caught up in changing international political and strategic contexts. With the Sandinista government voted out of office in Nicaragua in early 1990, the U.S. program to contain Communist influence in the region lost its raison d'être. Coupled with further threats of a suspension of U.S. economic and military aid, the Cristiani government and the FMLN were pressured to reassess their orientations and policies and to reach a negotiated settlement to the civil war.[22]

On December 15, 1992, the final stages of the ceasefire resulted in a nascent but real peace process. The key provisions of the peace accord included wide-ranging reforms in the military, national civilian police, the judiciary, elections, and the social sectors. Implemented properly, these provisions would redefine the future of civil-military ties. The military reforms of the armed forces stress democratic values and prohibit an internal security function, except under certain circumstances; a new civilian intelligence service is to be placed under the president's authority with legislative oversight; paramilitary groups are to be banned, civil defense forces disbanded, and forced recruitment ended. Many worried that the government would allow the members of National Police (PN) to join the reformed police force. A 1994 Human Rights Watch/Americas report warned that "contamination of the new police force [National Civilian Police—PNC] with existing police units notorious for abuse poses a serious and potentially permanent problem."[23]

Some of the reforms ordered by the 1992 peace accord have been upheld. Leaders of the former rebels participated in the 1994 elections and won one-quarter of the seats in the national assembly. The National Police is being replaced by a new police force. However, land reform lags behind, and the justice system remains vulnerable to manipulation by the bureaucracy and unchecked corruption. An investigative panel, officially known as the Joint Group, composed of government appointees and a representative of the UN secretary-general found "serious indications" that many of the same people who organized or covered up the activities of death squads during the civil war were involved with organized criminal groups. A report by the panel said the groups included members of the military and police as well as government officials and wealthy individuals. The panel, which suggested that the government was serious about fighting such organizations, cautioned that the "justice system, by action or omission, continues to give the margins of impunity that these organizations require." An essential step, however, was taken in the summer of 1994 to reform the judicial system with the naming of a new supreme court, which controls the entire judiciary.[24] The troubling issue still concerns the dismantling of the death squads. Many reports indicate that there are still powerful political figures, associated with the death squads, who belong to the ARENA party. Judicial and police reforms must be carried out by a president whose own party has been linked to the death squads. It remains to be seen whether Salvadoran president Armando Calderón Sol has the political determination to sustain such reforms and keep the country moving toward national reconstruction.

In the social domain, the government is to implement existing land reforms; special treatment is to be accorded to former combatants from both sides in the distribution of state-owned land; and the government is committed to financing long-term, low-interest loans for land purchases.[25] Understandably, any success in these areas would give rise to optimism that El Salvador's peace plan is viable. The national reconciliation initiatives and the peace talks notwithstanding, many tensions regarding the future role of the armed forces in the country linger. The extent to which the military's subordination to civilian rule will become a reality is a major question. It remains to be seen whether a substantive change in the previous patterns of civil-military relations will endure—or even be made.

Abortive Attempts at Democratization

The first, brief, experiment with free elections in El Salvador took place in 1930, when Manuel Araujo won the support of the small middle class. The short-lived experiment was undermined by the global financial disaster in 1931–1932. General Maximiliano Hernández Martínez took office via coup in December, 1931. A degree of democracy returned to El Salvador in 1950 when the relatively free election of Oscar Osoria as president spawned new hope for the middle classes, but the administration of José María Lemus ended this phase. During the 1960s and 1970s, the regimes of Julio Rivera, Armando Molina, and Carlos Humberto Romero attempted to appease the middle classes with plans for synoptic agrarian reforms, but plans of effective scope were not implemented: the armed forces' alliance with the coffee barons preempted them. The consequence in civil society was growing penetration of and support for leftist guerrilla activities.

Rise of the Christian Democratic Party

By the early 1980s, the survival of the so-called tripartite alliance between the military, the PDC, and the United States rested upon the practice of free elections in El Salvador. It appeared highly unlikely that the previous levels of U.S. foreign aid to El Salvador would continue. The 1982 constituent assembly election, in which the PDC won 40 percent of the votes (twenty-four seats), was partly free. In addition to relatively free media and party politics, "the intermediary groups such as unions and business associations, which are quite well developed in El Salvador, were active in the campaign both as supporters of various parties and as pressure groups."[26] But these elections were held during the time of greatest death squad activity. Thus, some argue, the elections were not free since opposition parties were not allowed to campaign openly and on an equal footing. Unions participated only insofar as they supported the business interests of elites. These elections were mainly used to rationalize, for the United States, the steady flow of U.S. military and economic assistance.

With active U.S. involvement directed at defeating Roberto D'Aubuisson, who represented the far right and some segments of the armed forces, as well as at promoting the regime of the Alberto Magaña (1982–1984), the March 25, 1984, presidential elections brought Duarte to power. Duarte's Christian Democratic Party subsequently gained a majority of the seats in the 1985 legislative elections. One observer notes that the previous elections (1982–1985) in El Salvador were called before basic consensus and compromise had emerged among social forces. Holding elections during a transition between regimes increased uncertainty because it was not preceded by a basic political accommodation. Unlike the 1994 election, the elections in 1982, 1984, and 1985 preceded political pacts. All the elections held in El Salvador between 1982 and 1985 emphasized the complex and at times contradictory relationship between democratization and the convocation of an election.[27] Although the primary function of the elections, as Terry Karl argues, was to deflect burgeoning pressure for a negotiated settlement, they were also integral to the general strategy for winning the war against the FDR-FMLN.[28] To the extent that external forces (e.g., the United States) imposed elections to sustain the civil war and to preclude any future truce with opposition forces, the election results during the 1982–1985 period effectively obstructed the political accommodation necessary for actual democratization. Thus, any growth of democratic institutions in the country was largely a consequence of the outcome of the war and of internal and international pressures for a negotiated regime transition, not of electoral politics.

Renewal of Civil Society

The resurrection of civil society in El Salvador was hampered by many difficulties. Opposition parties representing labor unions, peasant organizations, or other popular organizations for many years were not allowed to exist. Manipulations and irregularities in electoral politics and accommodations with the military and economic elites marginalized attempts at effective political participation by popular groups.[29] Nonetheless, as pointed out earlier, the economic and political liberalization of the early 1980s had increased the space for popular organizations, albeit only slightly. The transition to electoral politics widened this space. For instance, the 1984 presidential election was preceded by a limited liberalization process that had lasted two years, making possible an increase in civil society. Terry Karl attributes the process to unintended consequences:

> By placing restrictions on the terrorist activities of the ultra-right, the Reagan administration helped to create a political opening in which labor and peasant unions, human rights groups, and other critics of the regime could become significantly more vocal. Open strikes, prohibited since the ferocious repression of 1980–1981, broke out in the Social Security Institute, the Salvadoran Teachers' Union, the textile industry, and several financial institutions. . . . The growing militancy of labor strengthened the UPD, the most important peasant and labor federation permitted to operate without repression. As a result of its growing strength, the UPD was able to strike a bargain with the Christian Democrats who agreed to support labor demands and dialogue in exchange for electoral support—a deal which temporarily pushed the party to the left.[30]

Unwilling to accept the economic policies of Duarte's regime, the U.S. administration tilted toward the right in the 1985 legislative and municipal elections. Between 1985 and 1989, the Duarte government undertook privatization and economic policies favored by Washington and by Salvador's internal business elites: "His administration devalued the *colón*, provided huge incentives to the coffee-growers, and channelled a major portion of development funds into the traditional private sector—measures contrary to the PDC's campaign promises of 1984–1985."[31] In the 1988 legislative and municipal elections, ARENA defeated the PDC. Nevertheless, the participation of the democratic left in the 1989 presidential elections paralleled a decrease in armed insurrections. A negotiated settlement became a real possibility after an announcement that guerrillas would negotiate with the government. To what extent previous liberalization programs affected the pace of the political transition is the subject of the next section.

Liberalization/Electoral Processes of the 1980s

Gary Bland argues that the liberalization process and thus political transition in El Salvador began tentatively, if not in earnest, in early 1984, when the campaign for presidency was won by José Napoleón Duarte. From 1984 through 1991, the liberalization process continued, despite the fact that the flimsy political openings and the electoral process were not themselves sufficient to constitute democratization.[32] The Salvadoran "democratization" lacked certain essential ingredients, of which the most conspicuous were the lack of minimal national consensus and institutional reforms. Duarte's initial economic and political liberalization, which began in 1984, precipitated, to some degree, the future transition to democracy. However, according to Bland, Duarte's tenure of office (1984–1989) prolonged the civil conflict and postponed the democratization process. This came about when Duarte drifted to the right and to a closer association with a U.S. admininstration that was primarily obsessed with the FMLN.[33] Democratization was also delayed by the corruption, inefficiency, and economic doldrums of his government.

In 1989, the return of "orthodox" economic plans and decentralization characterized the Cristiani government's approach. Despite intimidation and continued human rights violations, the overall political climate improved. Some reports suggest that the Salvadoran media was one of the most freely operating in Central America: Salvadorans were relatively free to organize and dissent.[34] The veracity of such reports can be questioned as media was controlled by right-wing forces. By 1991, the Salvadoran Legislative Assembly had been expanded to give smaller political parties greater opportunity to gain formal access to the legislative process. Results of elections to the legislature for the period 1985–1991 reveal the expansion of representation (see Table 7.1). Although the 1992 peace accords were fundamental to democratization, what proved most relevant for the political transition were gradual measures of liberalization adopted during 1984–1991. These were, in Bland's words, "quasi-institutionalized to the extent that it became costly to eradicate them, the price being . . . a loss of vital U.S. military support and international

Table 7.1 Legislative Assembly Elections, El Salvador, 1985—1991

Party	1985	1988	1991
PDC	33	23	26
ARENA	13	30	39
PCN	12	7	9
CD	—	—	8
UDN	—	—	1
AD	1	0	—
PPS	0	0	0
POP	0	0	—
PAISA	1	0	—
Total	60	60	83

Source: Louis W. Goodman, William M. LeoGrande, and Johanna Mendelson Forman, eds., Political Parties and Democracy in Central America, Boulder, CO: Westview, 1992: 375.

condemnation."[35] The implications of the peace process for democratization merit serious consideration.

The Peace Process

With the formal end to the civil war on December 15, 1992, and the ensuing peace process, two commissions were created. The Truth Commission, sponsored by the United Nations, was set up to investigate, collect, and reveal evidence of human rights violations and the war's atrocities. The ad hoc commission was charged with identifying names of army officers to be purged from the armed forces. In its 800-page report, the Truth Commission verified that 85 percent of the crimes and violations were perpetrated by government-directed anti-Communist forces, among them the Salvadoran army and right-wing death squads, backed in some instances by the oligarchy. However, the Salvadoran national assembly opted for general amnesty for the accused in the interest of promoting national reconciliation.[36]

Prospects for the consolidation of a civilian democratic regime are overshadowed by the legacy of sixty years of military domination of politics. This domination consolidated the military presence in the state, expanded paramilitary networks in rural areas, and maintained the military's institutional autonomy.[37] Moreover, the peace accords of the 1990s have not adequately addressed several areas in which the military retains influence: telecommunications, transportation, the census bureau, customs, civil aeronautics, and the postal service. Knut Walter and Philip Williams argued in 1993 that the accords fall short of providing sufficient provisions for civilian oversight of the military as an institution. The peace agreements offer no detailed process for legislative oversight of the military; nor do the accords go far enough in abolishing the paramilitary networks in the countryside.[38]

1994 Elections: Permanent Peace or New Uncertainties?

The 1994 elections for president, 84 national legislators, and 262 mayors were conducted in two rounds of balloting (March 20 and April 24). The results showed that Armando Calderón Sol, of the conservative Republican Nationalist Alliance (ARENA), won 641,108 votes (49 percent) on March 20 and 813,264 votes (68 percent) on April 24, and altogether 39 seats in the National Assembly. Zamora and the FMLN, known as the Coalition, won 325,582 votes (25 percent) on March 20 and 378,980 votes (32 percent) on April 24, and altogether 22 seats in the National Assembly.[39] Many observers believe that people voted for Armando Calderón Sol out of fear that if the left were to win, the country would become destabilized, the economy would suffer from capital flight, and the army would not be willing to let the opposition rule. One analyst summarizes the consequence of such a fear aptly: "When stability becomes the principal value, this can cause people to vote for those who are capable of causing violence and destabilization if they lose."[40]

Nevertheless, these first free elections in twelve years marked the culmination of a two-year-old peace pact. A *Monitor* report in early 1994 thought it was still too soon to answer questions such as whether or not civil war would actually end and whether the election results would promise long-term peace, tranquillity, and jobs.[41] Calderón Sol's connections with hard-line members of ARENA raise serious questions about his commitment to the broad political and judicial reforms advocated in the UN-brokered peace accords.

The gravity of the country's economic and political crisis might well compel Calderón Sol to work with the opposition. He cannot afford strikes and turmoil at a time when the country needs rebuilding and fast recovery following the war (and with dwindling foreign aid).[42] Calderón Sol has been careful to strike a conciliatory tone, but many in ARENA appear to be resistant to sweeping reforms and changes.[43] In late 1994, the peace seemed tentative. People familiar with war-torn rural El Salvador continued to view with skepticism the transition to democracy.[44]

Economic Restructuring

Several factors crippled the Salvadoran economy in the 1980s. War-related damage to the economy caused by guerrilla destruction is estimated to be over $2 billion—approximately the same amount that the U.S. Agency to International Development (AID) has pumped into El Salvador for economic stabilization.[45] The balance of trade dropped sharply, from a positive $112 million in 1980 to a negative $515 million in 1989. A sharp drop in coffee exports, coupled with an accompanying fall in coffee prices in 1989, generated widening trade imbalances at the end of the decade.[46] Declining export income, rising debt service, and foreign assistance tied to stabilization—not investment—contributed greatly to the economy's inability to afford imported intermediate goods such as raw materials, semiprocessed goods, agricultural inputs, and capital goods such as machinery.[47] The absence of investment, persistent budget deficits, external debt—notwithstanding the continued flow of U.S. economic aid—devalued currency, and deepening poverty intensified the precarious state of the economy in the late 1980s.[48]

Vagaries of Economic Policies

The economic policies of the 1980s were shaped largely by two contrasting economic orientations. The first orientation was the "structural reform model." It was introduced with support from the United States and was closely linked to a global counterinsurgency strategy.[49] The supporters of this orientation were found mostly in the PDC and a faction of the armed forces, some of the minor parties, and the reformist wing of the Popular Movement. The second orientation, the "productive adjustment model," was advanced by the International Monetary Fund and the World Bank. This model was supported by the oligarchy and its coalition of trade associations, right-wing political parties, other factions of the armed forces, and technocrats.[50] In the early 1980s, economic policymaking under the juntas and the government of national unity promoted "adjustments," with the result that there were immense economic gains for the oligarchy, intensification of the civil war, and escalating U.S. intervention.

The Duarte administration, which for a brief period (1984–1985) broke with the prior stabilization program, introduced unorthodox reformist policies. The result was an increase in both government intervention and U.S. participation in managing the country's economy.[51] Although the Duarte administration during this period was fairly effective in curbing the deterioration of some macroeconomic conditions, it fell well short of stemming the loss in purchasing power and stopping the plummeting standard of living. The war strategy of the government was a function of its new economic orientation. A strategy of low-intensity warfare, wrote Pelupessy, altered "the nature of repression from open, or indiscriminate, to selective."[52]

However, between 1986 and 1989, the Duarte government edged toward orthodox adjustment policies. These were principally aimed at enhancing the supply of export goods and curtailing the government's role in economic decisionmaking. Many difficulties complicated the so-called reformist approach of the Duarte administration. One was the inability of the government to gain support of private capital. A second was the inconsistency of U.S. attitudes concerning economic decisionmaking and concerning USAID policy toward proposals from the international financial organizations. A third was the imperatives of the war. A fourth—to name one more—was the inability of the government to secure a wide base of support for the "reformist" orientation.[53]

Predictably, the Cristiani government opted for the adjustment approach—plans that were immediately supported by the international financial institutions. The IMF approved a twelve-month standby agreement that led to a rescheduling of $135 million of El Salvador's Paris Club debt with official creditors. The World Bank also approved a $75 million loan for structural adjustment programs. In May 1991, members of the General Agreement on Tariffs and Trade (GATT) approved El Salvador's membership. Several bilateral and multilateral donors have pledged $1 billion under a national reconstruction assistance package. To promote judicial reform, USAID officials in El Salvador signed a grant agreement with the government of El Salvador in September 1992. The five-year, $15 million judicial reform agreement obligates the government of El Salvador to budget sufficient funds for the institutions targeted for assistance before U.S. funds are released.[54] In December 1992, while using the provisions of the Enterprise for the Americas Initiative, the U.S. government reduced El Salvador's debt by 75 percent from

$617 million to $151 million.[55] In March 1992, El Salvador and Guatemala entered into a free trade agreement with a view to creating common external tariffs and export tax systems. Similar pacts are expected to be concluded with Honduras.[56] The Clinton administration slashed aid to El Salvador by almost 60 percent, from $230 million to about $94 million in 1994, the rationale being that with a peace agreement in effect and the economy on the recovery, the foreign aid to El Salvador at the previous levels is no longer justifiable.[57] Some question such an analysis, arguing that the future of democracy in El Salvador hinges upon economic development. Although the currency has been stable at 8.7 to the U.S. dollar and government investment in infrastructure has continued, as evidenced by the new four-lane highways under construction linking the capital city to the port of Acajuita, proponents of higher levels of aid feel that sharp reductions could reverse the gains of the peace process.[58]

The return to "adjustment" by the Cristiani administration, however, has brought little solace to the poor majority. Poverty has deepened. In the 1990s, the biggest economic problems of the previous two decades—that is, tenuous export revenues and deep structural inequities—continue to mark the troublesome economic landscape of El Salvador. The most compelling question now is whether democratization can be translated into a better distribution of national wealth and law. Thus far the answer has been negative. Several elections in the 1980s proved inadequate to effect justice and equity for the great majority of Salvadorans. Constructing a democratic society in El Salvador by building a civil society is now the pivotal element of the negotiation process. In the absence of such a construction, the regularity with which elections take place is unimportant.

Human Rights Setbacks

Despite the electoral politics of the 1980s, El Salvador remained a nation in which egregious abuses of human rights were common. The army, death squads, and security forces perpetrated the most serious human rights violations in the history of the nation. The slaying of Archbishop Oscar Arnulfo Romero; the brutal rape and murder of four American churchwomen in 1980; the 1981 El Mozote massacre in which more than seven hundred civilians were killed by the armed forces;[59] and the killing of six Jesuit priests, their housekeeper and her daughter in 1989 are examples of the atrocities.[60]

In the aftermath of the signing of the peace agreement of January 16, 1992, the United Nations Observer Mission in El Salvador (ONUSAL) began monitoring the human rights situation. With over one hundred observers and six regional and subregional offices in El Salvador, ONUSAL has had a tangible impact on the observance of human rights in the country. It is premature to contend that ONUSAL's presence will spur Salvadoran governmental institutions, including the courts, effectively and at all times to

perform their central role in human rights protection.[61] The Truth
Commission's findings strongly reinforced the widely held view that the
Salvadoran government was largely responsible for blatant human rights
abuses. This recognition was important, but punishment was compromised in
the name of national reconciliation.[62]

The most nagging questions in the current peace negotiations concern the
issue of military impunity and official disregard for human rights violations
and the need for a truly independent judiciary that could control the unlawful
powers of the socioeconomic and political elite. In general, political rights have
been expanded in recent years. Major improvements include the return of
left-wing political exiles in 1987, the expansion of political parties, the recognition of the FMLN as a political party in the 1994 election, and the creation
of a new, five-member national electoral commission.[63]

Through mid-1994, reports indicate that the paramilitary death squads
remain, though their structures have changed. They have become more
decentralized and have extended into organized crime. Some members of the
armed forces and national police appear to be involved. Many abuses reflect
the failure of El Salvador's judicial system to prosecute those responsible for
human rights violations.[64] Some union leaders have been denied permission to
exit the country.[65] One study shows that the labor unions—organizations of
campesinos and other workers—that are members of the UNTS (National
Unity of Salvadoran Workers) were special targets for government repression
during the 1980s. Although human rights organizations have augmented their
work and improved their methods, and although more cases were brought
before the courts and international forums during the Duarte term, relatively
little was accomplished in terms of investigating government abuses.[66]

Americas Watch reported in 1991 that the pattern in the later years of the
1980s was one of selective killing rather than mass killings of labor and peasant
leaders and members of their organizations. The frequent attacks and bombings
of the offices of FENASTRAS, the National Federation of Salvadoran
Workers, during 1989 were typical. The slaying of Archbishop Oscar Arnulfo
Romero on March 24, 1980, was the first of several targeted attacks on church
officials and religious workers. The case of the 1989 slaying of six Jesuit priests
and two women domestics displayed the military's intention to limit the role
of the church in civil society. Similar assaults were directed at leftist
politicians, journalists, students, and teachers. It is estimated that thirteen
university faculty members, students, and workers were killed in 1989, most
of them at the hands of the armed forces. Similarly, health workers, human
rights monitors, founders of the nongovernmental Human Rights Commission
of El Salvador (CDHES), judges, and lawyers were victims of violent assaults
throughout the 1980s.[67]

All this indicated that the holding of elections after 1984 had resulted
neither in civilian control of the military nor in the prevalence of a rule of law.
In short, electoral politics had failed to restructure a dysfunctional and abusive

system. The impact of external pressures in such a process, although considerable, had not been steadily effective. Americas Watch reported in 1992 that the government's ongoing failure to investigate violent crimes and attacks—unless pressured to do so by ONUSAL—had contributed to polarization and mistrust.[68]

In 1992, U.S. support for the Salvadoran armed forces faced congressional opposition. According to Americas Watch, Congress directed most of the administration's request for $85 million in military aid to a fund for the demobilization, retraining, and reemployment of former combatants from both sides. The remaining $21.3 million in military aid was restricted to nonlethal items. Congress adopted cuts (similar to those of fiscal year 1992) in the administration's $40 million request for fiscal year 1993. Congress approved $11 million in nonlethal military assistance and $29 million for the demobilization fund. It also specified that of $1.4 million in military training funds, 75 percent was to be used to establish an effective judicial system and code of conduct, as well as to conduct training in the observance of internationally recognized human rights. Nevertheless, the Bush administration's limited cooperation with both the Truth and ad hoc commissions, which have sought the further release of important information from U.S. governmental files, displayed a lack of serious commitment on the part of the U.S. government to reforms in the armed forces.[69] Under congressional pressures, the Clinton administration declassified documents pertaining to cases examined by the Truth Commission. Over 12,000 documents were released in November 1993, identifying several ARENA leaders who had links to death squad activities. Those documents also confirmed that the U.S. government was aware of the magnitude of the death squad operations. The Clinton administration pressured the military to comply with the recommendations of the ad hoc commission; it also quietly suspended $11 million in U.S. military aid earlier in 1993, when the army high command failed to enact the purge mandated by the peace accords. The funds were released later that year. The U.S. government also condemned the October murder of FMLN party leader Francisco Velis Castellanos and consented to lobby for a swift resolution of the investigation of the murder.[70]

More positively, and in compliance with the 1992 UN-brokered peace pact, the purge of Salvadoran army commanders continued in 1993. General René Emilio Ponce, a former defense minister responsible for several wartime human rights violations, and seventeen other officers stepped down on July 1, 1993. Prominent among those replaced were General Juan Orlando Zepeda, deputy defense minister; General Gilberto Rubio, chairman of the joint chiefs of staff; General Mauricio Vargas, joint chiefs vice-chairman; and the commanders of the air force and navy.[71] The key question in the aftermath of the military purge is whether the new military command will come under full civilian authority.

In certain areas, the social and economic rights of the Salvadoran people deteriorated considerably in the 1980s. The percentage of the population with access to safe water dropped from 53 percent during the 1975–1980 period to 41 percent during the 1988–1990 period.[72] Public expenditure on education as a percentage of the GNP declined from 2.3 percent in 1960 to 1.8 percent during the 1988–1990 period.[73] The annual growth rate of earnings per employee fell sharply from 2.4 percent during the 1970–1980 period to –9.4 percent during the 1980–1989 period.[74]

Conclusion

El Salvador's democratic experiment was made possible by mounting international, regional, and internal pressures after some sixty years of military rule and a civil war. By the end of the 1980s, it was clear that the ARENA government and the FMLN were locked in a bloody, dead-end struggle with neither side capable of defeating the other. The ARENA government's vows to narrow the country's political and economic divisions, to put an end to civil war, and to continue on the path to economic modernization were not fulfilled. Similarly, the FMLN's mass-based revolution was stifled by the United States–backed Salvadoran army and right-wing forces. With the end of the Cold War and a vastly different international political climate, it became evident that the U.S. counterinsurgency strategy had run its course, as had external military and political support for the FMLN guerrillas. The dismal state of the economy, the failure of the ARENA government to broaden its political base, and divisions between the country's oligarchy and the military resulted in lessened support for a military solution. The guerrilla opposition jumped at the opportunity to carve out for itself an active part in the process of democratic transition.

Perhaps one of the most significant factors in this process was the quasi-institutionalized civil society that developed in the 1980s, despite the prevailing political repression. Pressure from the United States to contain ultra-right violence led to the unintended consequences of widening the political space and the outburst of popular organizations throughout the 1980s. The role of popular organizations in postwar economic and political structures is expected to increase as the transition to demilitarization unfolds.

The path toward democratization will be difficult. El Salvador has never experienced a sustained democratic administration. With the new political processes established in the immediate aftermath of the cease-fire, hopes for a well-constructed democracy remained high.[75] Today, however, El Salvador falls well short of representing a country in which a democratic process has strengthened democratic institutions. The politically motivated violence continues to plague El Salvador, a violence that is carried out by a broad criminal network. Too often, this network involves members and officials of the armed forces and the national police. To avoid direct intervention in politics by the armed forces, it is essential to build a civil society with transformed civil-military relations. The transition from liberalization to democratization depends on whether structural reforms in the military, the national civilian police, the judicial and political systems, land tenure, and civil society continue unimpeded in the post-1994 political reconciliation.

The fate of civil-political rights in El Salvador also remains closely tied to the strengthening of judicial process and autonomy. And the future of socioeconomic rights hinges, to a great extent, upon the government's ability to implement land reform programs and reduce income inequalities, thereby improving the abysmal living conditions of the masses. Elections in the 1980s and 1990s have not substantially improved the standard of living of most Salvadorans. Many doubt that political violence will soon be over. Most Salvadorans remain, and rightly so, uneasy about the prospects for democracy and judicial, economic, and political reforms in their country following the 1994 elections. Elections without a minimal national consensus on the prevalence of the rule of law, without basic politicoeconomic accommodations among social forces, and without real economic change will not sustain democracy.

Notes

1. U.S. State Department, *Background Notes: El Salvador*, Vol. IV, No. 2, February 1993, pp. 1–8. See p. 2.
2. See Richard A. Haggerty, ed., *El Salvador: A Country Study*, Washington, D.C.: U.S. Government Printing Office, 1990, p. xix.
3. See Booth and Walker, eds., *Understanding Central America*, p. 32.
4. Ibid.
5. Ibid., p. 34.
6. Richard A. Haggerty, op. cit., p. xx.
7. U.S. State Department, op. cit., p. 3.
8. Ibid., p. 3.
9. Ibid., p. 5.
10. See Fitch, "Democracy and Armed Forces," p. 200.
11. Rex A. Hudson, "National Security," in Haggerty, op. cit., pp. 197–260. See p. 200.
12. See Blee, "The Catholic Church," p. 59.
13. Ibid., p. 60.
14. Hudson, op. cit., p. 201.
15. Ibid., p. 202.
16. Petras and Molley, *U.S. Hegemony*, pp. 128–129.
17. Ibid., p. 129.
18. Ibid., 131.
19. See Blachman and Sharpe, "Transition," pp. 38–39.
20. Fitch, "Democracy and Armed Forces," p. 186.
21. See Walter and Williams, "The Military and Democratization," pp. 39–88. See pp. 57–63.
22. Fitch, "Democracy and Armed Forces," p. 186.
23. *Christian Science Monitor*, March 23, 1994, p. 2.

24. *New York Times,* Sept. 11, 1994, p. 12.
25. U.S. State Department, op. cit., p. 5.
26. See García, "El Salvador," pp. 71–72.
27. See Karl, "Imposing Consent?" p. 12.
28..Ibid., p. 17.
29. Blachman and Sharpe, "Transition," pp. 41–42.
30. Karl, "Imposing Consent?" p. 27.
31. Ibid., p. 33.
32. See Bland, "Assessing the Transition," p. 164.
33. Ibid., p. 172.
34. Ibid., pp. 186–187.
35. Ibid., p. 197.
36. *Time,* March 29, 1993, p. 14.
37. Walter and Williams, "The Military and Democratization," p. 41.
38. Ibid., pp. 67–69.
39. *Los Angeles Times,* April 30, 1994, p. A2.
40. *Christian Science Monitor,* April 28, 1994, p. 6.
41. *Christian Science Monitor,* March 18, 1994, p. 7.
42. *Los Angeles Times,* April 30, 1994, p. A2.
43. Ibid.
44. *Washington Post,* March 20, 1994, pp. A31 and A33.
45. Tom Barry, *El Salvador: A Country Guide,* Albuquerque, NM: Inter-Hemispheric Education Resource Center, 1990, p. 69.
46. Ibid., p. 71.
47. Ibid.
48. Ibid., pp. 71–75.
49. See Pelupessy, "Economic Adjustment Policies," p. 48.
50. Ibid., pp. 48–49.
51. Ibid., pp. 64–70.
52. Ibid., p. 76.
53. Ibid.
54. GAO/NSIAD-93-149, *Foreign Assistance: Promoting Judicial Reform to Strengthen Democracies,* Washington, D.C.: United States General Accounting Office, September 1993, pp. 1–49. See p. 15.
55. U.S. Department of State, op. cit., p.7.
56. Ibid.
57. *Wall Street Journal,* Jan. 17, 1994, p. 6.
58. *Wall Street Journal,* Aug. 19, 1994, p. 11.
59. Investigators have uncovered the remains of a horrible crime—a crime that the Reagan administration vehemently denied—in a remote corner of El Salvador: the El Mozote village, where, in December 1981, hundreds of the villagers were massacred by the Salvadoran army. Many villagers seemingly had believed that the army would protect them as they were caught in crossfire in the war between the guerrillas and the army. Mark Danner maintains that the story of the massacre at El Mozote stands as a central parable of the Cold War, happening as it did under the mask of the anti-Communist crusade. For more information on the related evidence and a wealth of testimony collected by the Truth Commission, see Danner, "The Truth of El Mozote," *New Yorker,* Vol. 69, No. 41, December 6, 1993, pp. 50–133. Americas Watch reports say that "up to one thousand civilians in ten or so hamlets and villages in Morazán Department were killed by the Atlacatl Battalion over about ten days in December 1981 (accounts differ as to exactly which days)." See *El Salvador's Decade of Terror: Human Rights Since the Assassination of Archbishop Romero,* Yale University Press, 1991, p. 49.
60. According to one account, some 42,000 people died between 1980 and 1982

and another 30,000 have died since. It is said that virtually all objective observers blame at least 80 percent of these deaths on the military, the police, and a rightist paramilitary organization with direct ties to public security forces known as Organización Democrática Nacionalista—ORDEN. For further information on this account, see Booth and Walker, *Understanding Central America,* pp. 85–86.

61. Cynthia J. Arnson, "Human Rights: Has There Been Progress?" in Tulchin and Bland, *Is There a Transition?* pp. 85–93. See p. 89.

62. Many Salvadorans have raised concerns over the issue of amnesty granted to the former security agents. Bitter controversy has also followed the failure to comply with some of the Truth Commission recommendations, including the call for the removal of all supreme court members. A growing number of Salvadorans have asked for foreigners to participate in the investigative groups. Many prominent figures continue to underscore the significance of the latest investigations into death squads. Archbishop Arturo Rivera Damás has stressed such concern, saying, "How can illegal armed groups be eliminated if we don't keep delving into the past until we find the roots of current violence?" See *Christian Science Monitor,* January 20, 1994, p. 7.

63. See McColm, *Freedom in the World,* p. 217.

64. *Human Rights Watch World Report 1994,* p. 94.

65. Ibid., p. 218.

66. Margaret Popkin, "Human Rights in the Duarte Years," in Anjali Sundaram and George Gelber, eds., *A Decade of War: El Salvador Confronts the Future,* New York: Monthly Review Press, 1991, pp. 58–82. See pp. 72–74.

67. See Americas Watch, *El Salvador's Decade of Terror,* pp. 41–80.

68. See *Human Rights Watch World Report 1993,* p. 109.

69. Ibid., p. 111.

70. Ibid., p. 97.

71. *Facts on File,* Vol. 53, No. 2748, July 29, 1993, p. 565.

72. United Nations Development Programme, *Human Development Report 1993,* Oxford: Oxford University Press, 1993, p. 144.

73. Ibid., p. 164.

74. Ibid., p. 168.

75. Unclés, "Redefining Democracy."

CHAPTER 8

Democratization, Liberalization, and Human Rights in Comparative Perspective

The transitional authoritarian regimes of the Third World are not likely to be replaced any time soon by robust democratic regimes capable of protecting human rights. The cases examined in the preceding chapters illustrated the constraints on democratization and human rights. If we treat liberalization as the single most important change, and democratization as a direct function of liberalization, we disregard the key role played by political leaders, the military, and external actors. Both *choice* and *structure* have a direct impact on the sustainability of democracy. Transition is influenced by the interplay between the two. This chapter compares the cases under review in order to better understand the interaction between choice, structure, and other factors. Four areas are important for this comparison: the military's political role, the external factors in electoral politics, human development conditions, and reform and its consequences. I close with comments on the prospects for democratization and human rights in a vastly changed world.

The Military's Political Role

The 1980s and early 1990s have been years of sweeping global democratization. Nonetheless, there have been military takeovers, interventions, and continuing pressures to end frail and restricted democratic regimes in some Third World countries. These justify skepticism about democratization in many Third World countries. Advocates of antidemocratic programs and ideologies argue that tackling socioeconomic problems requires decisive, direct, and forceful measures. Without necessary economic reforms and adjustments—this argument goes—the process of democratization will not create stability. Decisive but undemocratic efforts have in some cases won the support of a public frustrated by poor economic conditions and disillusioned by the failure of a "democratic" government to curb political corruption, economic decay, and inefficiency. Given the fact that many Third World societies lack mechanisms for orderly bargaining and consensus building—the two essential ingredients for a civil society—it is easy to understand why the public in these countries have at times embraced praetorian politics.

Historically, nationalism has perpetuated the legacy of praetorian rule. In all four cases reviewed here—Algeria, El Salvador, Pakistan, and Peru—the participation of military leaders in wars of independence was the route by which the military became involved in politics. The estrangement of the colonial aristocracy from such wars left the armed forces as arbiter of their countries' political fate. Today, the active support or acquiescence of the military is the key to any viable and sustained political transition to democracy in these countries. In each case, the military has traditionally been either the dominant player or at least a key player in political pacts with other elite groups. These political pacts helped define the military's interests and involved triple alliances in all of these cases: FLN/state/army in Algeria, president/prime minister/army in Pakistan, landowners/state/army in Peru, and coffee barons/state/army in El Salvador.

In Algeria, the army traditionally played a progressive role, supporting secular regimes and their orthodox and unorthodox economic reforms and even some degree of political opening. In Pakistan, the army proved to be very conservative: only recently (in the post-Zia era) has it shown some tolerance for economic reform and political opening. In Peru (1968–1980) we find the most reformist and progressive army among these four cases. The Peruvian junta's reforms and economic modifications created a new, entrepreneurial, nationalist, and developmentalist elite, which pushed the older oligarchy to the margins. These reforms expanded the educated middle class and contributed substantially to ensuing democratic openings in the late 1970s and early 1980s. The initial manifestations of a move toward civil society became evident in 1975 under the Velasco government. Recently, the military has supported Fujimori's coup after democratic rule proved volatile.

In El Salvador we find the most notoriously conservative and least progressive of the four armies. The Salvadoran military's association with right-wing forces and death squads and its alliance with the coffee producers has been exploitative and repressive. The importance of export crops and the need to suppress peasant rebellions in the coffee-growing areas of western El Salvador led the landed oligarchy to an alliance with the army. From the 1932 Hernández coup until 1980, all presidents but one were army officers who helped sustain this uneasy and sometimes shaky oligarchy/military alliance. The triangle of church/army/oligarchy was the basis of power in El Salvador until Oscar Arnulfo Romero removed the church from the triangle in the late 1970s. Nationally, the armed forces may have subsequently appeared more independent, but that is probably because their power increased relative to the oligarchy and the church. In both El Salvador and Peru, counterinsurgency measures against indigenous guerrilla movements and civilians expanded the army's involvement in brutal operations. These activities, involving flagrant human rights abuse, were often beyond the state's control.

In Pakistan, and to a lesser extent in Algeria, ethnic minorities and insurgencies posed challenges to the central government and helped to prolong the army's politicized role. In Pakistan, the army's efforts to stifle ethnic insurgency in Sind, for example, has frequently led to excessive violence. Since the early 1980s in Algeria, Berber minority groups have been the object of government repression. Following the riots at Tizi-Ouzou in March and April of 1980, in which thirty-two Berbers were killed and two hundred injured, the Algerian army and security forces have suppressed the Berbers' calls for cultural autonomy and have viewed them as cultural separatists intent on threatening Algeria's national security.[1]

External Factors and Electoral Politics

In each of the four case, the society and politics of the country has been shaped by external factors. Since their independence from colonial control, whether by the British, French, or Spanish, these countries have been influenced by a myriad of bilateral and multilateral activities. The most significant influences have been foreign aid and structural adjustment. Immediately after World War II, foreign aid was not directly linked to democratization efforts in the Third World. In the post–Cold War era, with the geopolitical calculations of the great powers of less importance, foreign aid and other multilateral assistance can be effectively utilized to promote economic liberalization and political openings.[2] Foreign aid and technical assistance ought to be directed at satisfying basic human needs and human rights considerations, especially in those Third World countries where economic liberalization is not accompanied and followed by political liberalization.

The tendency to emphasize foreign aid for nations that have had or will have elections runs the risk of pressing these nations toward conducting either restricted and closely monitored elections, in which case the old power relationships and social pacts remain intact, or conducting democratic elections with results that could very well jeopardize the democratization experience itself. Foreign aid alone hardly ever brings about a desirable change in the economic and class structure of a recipient country. Below I give case histories of each of the four countries selected for study.

El Salvador

During the 1980s, U.S. foreign aid to El Salvador (military and otherwise) helped to increase the military's coercive power and control. By turning to authoritarian and restricted electoral politics, the military managed to control electoral results and thus gained more U.S. support. The threat of change from below was firmly contained as electoral mobilization defused, to some extent, social pressures.[3] To the extent that elections imposed by the United States and others sustained the civil war and precluded a truce with opposition forces, the 1982–1985 elections actually blocked the national accommodation vital for effective democratization. The resort to a negotiated political transition and democratization in the late 1980s and early 1990s was clearly a consequence not of electoral politics per se but of international pressures for an end to violence.

Algeria

In Algeria, internal and external pressures forced President Chadli Bendjedid to unleash a swift process of political liberalization and multiparty elections (1991–1992). This led to the polarization of Algerian society into two non-democratic alternatives: military rule or theocratic rule. With the military at the helm (1992), the brief period of democratization came to an abrupt halt in an environment of violence and repression.

Pakistan

In Pakistan, the death in 1988 of the military ruler, General Zia, was followed by multiparty elections. Pakistanis have since seen a liberal interregnum under Benazir Bhutto, a return to traditional politics under Nawaz Sharif, and a further period in office of Bhutto. Since 1985, Pakistan's several elections have done little to cope with the socioeconomic and political ills of the country. Following the Soviet withdrawal from Afghanistan in the late 1980s, the massive infusions of foreign and military aid into Pakistan stopped. Further- more, U.S. administrations since then have attempted to link U.S. foreign aid to Pakistan's progress in phasing out its nuclear program. The nation's economy has deteriorated, drug trafficking has increased enormously, and sectarian splits have become more frequent. The presidential powers enumerated in Pakistan's constitution often led to the dismissal of elected prime ministers and reflect Pakistan's uneasy embrace of democracy.

Peru

In Peru, a frail democratic order became a new target of authoritarian populism in 1992. President Fujimori ended twelve years of electoral politics (1980– 1992) by pulling off an executive coup (the *autogolpe*). After the first presiden- tial elections were held in the 1980s, Peruvian living standards plummeted and guerrilla-related violence escalated. Not surprisingly, Fujimori's neoliberal, autocratic rule enjoyed great popular support. The crumbling economy and the lack of a sense of community severely undermined popular support for democracy in Peru. To make elections or democratization a condition for further foreign aid to Peru is, in light of the country's poverty, deprivation, and civil war, an error. Although a strong case can be made for development aid and democratization, Peru operates under strong constraints. In some cases, political and economic realities prevent the linkage of foreign aid to democratization. In other cases, such linkages may be instrumental in creating constructive change. This view does not demean democracy or express a nostalgia for authoritarianism. Democratic measures alone will not improve an ailing economy. Economic liberalization and reforms must be vigorously pursued in order to establish the base necessary for democratization. Without a gradual buildup of civil society, the Peruvian government cannot survive the political fallout of reform.

In addition to foreign aid, structural adjustments initiated by international financial institutions must deal with the expanded role of the state in social welfare. Structural adjustments, especially at earlier stages, require strong government actions and may also require the imposition of heavy-handed economic programs. In some cases, such measures have won the approval of the public. In Pakistan, Qureshi's neoliberal economic measures gained the respect and support of many Pakistanis.[4]

Peru's Fujimori has been quick to curb the inflation rate and his orthodox economic policies have been widely supported by a large segment of the Peruvian public. Many have put their hopes in the hands of the decisive El Chino (the Oriental). It is easy to understand this in light of the fact that many popular uprisings in Peru have reflected economic grievances. Although many Latin American countries have ushered in democratic reforms, a new breed of strongman has evolved in some of these countries. The new brand of authoritarian populism couched in nationalistic terms appears to be tolerable for the people it governs so long as it fosters economic prosperity and guarantees law and order.[5] This could in many respects pave the way for elite-initiated liberalization programs.

In Algeria, the economic uncertainties caused by a sluggish process of economic liberalization were exacerbated by poor management and implementation, but they were finally made intolerable by a natural disaster and a long period of political decay that stunted the growth of civil society. By contrast, the fate of economic restructuring and adjustments in El Salvador became closely linked with the United States and the Salvadoran army's counterinsurgency strategies during the civil war. The Duarte administration, which first introduced unorthodox reform policies during the 1984–1985 period, failed to gain wide popular and private-sector support for its approach. The imperatives of civil war and the U.S. government's commitment to a military victory and to preserving the basic socioeconomic and political power structures (and its capricious attitudes toward El Salvador's economic difficulties in the 1986–1989 period) compelled the Duarte government to adopt orthodox policies of structural adjustment.[6] The Cristiani administration (1989–1994) opted for orthodox policies and immediately gained the support of the international financial institutions. However, the adherence to orthodox policies by the

Cristiani administration deepened the country's poverty and inequity. Cristiani's policies did not affect the core issues of socioeconomic inequality and political stability in El Salvador. As stated earlier, liberalization measures that overlook equality are certain to accentuate the problems of distribution.[7] El Salvador is typical.

The hopes for improvements in human rights and democratization in El Salvador now rest with the peace process and its prospects for better distribution of national wealth and better execution of law. Between 1982 and 1993, El Salvador had six elections, some fraudulent, others restricted. Those elections proved inadequate to create equity or increase the welfare of the great majority of Salvadorans. They produced governments without power to govern on behalf of the people. There are still legitimate doubts about whether the 1994 elections, the first free and fair elections in El Savador's postindependence history, produced a different outcome. Elite-oriented military establishments continue to function as the real "regimes" with veto power over key policy issues.[8] The success of present and future economic reforms will hinge upon the peace process and concomitant reforms in civil society. Without an effective peace process and reforms, the main beneficiary of orthodox economic policies will again be the oligarchy and its coalition of trade associations, right-wing factions, the armed forces, and state technocrats.

Human Development Conditions

The human development index (HDI), constructed by the UN Development Programme since 1990, measures standards of living and presents a normative way to assess them. There are some reservations concerning some of its indicators—for example, that income is a measure of well-being—but HDI addresses many relevant concerns, such as lifespan, infant and child mortality, illiteracy, freedom from hunger and undernourishment, and personal liberty. These are the essential components of well-being and make the individual the measure of all development activity. The HDI includes three key components: longevity, knowledge, and income. These are combined to create an average deprivation index. Longevity is measured by life expectancy at birth; knowledge is measured by two educational variables, adult literacy and the mean number of years of schooling. Income is measured by real GDP per capita in purchasing power parity dollars.

HDI is a measure of comparing and contrasting different countries to identify sources conducive to political instability and economic strain. As Table 8.1 reveals, of the four cases under consideration, Peru in 1990 topped the HDI rankings.

Table 8.2 shows why both Peru and Algeria (ranked above El Salvador and Pakistan in HDI) in recent years have experienced social unrest and political upheavals. The trends in economic performance of Peru and Algeria

Table 8.1 Human Development Index: Selected List

	HDI world ranking	Life expectancy in years at birth 1990	Educational attainment	Adjusted real GDP per capita	HDI[a] 1990
Japan[b]	1	78.6	2.87	5,049	0.983
Peru	95	63.0	2.17	2,622	0.592
Algeria	107	65.1	1.17	3,011	0.528
El Salvador	110	64.4	1.68	1,950	0.503
Pakistan	132	57.7	0.55	1,862	0.311
Guinea[b]	173	43.5	0.20	501	0.045

Source: Figures from United Nations Development Programme, *Human Development Report 1993*, Oxford: Oxford Univ. Press, 1993: 135–137.
[a]The closer HDI is to 1, the better the ranking.
[b]Japan and Guinea are cited to provide comparisons.

in terms of the GNP per capita annual growth rate and average annual rate of inflation in 1991 reflect these countries' dismal economic situations. The broad appeal of the Islamic Salvation Front (Front islamique du salut—FIS) in Algeria in the early 1990s developed amid economic decline. The inflation rate jumped from 6.6 percent a decade ago to 50 percent in 1991. In Peru, the inflation rate increased from almost 234 percent during the period of 1980–1990 to 386 percent in 1991 (see Table 8.2). This made it possible for Fujimori to engineer his coup with considerable public support. At a time of dismal economic conditions, Fujimori's actions were met with a degree of understanding.

A comparison of the progress in human development in these countries (see Table 8.3) shows that Peru's economic and welfare decline were bound to pose obstacles to the continuation of democratic rule. The HDI registered a negative rate of –0.003 during the 1970–1990 period. El Salvador showed a

Table 8.2 Trends in Economic Performance

HDI rank	GNP per capita annual growth rate (%)		Average annual rate rate of inflation (%)	
	1965–80	1980–90	1980–90	1991
95 Peru	0.8	–2.0	233.7	386.0
107 Algeria	4.2	–0.3	6.6	50.0
110 El Salvador	1.5	–0.6	17.2	11.9
132 Pakistan	1.8	2.9	6.7	10.7

Source: The United Nations Development Programme, *Human Development Report 1993*, Oxford: Oxford Univ. Press: 188–189.

Table 8.3 Changing HDI over Time

Country	HDI 1970	HDI 1990	Difference 1970–90
Algeria	0.358	0.528	0.170
Pakistan	0.226	0.311	0.085
El Salvador	0.483	0.503	0.020
Peru	0.595	0.592	−0.003

Source: The United Nations Development Programme, *Human Development Report 1993*, Oxford: Oxford Univ. Press, 1993: 103.

negligible improvement (0.020) and Pakistan a less than substantial one (0.085). In marked contrast, Algeria displayed a noticeable degree of improvement. Its ranking, based on a 0.170 improvement, moved out of the "low" category to the "medium" group. This occurred despite the fact that Algeria did not have free, fair, and competitive elections.

The evidence presented in Table 8.3 suggests that Algeria's socioeconomic improvement in certain areas made it possible for the country to experiment with some degree of political transition. Nevertheless, the country was not prepared for an abrupt transition. This evidence suggests that socioeconomic development alone may not lead to the emergence of democracy. What really makes such a transition possible is the balance in measures of liberalization in both economy and polity. Economic growth, development, or even welfare cannot thrust a nation into steady democratization. For the latter to happen, economic development must be based on a gradual and measured political and economic liberalization. Despite its utility as an indicator of quality of life, HDI alone fails to account for the state of liberalization in each country. It would be useful to combine HDI with other supplementary indicators better to account for the state of liberalization and the standard of living.

Fix-it Democratization or Balanced Liberalization?

Fix-it democratization has failed to change the practice of military and authoritarian rule in Algeria, El Salvador, Pakistan, and Peru. The political leaders of these countries, besieged by superpower-client relations, economic uncertainties, corruption, ethnic strife, guerrilla warfare, and in some instances drug trafficking, have found this modus operandi to be highly destabilizing.[9] Algeria's leaders, for example, buffeted by a natural disaster, food riots, and degenerating economic performance at the end of the 1980s, encouraged the consideration of political liberalization, but President Bendjedid's swift, tactical transition to a multiparty system polarized the society. Thus, the political liberalization itself led to the cancellation of a second round of elections, after the Islamic Salvation Front (FIS) had swept the December 1991 first-round contests. The accompanying coup forced the resignation of Bendjedid and dissolution of the National Assembly.

In Pakistan the post-Zia era marked the end of twenty-five years of military dictatorship. Several elections have since taken place, yet Pakistan's economic conditions have improved only marginally. In Peru, in 1990, the country's third election since 1980 paved the way for a presidential coup—a unique takeover with significant implications for the nation's prospects for democratization. In El Salvador, electoral politics during the 1980s failed to bring popular legitimacy to political regimes. In the mid-1990s, political regimes will be judged both by their political legitimacy and their performance legitimacy.

Elected democracies have proved just as capable of withstanding the pressures of transition as have traditional and modernizing authoritarian systems. This is not to argue that the democratization tides, to use Huntington's metaphor, will be reversed; rather, it suggests that a realistic pace of change, with balanced liberalization, is essential for sustained reform. The choices and political will shown by the leaders are important, but an abrupt democratization will not fundamentally alter the course of these countries' transitions from authoritarianism.[10]

While there are cultural impediments to democratization in many Third World countries, cultures are not immutable. They can and do evolve.[11] The process of liberalization is a legitimate median between swift, full-scale democratization and traditional authoritarian governance. This intermediate stage is warranted as a prelude to a gradual broadening of civil society. Sudden democratization in the form of electoral politics proved counterproductive and highly destabilizing in Algeria under Bendjedid, and in Pakistan under Benazir Bhutto (1988–1990), and are so doing in Peru under Fujimori. In El Salvador, the political elites used liberalization to keep their political pacts intact; and the quasi-institutionalized civil society, which showed signs of new life in the 1980s, coupled with U.S. pressure to contain ultra-right violence, produced, however inadvertently and inadequately, a semi-civil society and a modicum of increase throughout the 1980s in popular organizations. By the mid-1990s, electoral politics in El Salvador had not culminated in the development of democratic institutions and reforms.

Reforms, Risks, Consequences

The conversion of a state-centered economy into a market-oriented economy carries many risks. It is clear that in many Third World countries, the requirement for adoption of a market economy is a strong state. Some have persuasively argued that a vast role for the state in a free-market economy in the less developed countries (LDCs) is legitimate and that privatization does not dismantle state operations in the economy; rather, it reasserts the partnership.[12] Iliya Harik points out that the state is expected to safeguard the public against the abuses of monopoly pricing and unfair business practices: "Should we consider Western democracies as our measuring rod, the likelihood that the state would abdicate its protective measures of citizen's rights in a market economy is quite slim."[13]

The success of capitalist development in Southeast Asia occurred in states that set conditions and pursued policies that shaped market premises and rules. Many have contended that government functions in areas such as social welfare need to be replaced by other institutions if the poor's suffering in an expanding private sector is to be frontally addressed. Amy L. Sherman asserts that Third World governments need not adopt a radical laissez-faire attitude during the transition to the market. The government's energies and activities can be shifted into areas that render market reforms beneficial to the truly vulnerable and disadvantaged. These reforms would entail "rebuilding infrastructure, clearly defining and defending property and contract rights, and funding preventive health care and primary education."[14] Sherman finds that the state-centered policies of populist regimes in the Third World have helped the urban middle and upper classes and hurt the poor. The two economic sectors most adversely affected are those in which the poor are most represented: the labor-intensive export sector and agriculture.[15] The responsibility for social welfare programs, Sherman adds, rests significantly with nongovernmental or quasi-governmental institutions: governments, she says, cannot provide this service. In contrast, Michael J. Francis views social welfare as an appropriate function of government and favors construction of and support for effective welfare systems.[16] The transition to more effective market-oriented policies demands an expanded role for the government to protect the poor from the painful effects of this change. Whether or not such a role could in the long run be consonant with democratization remains subject to debate.

From the perspective of political elites, market reforms and structural adjustment programs pose serious risks. Economic reforms inevitably are accompanied by political friction, leading as they do to the redistribution of resources, growth in the activity of nongovernmental actors, and the expansion of civil society. "Without a well-developed civil society," Joseph E. Ryan writes, "it is difficult, if not impossible, to have an atmosphere supportive of democracy. A society that does not have free individual and group expressions in nonpolitical matters is not likely to make an exception for political ones."[17] A developing civil society leads to demands for social opportunities and mobility, basic rights, and political openings. If market reforms are to produce desirable long-term results, many reform programs must be implemented: the introduction of civil rights is prudent government.

In Algeria, economic liberalization in the 1980s was not accompanied by a balanced expansion of civil society. Bendjedid's introduction of radical changes and swift reforms almost a decade after limited economic liberalization was inept. The last-resort democratization further polarized the political climate and the army's takeover showed that the military was not prepared to accept the consequences of political reforms.

In Pakistan, a wretchedly poor land, the continuation of economic reforms was largely eclipsed by the political and constitutional crises over the boundaries of presidential power. Democratization and its complex dynamics have caused several government turnovers and a deterioration in economic conditions for most Pakistanis. In Peru, the risks and costs associated with political liberalization and democratization compelled Fujimori to adopt repressive revisionist measures. El Salvador, emerging shakily from civil war, has experienced no major socioeconomic reforms. Constrained largely by the civil war and counterinsurgency measures, reforms were regarded as threatening to the vested interests of the oligarchy and parts of the army.

Prospects for Democratization and Human Rights

The collapse of the Soviet bloc and the subsequent surge in electoral politics and multiparty systems in Third World countries have created an erroneous assumption: that democratization will solve many Third World problems. Several false premises stymie the debate regarding the prospects for democratization.

First, it is argued that the process of democratization (as defined in terms of electoral competition) is a necessary condition for protecting basic economic rights and needs. It follows that only after democratic structures of government are established will basic economic rights and needs be realized. While refuting a general trade-off between democracy and development, some argue that "transitions toward democracy do not guarantee a promised land of rapid economic development and a vastly improved human rights situation."[18]

Electoral compromises may prove to be short-lived tactical ploys of leaders who seek to derail genuine drives toward reform while offering token responses to internal and external pressures. Lack of economic endowments, of appropriate social structures, of alternative political values, and, most importantly, of a viable economic base can render transitions to democracy impractical.

In Africa, for instance, as Bratton and Van de Walle point out, "the opportunism of opposition political leaders, their patronage followings, and their links with current state elite, all suggest that a change of leaders would probably perpetuate a clientelistic pattern of politics as usual."[19] Democratization has no essential link to the protection of human rights in those Third World countries that lack a gradual preparation for and exposure to a mature or prolonged process of liberalization. The emergence of freely elected autocrats and authoritarian factions in some Third World nations illustrates this point.

The idealism of the post–Cold War world must take into account the still extant, even if not dominant, antidemocratic realities of Third World politics.[20]

Second, as a corollary, it is assumed that democratization will generate peace and prosperity and enhance living conditions in Third World societies. Robert L. Rothstein questions this, arguing that weak and potentially fragile democracies of the Third World will not necessarily promote peace and prosperity. Comparing weak democracies with benign authoritarian regimes, he notes:

> One has here democracies with an important degree of normative legitimacy and a much lower degree of performance legitimacy matched against authoritarians with a substantial degree of performance legitimacy and a marginal degree of normative legitimacy. There is no abstract way at any particular moment to choose which of these regimes is preferable because each fulfills important public needs.[21]

Although it can be argued that weak and unstable democracies are preferable to the authoritarian regimes of Third World countries, one cannot be sure that electoral politics and some related policy adjustments will, when the proper structural foundations and resources are absent from these societies, in the long run produce sustainable democracies.

Invariably, I am reminded of the conditions surrounding the creation of the Weimar Republic (1919–1933) where the German political regime was, on the surface, swiftly transformed from one of Europe's most authoritarian into one of its most democratic. Elections allowed extremist parties (including the Nazi party) to gain access to parliament, helping to create for Weimar Germany an extremely polarized party system. The Weimar constitution might have worked in a country with considerable democratic experience and relatively subdued ideological fragmentation, but that, as Charles Hauss points out, surely was not Germany in 1919.[22] The economic and political difficulties of the 1920s and early 1930s rendered effective governance impossible. A little-known nationalist, Adolf Hitler, who led the Nazis (National Socialist Democratic Workers Party), came to control a majority in the Reichstag. "Contrary to the expectations of the more conventional politicians," Hauss writes, "Hitler used that majority to pass legislation that turned the Weimar Republic into the Third Reich [1933–1945], probably the most repressive and reprehensible regime in history."[23]

Circumstances in today's Third World are of course different from those of the postwar Weimar Republic: the latter was handicapped by the political legacy of the Versailles Treaty, which crippled Germany's economy. However, the failure of the Weimar parliamentary democracy is in some ways analogous to the experiences of some Third World nations.

Third, it is assumed that the promotion of an all-encompassing, market-oriented, and swift democratization—as standardly prescribed by neoliberals—is a viable option for Third World countries grappling with the difficulties of transition. This assumption has been challenged from several standpoints. Stephan Haggard argues that the success of market-oriented reforms by the authoritarian governments of South America (Argentina, Brazil, Chile, Uruguay), Turkey, the NICs of East Asia, and the social democratic government of India, refutes the claim of neoliberals that democratization is essential to economic success.[24] Haggard concludes:

> But are the economic and political conditions ripe in the developing world for such social-democratic governments? Perhaps not, but the supply of enlightened despots is equally scarce. It is thus not an altogether pious hope to think that the poor will fare better under newly-emerging democratic governments than they have under governments that systematically excluded them.[25]

Haggard is right in arguing that the success of market-oriented reforms under those governments of Third World countries that are authoritarian indicates that abrupt political changes in fragile democracies might be counterproductive, in an economic sense. But gradual, protracted adjustment might not necessarily be inconsistent with long-term democratization, were leaders to give it serious consideration. The transitions toward democracy in South Korea, Taiwan, and Chile indicate that prolonged and gradual liberalization may indeed be the key to successful transition. In the long run, the main concern does not need to be the promotion of more stable democracies in the Third World, but the creation of conditions in which progressive transition can be sustained.

Assessing the alternatives to so-called liberal democracy in Latin America, Laurence Whitehead argues that many kinds of authoritarian experiments have been attempted and failed—reformist, populist, socialist, and reactionary. Likewise, neoliberal projects, even if successful (as in contemporary Chile), can face substantial and potentially destabilizing countercurrents. In the neoliberal "depoliticized democracies" there is typically a considerable amount of interim illiberalism and disregard for the legitimate interests of certain groups; there are intolerant styles of policymaking, and lack of full regard for participatory democracy.[26] Nevertheless, Whitehead writes, the neoliberal approach to democracy has many advantages—the possibility of eventually arriving at a stable, viable, liberal regime, that is, democratic "consolidation." Whitehead's reasoning is compelling:

> The alternative of permanent crisis and insecurity under "unstable populism" seems unable to offer any such prospect. In fact it is the poorest, the most vulnerable, the racially subordinate and so forth who suffer most under erratic populism, despite intermittent rhetoric in their favor. . . . Most of the now quite abundant literature criticizing Latin America's democratization as elitist and unconnected with the lived experience of the mass of the population (the

"social movements" perspective) fails to distinguish adequately between neo-liberal and paternalist (or clientelist) strategies of democratization. Both may be opposed to autonomous participation from below, but only the neo-liberal strategy (extending the role of the market) seems capable of leading to regime consolidation.[27]

In tempestuous Third World politics, it may not be possible to encourage building democracy and a free market at the same time. James A. Dorn, who examines the role of government and the market in the successful postwar development experiences of East Asian countries, attributes the rapid growth of East Asian economies to more open civil society—a situation in which personal as well as economic liberties are protected. Dorn observes that "political democracy is neither necessary nor sufficient for economic democracy [or economic liberalization] and a spontaneous market order."[28] "Economic democracy," he adds, "is the natural outcome of consumer sovereignty and economic liberty; it is not dependent on political democracy."[29] But, citing the experiences of Taiwan and South Korea, where economic liberalization and its ensuing prosperity have led to political liberalization, he also contends that free markets and economic liberalization spur political democracy:

> Economic freedom and political freedom cannot long be separated without damaging the fabric of civil society. People's right to govern themselves in the open market is simply a reflection of an individual's right to be left alone, that is, the right to self-governance. Ultimately, the thirst for economic freedom will spill over into the thirst for political freedom, democracy, and a rule of law.[30]

From a different perspective, some have argued that the simplistic and mechanical assumptions of Western intellectual orthodoxy regarding the dogmas of the free market are a problem. Zbigniew Brezezinski wrote that "unless democratic practice, and especially the economic performance of the free market system, leads to a demonstrable improvement in social conditions, it is only a question of time before a negative reaction to these concepts [democracy and the market economy] sets in."[31] The prospects for sustainable democratization in many Third World countries are grim because, in part, the democratic path to stability and prosperity has thus far led to instability and poverty. Democratic institutions continue to be highly vulnerable during the painful process of economic restructuring as well as during the gradual diminishing of massive state control.

In the final analysis, some say, the prospects for democratization lie in the attempts of political leaders to create a sense of citizenry in their people.[32] Without such a sense, Peru's highland Indians will turn toward Sendero Luminoso, Salvadorans will drift toward the FMLN, Algeria's youth will be attracted to the FIS, and Pakistan's political polarization and sectarian rifts will further deepen. The ability of governments to work in the interests of a vast majority of their citizens hinges upon gradual, effective economic and political liberalization.

The key question deals with the modus operandi: How economic and political liberalization can effect the necessary reforms and initiatives. The consensus is that states that liberalize, reducing economic involvement and regulatory powers, might be less inclined to resort to repressive measures. It is reasonable to conclude that liberalized Third World systems are likely to move toward and attain some measure of democratic governance more than are traditional authoritarian countries. The point to bear in mind is that economic reforms are crucial for a political transition toward democracy. A successful economic program and consensus promoted democratic transition in Chile; similarly an effective economic consensus might well be a sine qua non for stable multiparty democracy in Mexico.[33] Mexico's new president, Ernesto Zedillo Ponce de León, is expected to turn to the social and political problems that top his priority list: poverty, income distribution, small and medium-sized business survival, judicial reform, and agricultural reforms, among other things. Zedillo would most likely follow along the path of economic transformation that reached its high point with President Salinas's drive for the North American Free Trade Agreement (NAFTA). One practical conclusion is that precipitous political liberalization and democratization, without a well-developed economic base, is likely to be unstable; to say the least, it lacks moral and practical justification. As is evident from the preceding arguments, those states that impose major barriers to and shun the expansion of civil society will perpetuate authoritarianism. Civil society is not bound to come about at all times. Nor do civic-minded elites, even under the best of circumstances, necessarily emerge from traditional political pacts to lead the society to democracy. But external actors—international development communities and financial institutions, regional and international organizations, the United States, the United Nations, and nongovernmental organizations—can propel, reinforce, and even compel the process.

To date, the direct influence of such outside forces has most often hindered rather than aided the development of democratic systems in the Third World. Robert A. Dahl underscores concern about this: "Probably American policy has done more harm to democratization in Latin America by assisting military establishments than any gain it has ever achieved through economic aid programmes."[34] The U.S. intervention in Haiti (Sept. 1994) could prove to be fruitless or even costly if the venture fails to effect meaningful change. Many uncertainties remain about Haiti's political future as the United States tries to implement a redefined role as peacekeeper. Some, who make a case for intervention in Haiti, maintain that this might help democracy flourish in that country. The Haiti intervention, however, is no indication of a major shift in U.S. policy. Such interventions in the past have been based on calculations such as acceptable costs and feasibility rather than on just-cause considerations (i.e., making the region safe for democracy). The case of Haiti seems no different. Furthermore, fundamental questions, like how to improve wealth disparities and living conditions, must be addressed if democracy is going to have a chance. After all, democracy cannot be granted to the Haitian people; it must be won through mobilization. It is not clear that this intervention in Haiti, unlike the previous one (1915–1934) will result in better understanding of the social problems of Haiti and its obstacles on the road to democratization.

Without material and moral support from industrialized democracies, nascent democracies confront unmanageable obstacles. But is it even possible, in these new, fragile democracies, for the financial and political support that external sources provide to be put to effective use? Jack Donnelly, who draws an important distinction between democratic and rights-protective regimes, sees an inherent difficulty in such a process. Donnelly's disclaimer is simple but telling:

> Human rights cannot be given. They must be earned—and maintained—through hard and persistent domestic political work. Rights-protective regimes are almost always the product of domestic, not international, political forces. . . . It is thus both relatively easy for a powerful outside actor to contribute in a major way to serious human rights violations and relatively difficult for both internal and international forces to establish rights-protective regimes.[35]

Donnelly, having questioned, from a human rights perspective, the virtues of elections and markets by arguing that free elections may bring rights-abusive governments to power and that markets are the lesser evil, not an intrinsic good,[36] proceeds to make his second point: democratization and the securing of internationally recognized human rights are not necessarily synonymous. While it is true that liberalized regimes may move toward a provisional and incomplete democracy—or what Laurence Whitehead labels "democracy by default"[37]—the alternative (that is, the interventionist or statist route) is utterly unattractive for many of these countries. Will the post–Cold War dynamics affect the level of international support for transitional democratic countries? Donnelly is cautiously optimistic:

> The post–Cold War reduction in foreign support for repression is a significant advance in the international struggle for human rights. This has opened political space for human rights advocates and helped to create a more level domestic political playing field. It will not, however, automatically result in comparable levels of international support for newly democratic countries.[38]

Donnelly's conviction that domestic forces are ultimately responsible for securing and maintaining human rights is both logically and intuitively compelling. But one should not lose sight of the fact that the fragile, poor, and vulnerable countries of the Third World are almost always dependent upon external forces. It is virtually impossible to envision improvements in the human rights situations of these countries without there being external support, a point that Donnelly addresses:

> The external economic dependence of many Third World countries is con-siderable. And the decade-long, continent-wide crisis in Africa powerfully illustrates the interaction of internal and external structural forces . . . with virtually all new democracies and recently liberalized regimes today facing severe economic problems, it would be dangerous to underestimate their vulnerability.[39]

There is, however, growing evidence that foreign aid to Third World nations will decline in the years to come.[40] It was reported early in 1994 that the year's U.S. military and economic aid to Latin America would decrease by at least 50 percent. "The era of U.S. foreign aid as a major factor in Latin American development is passing," said Carol Lancaster, deputy director of the U.S. Agency for International Development (USAID).[41] But there must be a minimum flow of foreign aid to the fledgling democracies and/or transitional democratic systems to promote civil rights in these societies.

Many observers have supported the view that certain civil liberties are integral to democracy and are likely to be institutionalized before others. Robert A. Dahl proposes a plausible sequence in which the right of access to alternative sources of information and a general freedom of expression must be established before freedom to organize and free and fair elections can be achieved:

> Except in countries already close to the threshold of democracy, therefore, it is a grave mistake to assume that if only the leaders of a non-democratic country can be persuaded to hold elections, then full democracy will follow. Other than in the near-polyarchies or the proto-polyarchies, elections should be seen as a critical stage following a process of liberalization, probably a lengthy process, in which the prior institutions and appropriate underlying conditions for stable democracy have developed.[42]

Such a sequence fits my general thesis that the existence of a supporting economic context is vital for effective and durable democratization in Third World countries. The fulfillment of socioeconomic needs and respect for rights is the backbone of any sustainable drive toward democratization. The tough policy choices ahead for Third World leaders must be understood in the context of an enormously complex sociopolitical climate and ongoing economic decline. To thrust democracy upon a country by various mechanisms, domestic and international, without the creation of a favorable civil society is bound to encounter many more difficulties than the already difficult process entails. In those cases where a country is not given the chance to develop democracy via gradual economic and political liberalization, the fate of democracy remains contingent on permanent external support.

Increasingly, scholars are convinced of the importance of prosperity during the transition to democracy. However, preoccupation with the economic aspects of liberalization to the exclusion of a broadening of civil society is to be intent on a fallacy. Economic liberalization and decentralization alone are not sufficient conditions for democracy. True, economic growth is likely to lead to democracy, as evidenced by the emerging trend that countries with burgeoning incomes have, in the past decade, become more democratic.[43] Ultimately, however, economic growth and prosperity, if upheld in a politically restrictive context, are unlikely to pave the way for a sustainable drive toward democracy. Douglass C. North, an economist, was reported saying, pithily: "Over the short run, dictators can always get good growth."[44] But clearly, in the long run, North adds, "if democratization does not begin to secure gains for all the people who have earned them as well as ensure millions of others the opportunity to do better, anything can happen: a change of regime, confiscation, rebellion, a reversal of fortunes." A reform strategy that focuses on both economic liberalization and the expansion of civil society will be the most viable. Proponents of either front ought to take a second look.

Notes

1. For further information on this, see Frederick Ehrenreich, "National Security," in Harold D. Nelson, ed., *Algeria: A Country Study,* Washington, D.C.: U.S. Government, 1986, pp. 293–347; esp. pp. 308–309.

2. For the serious reservations held by some Third World countries regarding the links between foreign aid and human rights, see Michael Vatikiotis, "Dollar Democracy," *Far Eastern Economic Review,* Vol. 153, No. 39, September 26, 1991, p. 35. Vatikiotis writes that the demise of Soviet Communism has promoted the United States to a preeminent strategic position in the Asia-Pacific region; and that it will allow a politically more assertive and economically powerful Europe to emerge. The European Union's insistence that human rights and environmental issues be written into the new generation of economic agreements has caused concern among Asian governments. Furthermore, it is not clear whether Asian countries will support putting pressure on China's Communist rulers to abandon their ideological postures. One irony, among many, about the end of the Cold War is that suspicion of Western intentions among some of Communism's traditionally staunchest enemies in Asia has deepened. Asian governments continue to be wary of aid and human rights linkage.

3. For an excellent account of transition to democracy in Central America and the related issues, see Blachman and Sharpe, "The Transition," p. 39.

4. Moeen Qureshi, a former World Bank vice president who was transitional prime minister after Sharif's abdication, initiated several economic policies between July and October of 1993. Those policies laid the ground for economic liberalization and reform and gained the respect of many Pakistanis.

5. *New York Times,* January 16, 1994, p. E4.

6. For further details regarding the impossibility of beginning socioeconomic reconstruction during Duarte's earlier months in office, see Liisa Lukkari North, "El Salvador," in Donnelly and Howard, *International Handbook,* pp. 117–134.

7. For an empirical account of a negative connection between inequality (indicators) and the prospects for stable democracies in the developing areas, see Arat, *Democracy.*

8. Booth and Walker, *Understanding Central America*, p. 109.

9. See the *Christian Science Monitor*, August 23, 1993, p. 22.

10. For a compelling argument on the role of leadership (the state), repression, and structural transformation within the context of the "trade-off debate," see Donnelly, *Universal Human Rights*, esp. Chapter 10. In this chapter, Donnelly argues that some repression (denial of civil and political rights) might be inescapable in any development strategy, but that does not render any repressive act or policy warranted, let alone necessary or unavoidable. Clearly, the intensity and the targets of repression are, to a large extent, matters of political choice. As such, "development strategies do in large measure reflect political regimes and the interests that underlie them, but not everything done to maintain a regime—let alone everything done to maintain political incumbents—is connected with the development strategy in question." Drawing on the experiences of South Korea and Brazil, Donnelly adds, "for example, the extensive use of particularly brutal forms of torture in Park's last years in South Korea had nothing to do with development; if anything, excessive repression in the late 1970s became economically dysfunctional. Similarly, much of the repression in Brazil and the Southern Cone countries in the 1970s was justified on political and ideological, not economic, grounds" (p. 189).

11. For a supporting argument on this subject, see Huntington, *The Third Wave*, OK: pp. 298–311. For a fundamentally different view, see Jack Donnelly, "Human Rights and Human Dignity: An Analytic Critique of Non-Western Human Rights Conceptions," *American Political Science Review*, Vol. 76, June 1982, pp. 303–316. Compare these perspectives with those of Adamantia Pollis, "Eastern Orthodoxy and Human Rights," *Human Rights Quarterly*, Vol. 15, No. 2, May 1993, pp. 339–356. Pollis argues, albeit in the European context, that the religious heritage of Eastern Orthodoxy practiced in the Balkans, Russia, and other East European states is not compatible with the Western conception of individual rights. The problem of institutionalizing democratic structures and processes is further complicated by the theology of Eastern Orthodoxy and the church's relationship to the state. Clearly, individual human rights cannot be derived from Orthodox theology: they stem from a substantially different worldview. A transformation of Orthodox thought is critical if Greece, the Balkans, and Russia are to be European. Take Greece as an example, for this country psychologically and culturally to assume a European identity (within the context of European integration) would necessitate a massive transformation of its worldview. If Orthodoxy is to become relevant to the realities of the European Union a reformation of the broad parameters of Orthodox theology seems inevitable. It remains to be seen whether Orthodoxy can face such mounting pressures and challenges.

12. For an excellent analysis, see Iliya Harik, "Privatization: The Issue, the Prospects, and the Fears," in Harik and Sullivan, *Privatization*, pp. 1–23. See p. 10.

13. Ibid.

14. See Sherman, "Rethinking," p. 39.

15. Ibid., p. 38.

16. See Michael J. Francis, "A Response to Rethinking Development," in Griffiths, *Third World*, pp. 40–42.

17. Joseph E. Ryan, "The Comparative Survey of Freedom—1992–1993 Survey Methodology," in McColm, *Freedom in the World*, pp. 77–82. See p. 81.

18. Sørensen, *Democracy and Democratization*, p. 89. Sorensen argues that stable and consolidated democracy correlates with a high respect for human rights in general, but transitions toward democracy themselves can create situations with a high degree

of human rights abuse (pp. 88–89).

19. Michael Bratton and Nicolas Van de Walle, "Toward Governance in Africa: Popular Demands and State Responses," in Hyden and Bratton, eds., *Governance and Politics in Africa*, Boulder, CO: Lynne Rienner, 1992, pp. 27–55. See p. 54.

20. See *New York Times*, January 12, 1992, p. E2. Also see Joseph S. Nye, Jr., "What New World Order?" *Foreign Affairs*, Vol. 71, No. 2, spring 1992, pp. 83–96. Nye draws attention to the dark side of the process of democratization, arguing that nationalism is becoming stronger in most of the world and thus a "policy of unqualified support for national self-determination would turn into a principle of enormous world disorder" (p. 91).

21. Rothstein, "Democracy, Conflict, and Development," p. 57.

22. Charles Hauss, *Comparative Politics: Domestic Responses to Global Challenges*, Minneapolis, MN: West, 1994, p. 134.

23. Ibid., p. 136.

24. See Haggard, "Markets, Poverty Alleviation," pp. 193–196.

25. Ibid., p. 196.

26. See Whitehead, "Alternatives To 'Liberal Democracy'," pp. 314–320.

27. Ibid., p. 320.

28. See Dorn, "Economic Liberty," p. 601.

29. Ibid., p. 602.

30. Ibid., p. 616.

31. Brzezinski, *Out of Control.*

32. See, for example, Rosenberg, "Beyond Elections."

33. See Baer, "Mexico's Second Revolution," p. 63.

34. Robert A. Dahl, "Democracy and Human Rights," pp. 235–251. See esp. p. 245. For a contrasting viewpoint, see Lars Schoultz, *Human Rights and United States Policy Toward Latin America*, Princeton, NJ: Princeton University Press, 1981. See especially Chapter 5. In this chapter, Schoultz states that, during the course of the 1960s and 1970s, the relationship between U.S. economic aid and human rights violations by the Latin American recipient governments underwent a drastic transformation: "While the aid program was regularly criticized as supportive of repressive Latin American governments throughout most of this period, by the late 1970s economic aid had become a principal foreign policy tool with which the United States was attacking the hemisphere's most repressive regimes" (p. 168). The implicit threat of aid reductions as a result of the U.S. Congress (subcommittee) interest may have helped to moderate some repressive measures and to forestall others (p. 195).

35. Donnelly, *International Human Rights.*

36. Ibid., pp. 149–156.

37. Whitehead, "Alternatives to 'Liberal Democracy'," p. 325.

38. Donnelly, *International Human Rights*, pp. 148–149.

39. Ibid., p. 158.

40. See *New York Times*, November 5, 1993, p. E5.

41. *Christian Science Monitor*, January 26, 1994, p. 4.

42. Dahl, "Democracy and Human Rights," p. 246.

43. Huntington's recent contribution, known as "the third wave," is based on this proposition. See Huntington, *The Third Wave*, esp. pp. 271–273.

44. Quoted in *Business Week*, June 7, 1993, p. 88.

Selected Bibliography

Adelman, Irma, and Cynthia Taft Morris. *Economic Growth and Social Equity in Developing Countries*. Stanford: Stanford Press, 1973.

Adrianzén, Alberto M. "Un Paso Atrás," *Quehacer*. Lima, June 17, 1993: 10–15.

Ahlluwalia, Montek S. "Inequality, Poverty and Development," *Journal of Development Economics*. Vol. 3, No. 4, 1976: 304–342.

Akacem, Mohammed. "Algeria: In Search of an Economic and Political Future," *Middle East Policy*. Vol. 11, No. 2, spring 1993: 50–60.

Alavi, Hamza. "Nationhood and Communal Violence in Pakistan," *Journal of Contemporary Asia*. Vol. 21, No. 2, 1991: 152–178.

Ali, Salamat. "Soldier's Solution," *Far Eastern Economic Review*. Vol. 156, No. 30, July 29, 1993: 15–16.

Americas Watch. *El Salvador's Decade of Terror: Human Rights Since the Assassination of Archbishop Romero*. New Haven, CT: Yale Univ. Press, 1991.

Americas Watch. *Human Rights in Peru: One Year After Fujimori's Coup*. New York: Human Rights Watch, 1993.

Amin, Tahir. "Pakistan in 1993: Some Dramatic Changes," *Asian Survey*. Vol. 34, No. 2, February 1994: 191–199.

Andreas, Peter R., and Kenneth E. Sharpe. "Cocaine Politics in the Andes," *Current History*. Vol. 91, No. 562, February 1992: 74–79.

Arat, Zehra F. *Democracy and Human Rights in Developing Countries*. Boulder, CO: Lynne Rienner, 1991.

Ascher, William L. "Democracy, Equity, and the Myth of the Welfare State in Developing Countries: The Case of Central America," in Kenneth E. Bauzon, ed., *Development and Democratization in the Third World: Myths, Hopes, and Realities*. New York: Taylor Francis, 1992: 221–236.

Ayoob, Mohammed. "The Security Problematic of the Third World," *World Politics*. Vol. 43, No. 2, January 1991: 257–283.

Baer, Delal. "Mexico's Second Revolution: Pathways to Liberalization," in Riordan Roett, ed., *Political and Economic Liberalization in Mexico: At a Critical Juncture*. Boulder, CO: Lynne Rienner, 1993: 51–68.

Bertsch, Gary K., Robert P. Clark, and David M. Wood. *Comparing Political Systems: Power and Policy in the Three Worlds*. New York: Macmillan, 1991: 588–590.

Bienen, Henry, and John Waterbury. "The Political Economy of Privatization in Developing Countries," in Charles K. Wilber and Kenneth P. Jameson, eds. Fifth edition, *The Political Economy of Development and Underdevelopment*. New York: McGraw-Hill, 1992: 376–402.

Blachman, Morris J., and Kenneth E. Sharpe. "The Transition to 'Electoral' and Democratic Politics," in Louis W. Goodman, William M. LeoGrande and Johanna Mendelson Forman, eds., *Political Parties and Democracies in Central America.* Boulder, CO: Westview, 1992: 33–52.

Bland, Gary. "Assessing the Transition to Democracy," in Joseph S. Tulchin and Gary Bland, eds., *Is There a Transition to Democracy in El Salvador?* Boulder, CO: Lynne Rienner, 1992: 163–206.

Blee, Kathleen M. "The Catholic Church and Central American Politics," in Kenneth M. Coleman and George C. Herring, eds. *Understanding the Central American Crisis: Sources of Conflict, U.S. Policy, and Options for Peace.* Wilmington, DE: Scholarly Resources, 1991: 55–75.

Booth, John A., and Thomas W. Walker, eds. *Understanding Central America.* Boulder, CO: Westview, 1989.

Bratton, Michael. "Beyond the State: Civil Society and Associational Life in Africa," *World Politics.* Vol. 41, No. 3, April 1989: 404–430.

Brzezinski, Zbigniew. *Out of Control: Global Turmoil on the Eve of the Twenty-First Century.* New York: Macmillan, 1993.

Chalmers, Douglas A. "The Politicized State in Latin America," in James M. Malloy, ed., *Authoritarianism in Latin America.* Pittsburgh: University of Pittsburgh Press, 1977: 23–45.

Cingranelli, David Louis. *Ethics, American Foreign Policy, and the Third World.* New York: St. Martin's, 1993.

Clark, Robert P. *Power and Policy in the Third World.* New York: John Wiley, 1986.

Claude, Richard Pierre, and Burns H. Weston, eds. *Human Rights in the World Community: Issues and Action.* Philadelphia: Univ. of Pennsylvania Press, 1989.

Crystal, Jill. "Authoritarianism and Its Adversaries in the Arab World," *World Politics.* Vol. 46, No. 2, January 1994: 262–289.

Dahl, Robert A. *Polyarchy: Participation and Opposition.* New Haven, CT: Yale Univ. Press, 1971.

———. "Democracy and Human Rights Under Different Conditions of Development," in Asbjorn Eide and Bernt Hagtvet, eds., *Human Rights in Perspectives: A Global Assessment.* Oxford: Basil Blackwell, 1992: 235–251.

Damrosch, Lori Fisler. "Politics Across Borders: Nonintervention and Nonforcible Influence over Domestic Affairs," *The American Journal of International Law.* Vol. 83, No. 1, January 1989: 1–50.

Deutsch, Karl W. *Tides Among Nations.* New York: Free Press, 1979.

Diamond, Larry, Juan J. Linz, and Seymour Martin Lipset, eds. *Democracy in Developing Countries.* Boulder, CO: Lynne Rienner, 1989, four volumes.

Donnelly, Jack. "Cultural Relativism and Universal Human Rights," in *Human Rights Quarterly.* Vol. 6, No. 4, November 1984: 400–419.

———. *International Human Rights.* Boulder, CO: Westview, 1993: 148.

———, ed. *Universal Human Rights in Theory and Practice.* Ithaca, NY: Cornell Univ. Press, 1989.

Donnelly, Jack, and Rhoda Howard. "Human Dignity, Human Rights, and Political Regimes," pp. 66–87 in Donnelly, *Universal Human Rights.*

———, eds. *International Handbook of Human Rights.* Westport, CT: Greenwood, 1987.

Dorn, James A. "Economic Liberty and Democracy in East Asia," *Orbis.* Vol. 37, No. 4, Autumn 1993: 599–619.

Douglas, Jack D. "Cooperative Paternalism versus Conflictual Paternalism" in Rolf Sartorius, ed., *Paternalism.* Minneapolis: Univ. of Minnesota Press, 1983: 171–200.

Eckstein, Harry, and Ted Robert Gurr. *Patterns of Authority: A Structural Basis for*

Political Inquiry. New York: John Wiley, 1975.

El-Kens, Ali. *Algerian Reflections on Arab Crises.* Translated by Robert W. Stookey, Austin: Center for Middle Eastern Studies, Univ. of Texas, 1991.

Enloe, Cynthia H. *Ethnic Conflict and Political Development.* Boston: Little, Brown, 1973.

Entelis, John P., and Lisa J. Arone. "Algeria in Turmoil: Islam, Democracy and the State," *Middle East Policy.* Vol. 1, No. 2, Spring 1992: 23–35.

Entelis, John P., and Phillip C. Naylor, eds. *State and Society in Algeria.* Boulder, CO: Westview, 1992.

Evans, Martin. "Algeria: Thirty Years On," *History Today.* Vol. 42, July 1992: 4–6.

Falk, Richard. *Human Rights and State Sovereignty.* New York: Holmes and Meier, 1981.

Fitch, J. Samuel. "Democracy, Human Rights, and the Armed Forces in Latin America," in Jonathan Hartlyn, Lars Shuldtz, and Augusto Varas, eds., *The United States and Latin America in the 1990s: Beyond the Cold War.* Chapel Hill: Univ. of North Carolina Press, 1992: 181–213.

Forsythe, David P., ed. *Human Rights and Development: International Views.* New York: St. Martin's, 1989.

Forsythe, David P. *Internationalization of Human Rights.* Lexington: D. C. Heath, 1991.

Franck, Thomas M. "The Emerging Right to Democratic Governance," *The American Journal of International Law.* Vol. 86, No. 1, January 1992: 46–91.

García, José Z. "El Salvador: Recent Elections in Historical Perspective," in John A. Booth and Mitchell A. Seligson, eds., *Elections and Democracy in Central America.* Chapel Hill: Univ. of North Carolina Press, 1989: 60–92.

Glewwe, Paul, and Dennis de Tray. "The Poor in Latin America During Adjustment: A Case Study of Peru," *Economic Development and Cultural Change.* Vol. 40, No. 1, October 1991: 27–54.

Gonzales, José E. "Guerrillas and Coca in the Upper Huallaga Valley," in David Scott Palmer, ed., *Shining Path of Peru.* New York: St. Martin's, 1992: 105–125.

Greenwood, Christopher. "Is There a Right of Humanitarian Intervention?" *World Today.* Vol. 49, No. 2, February 1993: 34–40.

Griffiths, Robert J., ed. *Third World: 94/95.* Guilford, CT: Dushkin, 1994.

Gurr, Ted Robert. *Minorities at Risk: A Global View of Ethnopolitical Conflicts.* Washington, D.C.: U.S. Institute of Peace Press, 1993.

———. "America as a Model for the World? A Skeptical View," *PS: Political Science and Politics.* Vol. 24, No. 4, December 1991: 664–667.

Haggard, Stephan. "Markets, Poverty Alleviation, and Income Distribution: An Assessment of Neoliberal Claims," *Ethics and International Affairs.* Vol. 5, 1991: 175–196.

Haggard, Stephan, and Robert R. Kaufman, eds. *The Politics of Economic Adjustment: International Constraints, Distributive Conflicts, and the State.* Princeton, NJ: Princeton Univ. Press, 1992.

Halperin, Morton. "Guaranteeing Democracy," *Foreign Policy.* No. 91, Summer 1993: 105–122.

Harik, Iliya, and Denis J. Sullivan, eds. *Privatization and Liberalization in the Middle East.* Bloomington: Indiana Univ. Press, 1992.

Hehir, J. Bryan. "The United States and Human Rights: Policy for the 1990s in Light of the Past," in Kenneth A. Oye, Robert J. Lieber, and Donald Rothchild, eds., *Eagle in a New World: American Grand Strategy in the Post–Cold War Era.* New York: Harper Collins, 1992: 233–255.

Henkin, Louis. "The Universality of the Concept of Human Rights," *Annals: AAPSS.* Vol. 506, November 1989: 10–16.

Henkin, Louis. "Law and Politics in International Relations: State and Human Values," *Journal of International Affairs*. Vol. 44, No. 1, Spring/Summer 1990: 183–208.

Hewlett, Sylvia Ann. "Human Rights and Economic Realities: Trade-Offs in Historical Perspective," *Political Science Quarterly*. Vol. 94, No. 3, Fall 1979: 453–473.

Horowitz, Irving Louis. "Political Legitimacy and the Institutionalization of Crisis in Latin America," *Comparative Political Studies*. Vol. 1, No. 1, April 1968: 45–69.

Howard, Rhoda E. "Cultural Absolutism and the Nostalgia for Community," *Human Rights Quarterly*. Vol. 15, No. 2, May 1993: 315–338.

Human Rights Watch: World Report 1993. New York: Human Rights Watch, 1992.

Human Rights Watch: World Report 1994. New York: Human Rights Watch, 1993.

Humana, Charles. *World Human Rights Guide*. Third edition, Oxford: Oxford Univ. Press, 1992.

Huntington, Samuel P. *Political Order in Changing Societies*. New Haven, CT: Yale Univ. Press, 1968.

———. "The Clash of Civilizations?" *Foreign Affairs*. Vol. 72, No. 3, Summer 1993: 22–49.

———. *The Third Wave: Democratization in the Late Twentieth Century*. Norman: Univ. of Oklahoma Press, 1991.

Huntington, Samuel P., and Joan M. Nelson. *No Easy Choice: Political Participation in Developing Countries*. Cambridge, MA: Harvard Univ. Press, 1976.

Janowitz, Morris. "Some Observations on the Comparative Analysis of Middle Eastern Military Institutions," in V. J. Parry and M. E. Yapp, eds. *War, Technology and Society in the Middle East*. London: Oxford Univ. Press, 1975: 412–440.

Kapur, Ashok. *Pakistan in Crisis*. New York: Routledge, Chapman & Hall, 1991.

Karl, Terry Lynn. "Dilemmas of Democratization in Latin America," *Comparative Politics*. Vol. 23, No. 1, October 1990: 1–21.

Karl, Terry. "Imposing Consent? Electoralism vs. Democratization in El Salvador," in Paul W. Drake and Eduardo Silva, eds., *Elections and Democratization in Latin America, 1980–1985*. San Diego, CA: Center for Iberian and Latin American Studies, UCSD, 1986: 9–36.

Kennedy, Gavin. *Military in the Third World*. New York: Charles Scribner's, 1974.

Kothari, Rajni. "Human Rights as a North-South Issue" in Richard Pierre Claude and Burns H. Weston, eds., *Human Rights in the World Community*. Philadelphia: Univ. of Pennsylvania Press, 1989: 134–142.

Lewis, John P. *Pro-Poor Aid Conditionality*. Washington, D.C.: Overseas Development Council, Policy Essay #8, 1993.

Lipset, Seymour Martin. "Some Social Requisites of Democracy: Economic Development and Political Legitimacy," *American Political Science Review*. Vol. 53, No. 1, March 1959: 69–105.

Lone, Salim. "Challenging Conditionality," *Africa Report*. Vol. 35, No. 4, September/October 1990: 31–32.

Loveman, Biran, and Thomas M. Davies Jr. "The Politics of Antipolitics," in Loveman and Davies, eds. *The Politics of Antipolitics*. Lincoln: Univ. of Nebraska Press, 1989: 3–13.

Marks, Stephen P. "Promoting Human Rights," in Michael T. Klare and Daniel C. Thomas, eds., *World Security: Trends and Challenges at Century's End*. New York: St. Martin's, 1991: 295–323.

Mayer, Ann Elizabeth. *Islam and Human Rights: Traditions and Politics*. Boulder, CO: Westview, 1991.

McClintock, Cynthia. "Peru: Precarious Regimes, Authoritarian and Democratic," in Larry Diamond, Juan J. Linz, and Seymour Martin Lipset, eds., *Democracy in Developing Areas: Latin America*. Boulder, CO: Lynne Rienner, 1988: 335–385.

———. "Peru's Fujimori: A Caudillo Derails Democracy," *Current History*. Vol. 92,

No. 572, March 1993: 112–119.
――――. "Peru's Sendero Luminoso Rebellion: Origins and Trajectory," in Susan Eckstein, ed., *Power and Popular Protest: Latin American Social Movements.* Berkeley: Univ. of California Press, 1989: 61–101.
McColm, R. Bruce. "The Comparative Survey of Freedom 1992–1993: Our Crowded Hour," in McColm, ed., *Freedom in The World: The Annual Survey of Political Rights and Civil Liberties, 1992–1993.* New York: Freedom House, 1993: 3–5.
Moore, Will H., and James R. Scarritt. "IMF Conditionality and Polity Characteristics in Black Africa: An Exploratory Analysis," *Africa Today.* Vol. 37, No. 4, 1990: 39–60.
Mortimer, Robert A. "Islam and Multiparty Politics in Algeria," *Middle East Journal.* Vol. 45, No. 4, Autumn 1991: 575–593.
――――. "Algeria: The Clash Between Islam, Democracy, and the Military," *Current History.* Vol. 92, No. 570, January 1993: 37–41.
Nasr, Seyyed Vali Reza. "Democracy and the Crisis of Governability in Pakistan." *Asian Survey.* Vol. 32, No. 6, June 1992: 521–537.
Nelson, Joan M., and Stephanie J. Eglinton. *Global Goals, Contentious Means: Issues of Multiple Aid Conditionality.* Washington, D.C.: Overseas Development Council, 1993.
Norton, Augustus Richard, "Future of Civil Society in the Middle East," *The Middle East Journal.* Vol. 47, No. 2, Spring 1993: 205–216.
Nyang'oro, Julius E. "The Evolving Role of the African State under Structural Adjustment," in Julius E. Nyang'oro and Timothy M. Shaw, eds., *Beyond the Structural Adjustment in Africa: The Political Economy of Sustainable and Democratic Development.* New York: Praeger, 1992: 11–27.
O'Donnell, Guillermo, Philippe C. Schmitter, and Laurence Whitehead, eds. *Transition from Authoritarian Rule: Prospects for Democracy.* Baltimore: Johns Hopkins Univ. Press, 1986, four volumes.
Organski, A. F. K. *The Stages of Political Development.* New York: Knopf, 1965.
Palmer, David Scott. "Peru, The Drug Business and Shining Path: Between Scylla and Charybdis?" *Journal of Interamerican Studies and World Affairs.* Vol. 34, No. 3, fall 1992: 65–88.
Park, Han S. *Human Needs and Political Development: A Dissent to Utopian Solutions.* Cambridge, MA: Schenkman, 1984.
Pastor, Manuel, Jr., and Carol Wise. "Peruvian Economic Policy in the 1980s: From Orthodoxy to Heterodoxy and Back," *Latin American Research Review.* Vol. 27, No. 2, 1992: 83–117.
Pease, Kelly Kate, and David P. Forsythe. "Human Rights, Humanitarian Intervention, and World Politics," *Human Rights Quarterly.* Vol. 15, No. 2, May 1993: 290–314.
Pelupessy, Wim. "Economic Adjustment Policies in El Salvador During the 1980s," *Latin American Perspectives.* Vol. 18, No. 4, Fall 1991: 48–78.
Petras, James, and Morris Molley, *U.S. Hegemony Under Siege: Class, Politics, and Development in Latin America.* London: Verso, 1990.
Pfeifer, Karen. "Economic Liberalization in the 1980s: Algeria in Comparative Perspective," in John P. Entelis and Phillip C. Naylor, eds., *State and Society in Algeria.* Boulder, CO: Westview, 1992: 97–116.
Pool, David. "The Links Between Economic and Political Liberalization," in Tim Niblock and Emma Murphy, eds., *Economic and Political Liberalization in the Middle East.* London: British Academic, 1993: 40–54.
Przeworski, Adam. *Democracy and Market: Political and Economic Reforms in Eastern Europe and Latin America.* New York: Cambridge Univ. Press, 1991.
Pye, Lucian W. "Armies in the Process of Political Modernization," in Jason L. Finkle and Richard W. Gable, eds., *Political Development and Social Change.* New York:

John Wiley, 1971: 277–283.
Radu, Michael. "Can Fujimori Save Peru?" *The Bulletin of the Atomic Scientists*. Vol. 48, No. 6, July/August 1992: 16–21.
"Régimen Económico," *Quehacer*. Lima, June 17, 1993: 22–24.
Renteln, Alison Dundes. "The Unanswered Challenge of Relativism and the Consequences for Human Rights," in *Human Rights Quarterly*. Vol. 7, No. 4, November 1985: 514–540.
Richards, Alan. "Economic Imperatives and Political Systems," *Middle East Journal*. Vol. 47, No. 2, Spring 1993: 217–227.
Richter, William L. "Pakistan Under Benazir Bhutto," *Current History*. Vol. 88, No. 542, December 1989: 433–436 and 449–451.
Rizvi, Hasan-Askari. "The Military and Politics in Pakistan," *Journal of Asian and African Studies*. Vol. 26, No. 1–2, 1991: 27–42.
Roberts, Hugh. "The Algerian State and the Challenge of Democracy," *Government and Opposition*. Vol. 27, No. 4, Autumn 1992: 433–454.
Rose, Leo E. "Pakistan: Experiments with Democracy," in Larry Diamond, Juan J. Linz, and Seymour Martin Lipset, eds., *Democracy in Developing Countries: Asia*. Boulder, CO: Lynne Rienner, 1989: 105–141.
Rosenberg, Tina. "Beyond Elections," *Foreign Policy*. No. 84, Fall 1991: 73–91.
Rothchild, Donald, and John Ravenhill. "Retreat from Globalism: U.S. Policy Toward Africa in the 1990s," in K. A. Oye, R. J. Lieber, and Donald Rothchild, eds. *Eagle in a New World: American Grand Strategy in the Post–Cold War Era*. New York: Harper Collins, 1992: 389–415.
Rothstein, Robert. "Democracy, Conflict, and Development in the Third World," *Washington Quarterly*. Vol. 14, No. 2, Spring 1991: 43–63.
Ruedy, John. *Modern Algeria: The Origins and Development of a Nation*. Bloomington: Indiana Univ. Press, 1992.
Sherman, Amy L. "Rethinking Development: A Market-friendly Strategy for the Poor," in Robert J. Griffiths, ed., *Third World: 94/95*. Guilford, CT: Dushkin, 1994: 36–40.
Shue, Henry. *Basic Rights: Subsistence, Affluence, and U.S. Foreign Policy*. Princeton, NJ: Princeton Univ. Press, 1979.
Sørensen, Georg. *Democracy and Democratization: Processes and Prospects in a Changing World*. Boulder, CO: Westview, 1993.
Swidler, Arlene. *Human Rights in Religious Traditions*. New York: Pilgrim, 1982.
Teson, Fernando R. *Humanitarian Intervention: An Inquiry into Law and Morality*. New York: Transnational, 1988.
Tomasevski, Katarina. *Development Aid and Human Rights*. New York: St. Martin's, 1989.
Tulchin, Joseph S., and Gary Bland, eds. *Is There a Transition to Democracy in El Salvador?* Boulder, CO: Lynne Rienner, 1992.
Unclés, Mario Lungo. "Redefining Democracy in El Salvador," *Social Justice*. Vol. 19, No. 4, Winter 1992: 110–125.
Vanhanen, Tatu. "Social Constraints of Democratization," in Tatu Vanhanen, ed., *Strategies of Democratization*. Washington, D.C.: Taylor & Francis, 1992: 19–35.
Walter, Knut, and Philip J. Williams, "The Military and Democratization in El Salvador," *Journal of International Studies and World Affairs*. Vol. 35, No. 1, Spring 1993: 39–88.
Weber, Max. *The Sociology of Religion*. Boston: Beacon, 1963.
Weiner, Myron. "Empirical Democratic Theory and the Transition from Authoritarianism to Democracy," in *PS: Political Science & Politics*. Vol. 20, No. 4, Fall 1987: 861–866.
Welch, Claude E., Jr. "The African Commission on Human and People's Rights: A

Five-Year Report and Assessment," *Human Rights Quarterly.* Vol. 14, No. 1, February 1992: 43–61.

Werlich, David P. "Fujimori and the 'Disaster' in Peru," *Current History.* Vol. 90, No. 553, February 1991: 61–64 and 81–83.

Wesson, Robert. *Democracy in Latin America: Promise and Problems.* New York: Praeger, 1982.

Whitehead, Laurence. "The Alternatives to 'Liberal Democracy': A Latin American Perspective," in David Held, ed., *Prospects For Democracy: North, South, East, West.* Stanford, CA: Stanford Univ. Press, 1993: 312–329.

Wolpin, Miles D. *Militarism and Social Revolution in the Third World.* Totowa, NJ: Allanheld, Osman, 1981.

World Development Report 1991: The Challenge of Development. Oxford: Oxford Univ. Press, 1991.

Zebiri, Kate. "Islamic Revival In Algeria: An Overview," *The Muslim World.* Vol. 82, Nos. 3–4, July-October 1993: 203–226.

Ziring, Lawrence. "Public Policy Dilemmas and Pakistan's Nationality Problem," *Asian Survey.* Vol. 28, No. 8, August 1988: 795–812.

————. "Pakistan in 1989: The Politics of Stalemate," *Asian Survey.* Vol. 30, No. 2, February 1990: 126–135.

Index

About the Book and Author

Abrupt democratization in Third World countries does not always result in enhanced human rights. Mahmood Monshipouri argues that human rights in fledgling democracies are most likely to be improved if the transition from authoritarianism is preceded by a process of economic liberalization, which works as a prelude to a gradual expansion of civil society.

Monshipouri bridges the gaps between democratization, liberalization, and human rights studies, using all three to explain the frequency with which democratic processes in the Third World have been aborted. He supports his analysis with a comparative assessment of the progress toward democracy in Algeria, El Salvador, Pakistan, and Peru.

Mahmood Monshipouri is associate professor of political science at Alma College.